State and Market in European Union Law
The Public and Private Spheres of the Internal Market before the EU Courts

Wolf Sauter and Harm Schepel

CAMBRIDGE
UNIVERSITY PRESS

CAMBRIDGE UNIVERSITY PRESS
Cambridge, New York, Melbourne, Madrid, Cape Town, Singapore,
São Paulo, Delhi

Cambridge University Press
The Edinburgh Building, Cambridge CB2 8RU, UK

Published in the United States of America by Cambridge University Press,
New York

www.cambridge.org
Information on this title: www.cambridge.org/9780521857758

First published 2009

Printed in the United Kingdom at the University Press, Cambridge

A catalogue record for this publication is available from the British Library

Library of Congress Cataloguing in Publication data
Sauter, Wolf.
  State and market in European Union law / Wolf Sauter and Harm Schepel.
    p.   cm. – (Cambridge studies in European law and policy)
  Includes bibliographical references and index.
  ISBN 978-0-521-85775-8 (hardback) – ISBN 978-0-521-67447-8 (pbk.)
  1. Trade regulation–European Union countries.   2. Freedom of
  movement–European Union countries.   3. Antitrust law–European Union
  countries.   4. Subsidies–Law and legislation–European Union countries.
  I. Schepel, Harm.   II. Title.   III. Series.
  KJE6415.S28 2009
  343.24′0721–dc22   2008039994

ISBN 978-0-521-85775-8 hardback
ISBN 978-0-521-67447-8 paperback

Contents

Acknowledgements

Various institutions have hosted this project for shorter or longer periods of time, sometimes unwittingly (in which case they won't be mentioned here by name). Hence we would like to express our thanks to the Centre for European Law and Policy (ZERP) Bremen, the law department of the University of Groningen, the Tilburg Centre for Law and Economics (TILEC), Kent Law School and the Brussels School of International Studies. In ways that are not always clear even to us, our common thinking on the subject has been shaped by the time we spent in Florence at the European University Institute (EUI) in the early 1990s, and we gratefully pay tribute to our teachers and fellow researchers there at what we consider to be a particularly exciting period in the history of the EUI law department.

We are grateful to John Bell, Christian Joerges, Claire Kilpatrick, Bernard Ryan and Ellen Vos for their comments on early and partial versions. Laura Pignataro has been kind enough to go through the full penultimate draft in painstaking detail: her comments have not just added valuable insights, but saved us from at least some embarrassment. Thank you for this. We would also like to thank Anne Witt for her research assistance; Tomáš Zlámal for his help in constructing the bibliography and the table of cases, and Kent Law School for funding their efforts. Our series editors, Jo Shaw and Laurence Gormley, deserve our warm gratitude for their patience and encouragement. Finally, the professionalism and dedication of the staff at Cambridge University Press, especially Jodie Barnes, Chantal Hamill, Sophie Rosinke and Richard Woodham, throughout the production process, has contributed greatly to its successful completion and made them a joy to work with.

Last but not least we would like to thank our loved ones for sacrificing time that could have been spent together instead and to apologise for having been absent-minded at other times when nominally we were present. We can only hope the result will find some merit in their eyes as well, and to do better next time.

Responsibility for the various views and errors in the text is, of course, ours alone. Although we have each taken the lead on drafting different parts of the text, these roles have swapped often enough for us to be jointly and severally responsible for the whole.

We have attempted to describe the law as it stood on 1 March 2008.

Wolf Sauter and Harm Schepel,
Brussels and Zoetermeer,
November 2008.

Abbreviations

AG	Advocate General
AJDA	*Actualité Juridique – Droit Administratif*
CDE	*Cahiers de Droit Européen*
CMLR	Common Market Law Review
CYELS	Cambridge Yearbook of European Legal Studies
EBLR	European Business Law Review
ECJ	European Court of Justice
ECLR	European Competition Law Review
ECR	European Court Reports
ECSC	European Coal and Steel Community
ELJ	European Law Journal
ELR	European Law Review
EPL	European Public Law
EuR	*Europarecht*
EuZW	*Europäische Zeitschrift für Wirtschaftsrecht*
ICLQ	International and Comparative Law Quarterly
LIEI	Legal Issues of European Integration
MLR	Modern Law Review
NJW	*Neue Juristische Wochenschrift*
OJ	Official Journal of the European Community
Ordo	*Jahrbuch für die Ordnung von Wirtschaft und Gesellschaft*
OUP	Oxford University Press
RMC	*Revue du Marché Commun*
RMCUE	*Revue du Marché Commun et de l'Union Européenne*
RMUE	*Revue du Marché Unique Européen*
RTDE	*Revue Trimestrielle de Droit Européen*
SEW	*Sociaal-economische Wetgeving*
YEL	Yearbook of European Law
ZHR	*Zeitschrift für das gesante Hardels- und Wirtschaftsrecht*

Table of Cases

European Court of Justice

Court of First Instance

1 Introduction

In this book we are concerned with one particular aspect of European economic law: the ways in which the European courts define and delineate the spheres of the 'market' and the 'State' in their various guises, and how they elaborate the relationship between these two categories. Hence, we deal with questions like the place of 'the State' in economic life, with the role of private actors and 'the market' in the provision of collective goods and, ultimately, with the relationship between economic freedoms and political rights. A large part of our enquiry will, inevitably, involve the question of whether (and if so, to what extent) EU internal market law reflects or propounds particular models of capitalism, such as neoliberalism or the 'European social model'.

The constitutional question at issue is not limited to the specific balance between the forces of the free market and public intervention at this one (or any other) time in the history of European integration: the fundamental question is not so much where European law sets these boundaries, but how they are set. At the extremes, two contrasting answers to this question are possible. The first answer recognises that the extent to which political decision-making can assert itself over the market is itself properly a political decision. In the other model, the legitimate sphere of government intervention is defined by market failure and hence limited to those activities or services that cannot be provided by the market mechanism.

Neither of these clearcut answers, of course, provides a viable course for European law. The first would render the very idea of the internal market nugatory; the second would turn the 'democratic deficit' of the Union into a constitutional value in and of itself. One would therefore expect to find less absolute, more pragmatic and infinitely more complex principles and mechanisms in the case law of the European courts. And so it transpires.

In this book we provide an analysis of the case law of the European courts concerning free movement and competition. This involves, on the one hand, those provisions that are formally addressed exclusively to either the Member States in their regulatory capacity or to private undertakings in their economic capacity. It also involves those provisions that explicitly recognise State intervention in the market and deal with public undertakings, monopolies, special and exclusive rights, and State aid. The focus is almost exclusively on primary Community law, although we have included discussion not only of especially significant secondary law, such as public procurement legislation, but also of some less significant secondary law, such as the VAT Directive, where we find the case law interesting for our purposes. The focus throughout is on instances of conflict between competing claims of market logic and discipline and the claims of primacy of political decision-making over the provision of collective goods. These are to be found in many and sometimes unexpected variations, but largely fall into two categories: interpretations of the scope of particular Treaty provisions on the one hand and substantive balancing of different values on the other.

In the remainder of this introductory chapter, we will both try to provide some context to our topic and set out the focus of our research. We will, first, discuss the rise and decline of European economic constitutionalism in the wider context of the process of European legal integration. Next, we will discuss the concept of the 'European economic constitution' itself in the light of two key approaches of particular relevance to our research: German *Ordo*liberalism and the French legal and political tradition associated with the notion of *service public*. These two diametrically opposed political and legal frameworks for European economic law and their ideological underpinnings will serve as ideal types for constructing our discussion. The subsequent section will discuss the reconfiguration of the public and private spheres following in particular the 1993 'November revolution' and outline the problems faced by the Court of Justice when dealing with these sensitive issues. Finally, we will identify the key variables of the substantive discussion in the subsequent chapters and formulate the research questions that we will address there.

1.1. The economy in European constitutionalism

The original EEC Treaty can be described as a system of 'embedded liberalism', a combination of external trade liberalisation and domestic interventionism.[1] EC law, after all, still explicitly acknowledges Member States' freedom to operate mixed economies in what is now Article 295 EC, according to which the Treaty 'shall in no way prejudice the rules in Member States governing the system of property ownership'. The absence of any provisions on social policy in the Rome Treaty, in this light, was not an unfortunate oversight and much less a policy choice in favour of economic liberalism, but could be construed as a fundamental decision in favour of domestic welfare states under direct democratic control.[2]

The process of constitutionalisation of the Treaty embarked upon by the Court of Justice kept this compromise largely intact. Thus, the canonical judgment in *Costa* v. *ENEL* found nothing in EC law to prevent Italy from nationalising its electricity industry, even while affirming the supremacy of EC law.[3] Even *Handelsgesellschaft* could be read in this way, protecting a decidedly illiberal Community regime of export controls against allegations of violating constitutionally protected 'economic liberty', even while affirming that respect for fundamental rights 'forms an integral part of the general principles of law' underpinning the Community legal order.[4] The Court's emphasis in its case law on free movement and competition law was squarely on market integration. The reference in the original Article 3(f) EEC to 'the institution of a system ensuring that competition in the common market is not distorted' was read in the key of terms of trade and not as an autonomous value.

Hence, in *Consten and Grundig*,[4a] the judgment that would define the objectives of EC competition law for decades, the Court made clear that even the anti-cartel provision Article 81 EC was concerned not so much with policing competitive markets, but with preventing fragmented markets. In disregard of the actual effects of the exclusive distribution agreement at stake, the Court noted:

What is particularly important is whether the agreement is capable of constituting a threat, either direct or indirect, actual or potential, to freedom of

---

[1] Applied to the Bretton Woods institutions, the term has been rendered famous by Ruggie, 'International Regimes, Transactions and Change: Embedded Liberalism in the Postwar Economic Order', (1982) 36 *International Organization* 379.

[2] For an elaborate reconstruction of the early years of European integration in this key, see S. Giubboni, *Social Rights and Market Freedom in the European Constitution – A Labour Law Perspective* (Cambridge University Press, 2006).

[3] Case 6/64 *Costa* v. *ENEL* [1964] ECR 585.

[4] Case 11/70 *Internationale Handelsgesellschaft* [1970] ECR 1133.

[4a] Joined Cases 56 and 58/64 *Consten and Grundig* v. *Commission* [1966] ECR 299.

trade between Member States in a manner which might harm the attainment of the objectives of a single market between States.[5]

This concern was later to be imported into the regime on the free movement of goods, finding its way into the famous *Dassonville* definition of measures having equivalent effect to quantitative restrictions in the free movement of goods.[6] It was here, of course, that the art of separation found its limits. One could argue that *Dassonville* and *Cassis de Dijon*[7] could still be fitted into the logic of free trade orthodoxy by representing an altogether classical shift from a concern with tariff barriers to non-tariff barriers. However, the sheer scope of free movement under Article 28 EC made it all but impossible to maintain a meaningful distinction between market integration and market regulation. That dilemma was to become all the more clear after the launching of the Single Market programme in the mid 1980s. In his history of European integration, John Gillingham claims:

> The adoption of the Single European Act was a choice for the market, a judgment on the part of the Member States to shift decision-making authority away from national political institutions as well as government-regulated economies and toward that abstraction, buyers and sellers. It represented an acknowledgement that the model of the national mixed-economy had had its day.[8]

On the basis of the actual text of the Act, of course, it was no such thing.[9] Economic context, political Zeitgeist and the focusing of energies on market integration have given the Single Act its status as a charter of the politics of deregulation and privatisation. To be sure, the Court and Commission responded in kind by making the most of the existing framework. The Court flanked its unfaltering vigilance under

---

[5] Article 81 EC prohibits anti-competitive agreements 'which may affect trade between Member States'. The Court reads this as a jurisdictional clause. On the contested objectives of EC competition law, see generally R. Wesseling, *The Modernisation of EC Antitrust Law* (Oxford: Hart, 2000), pp. 77 ff.

[6] Case 8/74 *Dassonville* [1974] ECR 837.

[7] Case 45/75 *Rewe* ('*Cassis de Dijon*') [1976] ECR 196.

[8] J. Gillingham, *European Integration 1950–2003 – Superstate or New Market Economy?* (Cambridge University Press, 2003), p. 294. There are useful antidotes to this 'From-Hayek-to-Thatcher' history of Europe. See B. Eichengreen, *The European Economy Since 1945 – Coordinated Capitalism and Beyond* (Princeton University Press, 2007); and, more generally, T. Judt, *Postwar – A History of Europe Since 1945* (London: Penguin, 2005).

[9] See e.g. the careful analysis in Craig, 'The Evolution of the Single Market' in C. Barnard and J. Scott (eds.), *The Law of the Single Market – Unpacking the Premises* (Oxford: Hart, 2002), pp. 1, 11 ff.

Article 28 EC with a 'public turn' in competition law, and the Commission started to make extensive use of its powers under the regime on State aid and Article 86 EC.[10] It was on this basis that Claus-Dieter Ehlermann (then director general of the European Commission responsible for competition policy) could famously proclaim the EC Treaty 'the most strongly free market oriented constitution in the world'.[11] Almost immediately afterwards, however, the balance swung back in the opposite direction with the 1993 'November revolution' set off by the *Keck*[11a] case. Before dealing with this reversal of the case law, we will briefly discuss the demise of embedded liberalism.

Embedded liberalism is, of course, in many ways a contradiction in terms and a compromise that is bound to fall victim to its own success to the extent that an international market is replaced by a internal market.[12] Two structural processes have been at work in the thirty-five years that separate the Rome (1957) and Maastricht (1992) Treaties. Jointly they explain the demise of embedded liberalism.

The first is simply the consequence of the fact that, ultimately, the separation of 'the market' from social and political life is artificial. As economic integration progresses, the processes of market building and political interventions in market processes will need to be coordinated somehow if they are to be effective. It is for this reason that the Single Market programme turned out to be as much an exercise in re-regulation as it was in deregulation: in highly complex societies, functioning markets require a regulatory framework.[13]

---

[10] See Gerber, 'The Transformation of European Community Competition Law?', (1994) 35 *Harvard International Law Journal* 25, and D. J. Gerber, *Law and Competition in Twentieth Century Europe – Protecting Prometheus* (Oxford: Clarendon, 1998), pp. 382 ff.

[11] Ehlermann, 'The Contribution of EC Competition Policy to the Single Market', (1992) 29 CMLR 257, at p. 273. Emphasis in original.

[11a] Joined cases C-267 and 268/91 *Keck and Mithouard* [1993] ECR I-6097.

[12] The institutional turn in political economy now associated with 'varieties of capitalism' would even seem to suggest that the separation of the production regime and the welfare-protection regime is dysfunctional in the light of the need for institutional complementarity. See e.g. J. R. Hollingsworth and R. Boyer (eds.), *Contemporary Capitalism: The Embeddedness of Institutions* (Cambridge University Press 1999); P. A. Hall and D. Soskice (eds.), *Varieties of Capitalism: The Institutional Foundations of Comparative Advantage* (Oxford University Press, 2001); and Rhodes, '"Varieties of Capitalism" and the Political Economy of European Welfare States', (2005) 10 *New Political Economy* 363.

[13] See e.g. Joerges, 'Markt ohne Staat? Die Wirtschaftsverfassung der Gemeinschaft und die regulative Politik' in R. Wildenmann (ed.), *Staatswerdung Europas? Optionen für eine Europäische Union* (Baden-Baden: Nomos, 1991), p. 225; and S. Weatherill, *Law and Integration* (Oxford: Clarendon, 1995).

Second is the process that emerged to remedy what Fritz Scharpf called the 'constitutional asymmetry' following from the combination of embedded liberalism (the 'political decoupling of economic integration and social-protection issues') and the constitutionalisation process:

At the national level, economic policy and social-protection policy had and still have the same constitutional status – with the consequence that any conflict between these two types of interests could only be resolved politically, by majority vote or by compromise. However, once the ECJ had established the doctrines of 'direct effect' and 'supremacy', any rules of primary and secondary European law, as interpreted by the Commission and the Court, would take precedence over all rules and practices based on national law, whether earlier or later, statutory or constitutional. When that was ensured, all employment and welfare-state policies at the national level had to be designed in the shadow of 'constitutionalised' European law.[14]

The Member States eventually woke up to the unintended realities of integration by European law as constitutionalised by the Court. In many ways, the Maastricht Treaty could be seen as an attempt to remedy this state of affairs. In the context of Economic and Monetary Union, Articles 2 and 3 of the EC Treaty became cluttered with a long list of objectives and activities that were in obvious need of political reconciliation and coordination – including social policy, environmental and consumer protection, 'economic and social cohesion' and industrial policy – while at the same time committing Member States to coordinate their economic policies 'in accordance with the principle of an open market economy with free competition' in Articles 4 and 98 EC.

The Community's economic framework had now arguably evolved into a system of contestable policy objectives. However, even as politics appeared on the European agenda, the Economic Community itself was shielded, notably by the Bundesverfassungsgericht (BVerfG). On the one hand, its Maastricht decision sparked off serious constitutional debate about political union and the feasibility of constitutionality and supranational democracy,[15] but on the other it protected the internal market and economic union from any such worries. As long as the

---

[14] Scharpf, 'The European Social Model', (2002) 40 *Journal of Common Market Studies* 645, pp. 646–7. Cf. F. W. Scharpf, *Governing in Europe – Effective and Democratic?* (Oxford University Press, 1999), pp. 43 ff.

[15] Suffice it to refer to the authoritative debate in Weiler, 'Does Europe need a Constitution? Demos, Telos, and the German Maastricht Decision', (1995) 1 ELJ 218; and Grimm, 'Does Europe need a Constitution?', (1995) 1 ELJ 282.

powers and competencies of the Community 'remain essentially the activities of an economic union', the BVerfG held that the Member States could continue to rely on their quality of sovereign power and their status of 'Masters of the Treaties'.[16] A new form of separation between the economic and the political spheres was thereby established. To paraphrase Christian Joerges, Europe could remain a 'market without a State' as long as its component members were content to be 'States without markets'.[17]

It was in the immediate aftermath of both the Maastricht Treaty and the BVerfG judgment that the European Court of Justice embarked on what Norbert Reich has called the 'November revolution', rejecting decisively the idea that the Treaty forms a neoliberal charter of economic freedom.[18] First, the Court's ruling in *Keck* did away with the assumption that the market freedoms serve the liberal pursuit of commercial freedom within individual Member States rather than merely regulating trade between Member States.[19] Next, the *Reiff/OHRA/Meng* trilogy definitively closed the door on the theory that the EC competition rules provide the exclusive yardstick by which Member States' social and economic policies are to be measured.[20]

The 'November revolution' was clearly a concerted effort by the Court to draw clear lines around the internal market, but the rationale behind it is all but self-evident. Several complementary interpretations can be, and have been, put forward, all in one way or another a response to the political signals sent out by the Maastricht Treaty:

---

[16] Bundesverfassungsgericht, *Brunner* v. *European Union Treaty*, 1 (1994), CMLR 57, paras. 54 and 55.

[17] Joerges, 'What is Left of the European Economic Constitution? A Melancholic Eulogy', (2005) 30 ELR 461, p. 475.

[18] Reich, 'The November Revolution of the European Court of Justice: *Keck*, *Meng* and *Audi* Revisited', (1994) 31 CMLR 459.

[19] Joined Cases C-267 and 268/91 *Keck and Mithouard* [1993] ECR I-6097. This is how Tesauro, 'The Community's Internal Market in the Light of the Recent Case-law of the Court of Justice', (1995) 15 YEL 1, at p. 5; and Möschel, 'Kehrtwende in der Rechtsprechung in der EuGH zur Warenverkehrsfreiheit', (1994) 47 NJW 429 both read the ruling, even if Möschel is decidedly less happy about the outcome than then Advocate General Tesauro.

[20] Case C-185/91 *Reiff* [1993] ECR I-4769; Case C-2/91 *Wolf W. Meng* [1993] ECR I-5751; and Case C-245/91 *OHRA Schadeverzekeringen NV (OHRA)* [1993] ECR I-5851. Again not amused, Möschel, 'Wird die Effet Utile Rechtssprechung des EuGH Inutile?', (1994) 47 NJW 1709, 1710 (to paraphrase, 'the economic constitution is about measuring politics to law. Is that what this was supposed to be about?'). For similarly grim case notes, see Bach, (1994) 31 CMLR 1357; and Van der Esch, 'Loyauté Fédérale et Subsidiarité', CDE 30 (1994), 523.

- *Subsidiarity:* First, it has been called 'subsidiarity' case law to highlight
  its implications for the vertical balance of powers: that between the
  Community and the Member States. In this reading, the Court
  'returns' to the Member States the power to decide on redistributive
  economic policies as long as these do not directly interfere with the
  internal market.[21]
- *Judicial formalism:* Second, the November revolution has been
  interpreted as the starting point of a retreat from judicial activism to
  formalism, with the Court insisting that the task of elaborating the
  principles of the economic constitution rests with the legislative
  institutions of the Community.
- *Loss of primacy of integration perspective:* Finally, the case law of the
  Court has been held against the light of the dynamics of market-
  building: now that the heroic days of establishing the internal
  market were drawing to a close, the purpose and scope of European
  economic law needed to be reconsidered. In this light, the brief
  flourishing of what has been called a neoliberal economic
  constitution (or *Wirtschaftsverfassung*) between the Single Act and the
  Maastricht Treaty was but a passing phase of forcing market
  integration by law.

There is a consistent body of case law from subsequent years that
confirms this line of line of thought – indeed, if the 'November
revolution' was considered bad, much worse was yet to come. In the
electricity monopoly cases of 1997, the Court held that discriminatory
practices prohibited by Article 31 EC itself could be covered by the
Article 86(2) EC exemption for services of general economic interest – a
concept largely defined at national level.[22] In *Altmark*, it held that the
Article 86(2) EC exception could save subsidies from the intrusions of
the State aid regime.[23] In the collective bargaining cases of 1999, it
settled the competing objectives of undistorted competition and social
policy in favour of the latter, inventing an exemption from the competition rules for anti-competitive measures resulting from collective

---

[21] Cf. Jickeli, 'Der Binnenmarkt im Schatten des Subsidiaritätsprinzips', (1995) 50 *Juristen Zeitung* 57; Rohe, 'Binnenmarkt oder Interessenverband? Zum Verhältnis von Binnenmarktziel und Subsidiaritätsprinzip nach dem Maastricht-vertrag', (1997) 61 *Rabels Zeitschrift* 1; and Winter, 'Subsidiarität und Deregulierung im Gemeinschaftsrecht', (1997) 31 EuR 247.

[22] Case C-157/94 *Commission v. Netherlands (Dutch Electricity Monopoly)* [1997] ECR I-5699; Case C-158/94 *Commission v. Italy (Italian Electricity Monopoly)* [1997] ECR I-5789; Case C-159/94 *Commission v. France (French Electricity and Gas Monopoly)* [1997] ECR I-5815; and Case C-160/94 *Commission v. Spain (Spanish Electricity Monopoly)* [1997] ECR I-5851.

[23] Case C-280/00 *Altmark Trans* [2003] ECR I-7747.

bargaining agreements.[24] In *Wouters* first and *Medina* later, the Court reversed decades of persistent case law by allowing corporatist arrangements to be justified under Article 81 (1) EC in a full-blown rule-of-reason test.[25]

On the other hand, there seem to be important contradictions as well, especially in the fields of free movement of services and capital. In a string of cases brought by the Commission against Member States retaining a measure of control over recently privatised or strategic industrial conglomerates, the Court has struck down the practice of 'golden shares'.[26] Starting with the 1998 cases of *Kohll* and *Decker*, the Court has subjected national social security systems to the discipline of the free movement regime, another nail in the coffin of embedded liberalism.[27] Furthermore, in December 2007, finally, it held collective action by trade unions against social dumping to be illegal under the provisions concerning the freedom of establishment and free movement of services.[28]

The ambiguity of these cases reveals the difficulties European economic law faces with the internalisation of competing objectives.[29] In that light, they clearly reflect the Maastricht Treaty with its plethora of goals. Recent amendments and Treaty revisions show that these problems have not yet been resolved. Thus, the ill-fated Constitutional

---

[24] Case C-67/96 *Albany International* [1999] ECR I-5751; Joined Cases C-115/97, 116/97, 117/97 and 119/97 *Brentjens Handelsonderneming* [1999] ECR I-6025; and Case C-219/97 *Drijvende Bokken* [1999] ECR I-6121.

[25] Case C-309/99 *Wouters* v. *Nederlandse Orde van Advocaten* [2002] ECR I-1577; and Case C-519/04 P *David Meca-Medina* v. *Commission* [2006] ECR I-6991.

[26] Case C-367/98 *Commission* v. *Portugal* [2002] ECR I-4731; Case C-483/99 *Commission* v. *France* [2002] ECR I-4781; Case C-503/99 *Commission* v. *Belgium* [2002] ECR I-4809; Case C-463/00 *Commission* v. *Spain* [2003] ECR I-4581; Case C-98/01 *Commission* v. *UK* [2003] ECR I-4641; Case C-174/04 *Commission* v. *Italy* [2005] ECR I-4933; Joined Cases C-282 and 283/04 *Commission* v. *Netherlands* [2006] ECR I-9141; and Case C-112/05 *Commission* v. *Germany* [2007] ECR I-8995.

[27] Case C-120/95 *Decker* [1998] ECR I-1831; and Case C-158/96 *Kohll* [1998] ECR I-1931. See e.g. P. Mavridis, *La Sécurité Sociale à l'Épreuve de l'Intégration Européenne* (Brussels: Bruylant, 2003); M. Dougan and E. Spaventa (eds.), *Social Welfare and EU Law* (Oxford: Hart, 2005); and G. de Búrca (ed.), *EU Law and the Welfare State: In Search of Solidarity*, (Oxford University Press, 2005). Cf. M. Ferrera, *The Boundaries of Welfare: European Integration and the New Spatial Politics of Social Protection* (Oxford University Press, 2005).

[28] Case C-438/05 *ITF* v. *Viking* [2007] ECR I-10779; and Case C-314/05 *Laval* [2007] ECR I-11767.

[29] Cf. Everson, 'Adjudicating the Market', (2002) 8 ELJ 152, especially at pp. 158 ff. Jürgen Schwarze has done the unthinkable in pulling together a systematic account of European economic law in his new tome: J. Schwarze, *Europäisches Wirtschaftsrecht. Grundlagen, Gestaltungsformen, Grenzen* (Baden-Baden: Nomos, 2007).

Treaty declared the Union's objectives to be 'to offer its citizens an internal market where competition is free and undistorted', while working for 'a highly competitive social market economy, aiming at full employment and social progress'.[30] The Lisbon Treaty retains the highly competitive social market economy, but has banished the system of undistorted competition that powers this economy to the legislative equivalent of a broom closet, a Protocol.[31] This new socio-economic settlement plays out in the shadow of political constitutionalism, complete with enhanced majoritarian politics, a Charter of fundamental rights, and notions of citizenship.[32]

Yet at the same time it evolves amidst the institutional and legal fragmentation launched by the 'new governance' of social Europe. This governance started gaining shape in the Treaty of Amsterdam, which inserted into Article 3 EC a reference to a 'coordinated strategy for employment' and was taken further by the Lisbon strategy. The result is the 'open method of coordination' (OMC), a contentious form of soft law outside the Treaty framework, far from the centralising tendencies of 'Brussels' and stretching out beyond employment strategies to the fields of education, health, pensions and social inclusion.[33] The re-coupling of economic integration and social welfare is thus accompanied by an exercise in decentralisation and dejuridification. That, in

---

[30] Article I-3(2) and (3). The Commission attributed the 'no' vote in France to 'the impression that the Constitution leant too much towards the liberal and not enough towards the social' in its Communication, *The Period of Reflection and Plan D*, COM (2006) 212, 1.

[31] Article 3, Treaty on European Union, as to be amended. In the Protocol on the Internal Market and Competition, the Contracting Parties 'consider' that the concept of the internal market includes a system of undistorted competition for purposes of competence under what is now Article 308 EC, to be renumbered as Article 352 TFEU.

[32] Cf. J. Schwarze (ed.), *Der Verfassungsentwurf des Europäischen Konvents-Verfassungsrechtliche Grundstrukturen und wirtschaftsverfassungsrechtliches Konzept* (Baden-Baden: Nomos, 2004).

[33] The literature is extensive. See e.g. Scott and Trubek, 'Mind the Gap: Law and New Approaches to Governance in the European Union', (2002) 8 ELJ 1; De Búrca, 'The Constitutional Challenge of New Governance in the European Union', (2003) 28 ELR 814; Trubek and Mosher, 'New Governance, Employment Policy and the European Social Model' in J. Zeitlin and D. M. Trubek (eds.), *Governing Work and Welfare in a New Economy – European and American Experiments* (Oxford University Press, 2003), p. 33; R. Dehousse (ed.), *L'Europe sans Bruxelles? Une Analyse de la Méthode Ouverte de Coordination* (Paris: L'Harmattan, 2004); O. De Schutter and S. Deakin (eds.), *Social Rights and Market Forces: Is the Open Coordination of Employment and Social Policies the Future of Social Europe?* (Brussels: Bruylant, 2005); Trubek and Trubek, 'Hard and Soft Law in the Construction of Social Europe: the Role of the Open Method of Co-ordination', (2005) 11 ELJ 343; and D. Ashiagbor, *The European Employment Strategy: Labour Market Regulation and New Governance* (Oxford University Press, 2006).

turn, makes the notion of a new European 'economic constitution' under the rule of law all the more elusive.[34] It is this concept of 'economic constitution' that will be elaborated on below.

1.2. Approaches to the European Economic Constitution

Although the term 'European Economic Constitution' has enjoyed wide currency in European legal thought since the earliest days of European integration,[35] its contours remain hazy. At a general level, it simply refers to the legal framework resulting from the combination of the constitutional doctrines of supremacy and direct effect on the one hand, and the substantive meaning given to the internal market rules on the other. In that sense, the 'constitutional' character of the internal market rules is fashioned wholly in instrumental terms to establish the parameters of their relationship with national regulatory frameworks.

In essence, the concept in this vein means little more than the observation that the internal market rules are forcefully imposed upon the Member States. The Court's own frequent use of the prefix 'fundamental' is almost invariably for this purpose. Thus, in *Forcheri*, the Court elevated Article 39 EC to the status of 'a fundamental right of workers and their families' as a build-up to extending the reach of the Treaty to access to education and vocational training.[36] In *Corsica Ferries France*, the point was made more bluntly: 'the provisions of the EEC Treaty concerning the free movement of goods, persons, services and capital are fundamental Community provisions and any restriction, even minor, of that freedom is prohibited'.[37] The Court has done much

---

[34] Christian Joerges finds in the OMC the death knell for constitutionalism, understood as law-mediated governance. See Joerges, 'What is Left of the European Economic Constitution? A Melancholic Eulogy', (2005) 30 ELR 461, pp. 478 ff.

[35] See e.g. J. Scherer, *Die Wirtschaftsverfassung der EWG* (Baden-Baden: Nomos, 1970); Constantinesco, 'La Constitution Économique de la CEE', (1977) 13 RTDE 244; and Zuleeg, 'Demokratie und Wirtschaftsverfassung in der europäischen Gemeinschaft', (1982) 16 EuR 21.

[36] Case 152/82 *Forcheri* v. *Belgium* [1983] ECR 2323, paras. 11 and 17. The Court has once applied the term to the free movement of goods, in the context of demanding effective judicial remedies against national authorities 'refusing the benefit of a fundamental right conferred by the Treaty'. Case C-228/98 *Dounias* [2000] ECR I-577, para. 64.

[37] Case C-49/89 *Corsica Ferries France* [1989] ECR I-4441, para. 8. The use of the term 'fundamental freedoms' to describe the free movement provisions is now so widespread as to make references seem redundant. It was used to spectacular effect in Case C-281/98 *Angonese* [2000] ECR I-4139, para. 35.

the same for Article 81 EC, declaring it to be 'a fundamental provision which is essential for the accomplishment of the tasks entrusted to the Community and, in particular, for the functioning of the internal market' in *Eco Swiss* and *Courage v. Crehan*.[38] The point here was to have national courts refuse to enforce arbitral awards contrary to the competition rules, and allow actions for damages between parties to anti-competitive agreements, respectively.[39]

Our concern with this instrumental use of the concept is simply that an emphasis on the *telos* of market integration overshadows profound political and ideological questions concerning the relationship between law, politics and the economy,[40] a tendency that is reflected in much, albeit not all, of the voluminous academic debate about the 'European Economic Constitution'.[41] However, not all thinking on the

---

[38] Case C-126/97 *Eco Swiss* [1999] ECR I-3055, para. 36; and Case C-453/99 *Courage v. Crehan* [2001] ECR I-6297, para. 20.

[39] This intrusion of constitutionalised internal market rules in private law relationships in the name of 'effectiveness' finds its mirror in Case C-194/94 *CIA Security* [1996] ECR I-2201, para. 40; and Case C-444/98 *Unilever Italia* [2000] ECR I-7535, para. 40; where the Court elevated the free movement of goods to 'one of the foundations of the Community' in order to force national courts not to entertain contractual claims based on national technical regulations that had not been duly notified to the Commission. Critically, Schepel, 'The Enforcement of EC Law in Contractual Relations: Case Studies in How Not to "Constitutionalize" Private Law', (2004) 12 *European Review of Private Law* 661.

[40] See Genschel, 'Markt und Staat in Europa', (1998) *Politische Vierjahresschrift* 55.

[41] See e.g. Mestmäcker, 'Zur Wirtschaftsverfassung in der Europäischen Union' in R. H. Hasse, J. Molsberger and Ch. Watrin (eds.), *Ordnung in Freiheit – Festschrift für Hans Willgerodt* (Stuttgart: Fischer, 1994), p. 263; Petersmann, 'Proposals for a New Constitution for the European Union: Building Blocks for a Constitutional Theory and Constitutional Law for the EU', (1995) 32 CMLR 1123; Everling, 'Wirtschaftsverfassung und Richterrecht in der Europäischen Gemeinschaft' in U. Immenga, W. Möschel and D. Reuter (eds.), *Festschrift für Ernst-Joachim Mestmäcker* (Baden-Baden: Nomos, 1996), p. 365; W. Sauter, *Competition Law and Industrial Policy in the EU* (Oxford: Clarendon, 1997); Sauter, 'The Economic Constitution of the European Union', (1998) 4 *Columbia Journal of European Law* 27; M. Poiares Maduro, *We the Court – The European Court of Justice and the European Economic Constitution* (Oxford: Hart, 1998); Cassese, 'La Costituzione Economica Europea', (2001) 11 *Rivista Italiana di Diritto Pubblico Comunitario* 907; J. Baquero Cruz, *Between Competition and Free Movement: The Economic Constitutional Law of the European Community* (Oxford: Hart, 2002); Hatje, 'Wirtschaftsverfassung' in A. von Bogdandy (ed.), *Europäisches Verfassungsrecht* (Berlin: Springer, 2003), p. 683; Schwarze, 'Das wirtschaftsverfassungsrechtliche Konzept des Verfassungsentwurfs des Europäischen Konvents- zugleich eine Untersuchung der Grundprobleme des europäischen Wirtschaftsrechts', (2004) EuZW 135; W. Schäfer (ed.), *Zukunftsprobleme der europäischen Wirtschaftsverfassung* (Berlin: Duncker & Humblot, 2004); and, appropriately last in the list, Joerges, 'What is Left of the European Economic Constitution? A Melancholic Eulogy', (2005) 30 ELR 461.

role of law in the economy has been predicated on market integration. Therefore we now turn to two national traditions that have had (and still have) a profound impact on European legal thought.

Ordoliberalism is an influential school of German economic and legal scholarship that originally emerged in academic isolation in Freiburg between the World Wars. Swept from relative obscurity to prominence by the post-war need for a coherent market-oriented perspective of the legal order, it has inspired the legal system of Germany as well as much of German legal thought on European integration.[42] Developed first in the context of the economic and political disintegration of the Weimar republic and later during the unspeakable degradation of the legal, political and economic systems by National Socialism, the overreaching concern of Ordoliberalism is with the ability of the legal system to prevent concentrations of both public and private power. If the programme was to avoid State planning, corporatism, cartelisation and monopolies of any kind, the chosen method to achieve this was the idea of the economic constitution.[43] The concept pulls together several threads of formal and substantive concerns and preferences in a systemic whole. Formally, constitutionalism is to be taken quite literally as an application to the economy of the core idea of political constitutionalism: a basic binding decision on the kind of economic system a community wants which will henceforth both legitimise and, more importantly, limit public intervention. Implicit in this is the recognition that a market economy, just like any other economic system, does not exist in a pre-political State of nature, but is crucially dependent on and embedded in the political and legal system. In Gerber's words:

---

[42] Especially in the German context, this had much to do with its successful alignment with the idea of the 'social market economy' which was to rise to ascendance in Christian-democratic politics. Important in both respects, A. Müller-Armack, *Wirtschaftsordnung und Wirtschaftspolitik. Studien und Konzepte zur Sozialen Marktwirtschaft und zur Europäischen Integration* (Freiburg im Breisgau: Rombach, 1966). A 'social market economy' in this context, though, bears little relation to the concept as enshrined in the Constitutional and Lisbon Treaties. Cf. Möschel, 'Competition as a Basic Element of the Social Market Economy', (2001) 2 *European Business Organization Law Review* 713.

[43] Good English expositions of Ordoliberalism are Joerges, 'European Economic Law, the Nation-State and the Maastricht Treaty' in R. Dehousse (ed.), *Europe after Maastricht* (Munich: Beck, 1994), p. 29; Gerber, 'Constitutionalizing the Economy: German Neo-liberalism, Competition Law, and the "New" Europe', (1994) 42 *American Journal of Comparative Law* 25; and D. J. Gerber, *Law and Competition in Twentieth Century Europe – Protecting Prometheus* (Oxford: Clarendon, 1998), pp. 232 ff.

The concept of an economic constitution turned the core idea of classical liberalism – that the economy should be divorced from law and politics – on its head by arguing that the characteristics and the effectiveness of the economy *depended* on its relationship to the political and legal systems. The ordoliberals recognised that fundamental political choices created the basic structures of an economic system.[44]

The substantive preference for a competitive market economy does perhaps not necessarily follow from the formal conception of a constitutionally ordered and protected economic system, but is directly related to it nonetheless. *Ordo*liberal obsession with competition law is, historically at least, not so much a function of a concern with aggregate economic performance and 'competitiveness' as it is a reflection of a concern with the perverse effects of concentrations of private economic power on the political system. The role of law in the *Wirtschaftsverfassung* is therefore both to shield the economy from political discretion and to protect the political system from succumbing to economic interests.

The *Ordo*liberals have cheered on the Court's progressive constitutionalisation of the market freedoms and the system of undistorted competition under the original Rome Treaty[45] and have protested bitterly against the 'interventionist' elements that were introduced by the Single European Act and the Maastricht Treaty.[46] The supranational

---

[44] D. J. Gerber, *Law and Competition in Twentieth Century Europe – Protecting Prometheus* (Oxford: Clarendon, 1998), p. 246. Emphasis in original.

[45] See e.g. Von der Groeben, 'Zur Wirtschaftsordnung der Europäischen Gemeinschaft' in H. von der Groeben, *Die Europäische Gemeinschaft und die Herausforderungen unserer Zeit* (Baden-Baden: Nomos, 1981), p. 201; E.-J. Mestmäcker, 'Auf dem Wege zur einer Ordnungspolitik für Europa' in E.-J. Mestmäcker, H. Möller and H.-P. Schwarz (eds.), *Eine Ordnungspolitik für Europa – Festschrift von der Groeben* (Baden-Baden: Nomos, 1987), p. 9; Th. Oppermann, 'Europäische Wirtschaftsverfassung nach den Einheitlichen Europäischen Akte' in P.-Ch. Müller-Graff and M. Zuleeg (eds.), *Staat und Wirtschaft in der EG* (Baden-Baden: Nomos, 1987), p. 53; Mestmäcker, 'Staat und Unternehmen im europäischen Gemeinschaftsrecht', (1988) 52 *Rabels Zeitschrift* 526; Von der Groeben, 'Probleme einer europäischen Wirtschaftsordnung' in J. F. Baur, P.-C. Müller-Graff and M. Zuleeg (eds.), *Europarecht, Energierecht, Wirtschaftsrecht. Festschrift für Bodo Börner* (Cologne: Carl Heymanns, 1992), p. 99; and J. Basedow, *Von der deutschen zur europäischen Wirtschaftsverfassung* (Tübingen: Mohr, 1992). The leading manifesto in English is Mestmäcker, 'On the Legitimacy of European Law', (1994) 58 *Rabels Zeitschrift* 615. Mestmäcker's work has been collected in E.-J. Mestmäcker, *Wirtschaft und Verfassung in der Europäischen Union* (Baden-Baden: Nomos, 2003).

[46] Behrens, 'Die Wirtschaftsverfassung der Europäischen Gemeinschaft' in G. Brüggemeier (ed.), *Verfassungen für ein ziviles Europa* (Baden-Baden: Nomos, 1994), p. 78; Mestmäcker, 'Zur Wirtschaftsverfassung in der Europäischen Union' in R. H. Hasse, J. Molsberger and Ch. Watrin (eds.), *Ordnung in Freiheit – Festschrift für Hans Willgerodt* (Stuttgart: Fischer, 1994), p. 263; and Streit and Mussler, 'The Economic

Wirtschaftsverfassung that appeared to emerge in the Court's case law until recently promoted the separation between markets and politics in line with the agenda of *Ordo*liberalism. Its contours neatly matched the normative parameters of *Ordnungstheorie*, with its emphasis on constitutional guarantees of competition and economic freedoms.[47] In this theory, far-reaching legal protection of private autonomy from public and private abuses of power alike results in convergence between 'objective' private and public interests: the public interest, objectively understood, is seen as resulting from strict curbs on public powers of economic intervention, which reduce the likelihood of policy capture by 'special interests'. In this sense, private law is endowed with normative superiority over public intervention, and the private law society with moral superiority over political decision-making procedures generally.[48] In the idealised view held forward by the *Ordo*liberals, negative integration and deregulation based on the superior economic rationality and supremacy of Community law opens up space for the *Privatrechtsgesellschaft* (private law society), as the public regulation struck down by the Court is replaced by private law, which in turn becomes the foundation of the Community legal order.[49]

Constitution of the European Community: From "Rome" to "Maastricht"', (1995) 1 ELJ 5. On the Constitutional Treaty, see e.g. Behrens, 'Das wirtschaftsverfassungsrechtliche Profil des Konventsentwurfs einer Vertrags über einer Verfassung für Europa' in A. Fuchs, H.-P. Schwintowski and D. Zimmer (eds.), *Festschrift für Ulrich Immenga zum 70. Geburtstag* (Munich: Beck, 2004), p. 21.

[47] Müller-Graff, 'Die wettbewerbsverfaßte Marktwirtschaft als gemeineuropäisches Verfassungsprinzip?', (1997) 31 EuR 422, attempts to establish these principles as a common constitutional core across the European Union. See also P.-Ch. Müller-Graff and E. Riedel (eds.), *Gemeinsames Verfassungsrecht in der Europäischen Union* (Baden-Baden: Nomos, 1998); and Drexl, 'Wettbewerbsverfassung- Europäisches Wettbewerbsrecht als materielles Verfassungsrecht' in A. von Bogdandy (ed.), *Europäisches Verfassungsrecht* (Berlin: Springer, 2003), p. 747. Cf. Feldmeier, *Ordnungspolitische Perspektiven der Europäischen Integration* (Frankfurt a.M.: Lang, 1993).

[48] The *locus classicus* is Böhm, 'Privatrechtgesellschaft und Marktwirtschaft', (1969) 17 Ordo, 75. Cf. Mestmäcker, 'Der Kampf ums Recht in der offene Gesellschaft', *Rechtstheorie* (1989) 20, 273. For critique, Günther, '"Ohne weiteres und ganz Automatisch"? Zur Wiederentdeckung der Privatrechtsgesellschaft', *Rechtshistorisches Journal* 11 (1992), 473; and Gerstenberg, 'Privatrecht, Demokratie und die lange Dauer der bürgerlichen Gesellschaft', (1997), 16 *Rechtshistorisches Journal* 152.

[49] Mestmäcker, 'Die Wiederkehr der bürgerlichen Gesellschaft und ihres Rechts', (1991) 10 *Rechtshistorisches Journal* 177, at 191. Cf. Rittner, 'Die wirtschaftsrechtliche Ordnung der EG und das Privatrecht', (1990) 42 *Juristen-Zeitung* 838; Schmidt-Leithoff, 'Gedanken über die Privatrechtsordnungen als Grundlage zum EWG-Vertrag' in M. Löwisch, Ch. Schmidt-Leithoff and B. Schmiedel (eds.), *Beiträge zum Handels- und Wirtschaftsrecht- Festschrift für Fritz Rittner* (Munich: Beck, 1991), p. 597; and E. Steindorff,

A radically different concept of the relationship between market and State, which leaves considerably less room for dynamic interaction with EU law, is based on the idea of *service public*. The legal construct of *service public* originated in French administrative law and from there largely constitutes what would elsewhere be called 'economic law'.[50] It is much more than a legal doctrine, however, having become a defining element of French political philosophy and an icon of national identity.[51] Indeed, in the influential writings of Léon Duguit, *service public* forms the very basis for the theory of the state and of public law. The State, in this account, exists simply to perform the tasks necessary for the promotion of 'social interdependence', the real basis for public law. Citizens have thus political rights to receive the services they need and the power of government derives solely from its duty to provide these: the idea of *service public* serves both to legitimise and limit the exercise of public power.[52] Much as Duguit, in Durkheimian fashion, may have believed in the 'social fact' of solidarity and in the objective scientific determination of society's needs, in practice this evolves through the notion of the 'general interest' that is defined through the political process and is to be protected from market forces by law. The *service public* view lifts public intervention in the economy – constrained by administrative law – to a higher plane in the legal order. By doing so it also relegates private-law mechanisms for resolving conflicts between competing interests to a role of secondary importance and of course limits the scope for market forces as such. Importantly, what follows from this view is that public action legitimised by the notion of *service*

EG-Vertrag und Privatrecht (Baden-Baden: Nomos, 1996). Cf. Joerges, 'The Impact of European Integration on Private Law: Reductionist Perceptions, True Conflicts and a New Constitutionalist Perspective', (1997) 3 ELJ 378.

50 See e.g. D. Linotte and R. Romi, *Services Publics et Droit Public Économique*, 5th ed. (Paris: Litec, 2003); and S. Braconnier, *Droit des Services Publics*, 2nd ed. (Paris: Presses Universitaires de France, 2007).

51 See e.g. Jourdan, 'La Formation du Concept de Service Public', [1987] *Revue de Droit Public* 89; Truchet, 'État et Marché', (1995) 40 *Archives de Philosophie du Droit* 314; Pontier, 'Sur la Conception Française du Service Public', [1996] *Recueil Dalloz* 9; Chevallier, 'Regards sur une Évolution', (1997) 23 AJDA 8; J.-P. Valette, *Le Service Public à la Française* (Paris: Ellipses, 2000); and J. Chevallier, *Le Service Public*, 6th ed. (Paris: Presses Universitaires de France, 2005). Critically, L. Cohen-Tanugi, *Le Droit sans l'État* (Paris: Presses Universitaires de France, 1985). Useful English exposition in T. Prosser, *The Limits of Competition Law – Markets and Public Services* (Oxford University Press, 2005), pp. 96 ff.

52 This summarises Martin Loughlin's summary in Loughlin, 'The Functionalist Style in Public Law', (2005) 55 *University of Toronto Law Journal* 361, pp. 368 ff. Duguit's *Les Transformations du Droit Public* was published in 1913 and translated into English, by Harold Laski, as *Law in the Modern State* (London: Allen & Unwin, 1921).

public should only be subject to a limited form of administrative law review under Community law.

Hence, pressures based on Community law to 'delegate' services of general interest to the private sphere meet with spirited resistance from the advocates of *service public*.[53] French legal scholarship has grown increasingly irritated by what are seen as continued 'attacks' of European competition law on this fundamental concept: European economic law has been described as the 'legal armour' of the 'ideology of the market', which is being turned into a 'war machine' against *service public*.[54] Fears of Court and Commission activism fuelled by complaints from private parties have led to a protracted effort to enshrine the *service public* in the Treaty itself (and to attempts to drown this effort in a series of papers by the Commission).[55] Consequently, the *service public* concept was written into the new Article 16 EC on services of general economic interest of the Amsterdam Treaty.[56] This ambiguous text reads:

---

[53] Cf. Treheux, 'Privatization and Competition versus Public Service', [1992] *Telecommunications Policy* 757; Devolvé, 'Les Contradictions de la Délégation de Service Public', [1996] AJDA 675; Auby, 'La Délégation de Service Public: Premier Bilan et Perspectives', [1996] *Revue du Droit Public* 1095; Symchowicz, 'La Notion de Délégation de Service Public', [1998] AJDA 195.

[54] Belloubet-Frier, 'Service Public et Droit Communautaure', (1994) 20 AJDA 270. See further Kovar, 'Droit Communautaire et Service Public: Esprit d'Orthodoxie ou Pensée Laïcisée', (1996) 32 RTDE 215, 493; Delacour, 'Services Publics et Concurrence Communautaire' [1996] RMCUE 501; and Lyon-Caen, 'Les Services Publics et l'Europe: quelle Union?', (1997) 23 AJDA 33.

[55] Cf. the barrage of communications from the Commission: *Services of General Interest in Europe*, OJ 1996 C281/3; *Services of General Interest in Europe*, OJ 2001 C17/4; *Report to the Laeken European Council – Services of General Interest*, COM(2001) 598 final; *Green Paper on Services of General Interest*, COM(2003) 270 final; *White Paper on Services of General Interest*, COM(2004) 374 final; *Implementing the Community Lisbon Programme: Social Services of General Interest in the European Union*, COM(2006) 177 final. The French senate in its report on services of general economic interest (most likely correctly) viewed Article 16 as a consolation prize ('une consolation'). *Rapport d'Information fait au Nom de la Delegation pout l'Union Européenne sur les Services d'Intérêt Général en Europe* (No. 82, 2000–2001 of November 2000, rapporteur Hubert Haenel), at 20, cited in Baquero Cruz, 'Beyond Competition: Services of General Interest and European Community Law' in G. de Búrca (ed.), *EU Law and the Welfare State: In Search of Solidarity* (Oxford University Press, 2005), pp. 169, 177.

[56] See Rodrigues, 'Les Services Publics et le Traité d'Amsterdam- Genèse et Portée Juridique du Projet de Nouvel Article 16 du Traité CEE', [1998] RMCUE 37; Ross, 'Article 16 and Services of General Interest: from Derogation to Obligation?', (2000) 25 ELR 22; and Baquero Cruz, 'Beyond Competition: Services of General Interest and European Community Law' in G. de Búrca (ed.), *EU Law and the Welfare State: In Search of Solidarity* (Oxford University Press, 2005), pp. 169 ff. Cf. e.g. L. Grard, J. Vandamme and F. van der Mensbrugghe (eds.), *Vers un Service Public Européen* (Paris: ASP Europe, 1996); Editorial, 'Public Service Obligations: A Blessing or a Liability?', (1996) 33 CMLR

Without prejudice to Articles 73, 86 and 87, and given the place occupied by services of general economic interest in the shared values of the Union as well as their role in promoting territorial and social cohesion, the Community and the Member States, each within their respective powers and within the scope of application of this Treaty, shall take care that such services operate on the basis of principles and conditions that enable them to fulfil their missions.

The ambiguity of Article 16 may come to be enhanced definitively by the following addition introduced by the Lisbon Treaty to what is now set to be Article 14 of the Treaty on the Functioning of the European Union:

The European Parliament and the Council, acting by means of regulations in accordance with the ordinary legislative procedure, shall establish these principles and set these conditions without prejudice to the competence of the Member States, in compliance with the Treaties, to provide, to commission and to fund such services.[57]

Meanwhile, the concept has likewise found its way into Article 36 of the Charter on Fundamental Rights:

The Union recognises and respects access to services of general economic interest as provided for in national laws and practices, in accordance with the Treaty establishing the European Community, in order to promote the social and territorial cohesion of the Union.

Both *Ordo*liberal universalism and *service public*-based statism continue to inform legal and political debate in the EU. Apart from their obvious ideological differences, these two schools of thought disagree fundamentally on the role they assign to the legal system. For *Ordo*liberalism, the law serves primarily to protect the market (and thereby the 'objective' public interest) from politics defined by narrow short-term private interests; in the *service public*-based view, the political realm is to be protected from market pressures by legal means, as it is legitimised by a democratic mandate. Yet although they appear to be logical opposites, both schools of thought are based on a strict distinction between the public and private spheres and consider such a distinction fundamental to legitimacy of the EU legal order. Herein lies the problem.

---

395. It is claimed that, as a manifestation of 'solidarity', the concept played a major role in the 'European model of society' that allegedly guided the Delors presidency. Cf. G. Ross, *Jacques Delors and European Integration* (Cambridge: Polity, 1995); and J. Delors, *Le Nouveau Concert Européen* (Paris: Odile Jacob, 1992).

[57] *Mutatis mutandis*, the paragraph is identical to Article III-122, Treaty establishing a constitution for Europe, OJ 2004 C310.

1.3. Blurring the distinction between the public and private spheres of the economy

It now seems clear that the processes of privatisation and trade liberalisation associated with what is commonly referred to as 'globalisation' do not lead to a wholesale 'retreat of the State' in favour of the creative destruction of market forces.[58] Instead, the consensus in the social sciences seems to point towards a transformation of the role of the State, a realignment of the public and private spheres, and enduring diversity between different national socio-economic systems.

The EU is perhaps the foremost example of an attempt to re-establish economic governance by pooling sovereignty in a context of economic globalisation. Increasingly, the economic policy-making powers of the Member States are coordinated, bound by common decision-making mechanisms and by legal rules. At the same time, in spite of the unprecedented economic policy convergence that started with the run-up to EMU, the degree and the means of State involvement in the economy continue to differ widely between the various EU Member States. Short-term political divisions over adjustment to common norms aside, the persistence of national peculiarities reflects fundamental differences in the general economic policy orientation and institutional frameworks of the individual Member States.[59] Even if general trends can be identified, patterns of realignment of the public and private spheres can diverge significantly not just between Member States, but across different sectors of the economy.

Privatisation itself has been a widespread feature of EU economies over the last two decades or so, causing major shifts of capabilities and resources to the private sector and a withdrawal of the State from direct

---

[58] Compare S. Strange, *The Retreat of the State – The Diffusion of Power in the World Economy* (Cambridge University Press, 1996); and P. Hirst and G. Thompson, *Globalization in Question. The International Economy and the Possibilities of Governance* (Cambridge: Polity, 1996).

[59] See e.g. V. A. Schmidt, *The Futures of European Capitalism* (Oxford University Press, 2002); and G. Menz, *Varieties of Capitalism and Europeanization: National Response Strategies to the Single European Market* (Oxford University Press, 2005). Cf. C. Crouch and W. Streeck (eds.), *Political Economy of Modern Capitalism: Mapping Convergence and Diversity* (London: Sage, 1997); B. Amable, *The Diversity of Modern Capitalism* (Oxford University Press, 2003); W. Streeck and K. Thelen (eds.), *Beyond Continuity: Institutional Change in Advanced Political Economies* (Oxford University Press, 2005); C. Crouch, *Capitalist Diversity and Change: Recombinant Governance and Institutional Entrepreneurs* (Oxford University Press, 2005); Crouch, 'Models of Capitalism', (2005) 10 *New Political Economy* 440; and J. Beckert *et al.* (eds.), *Transformationen des Kapitalismus* (Frankfurt a.M.: Campus, 2006).

intervention in the economy. The provision of hitherto traditional 'public goods' – such as water, transport, energy, communications, health care, refuse collection and even prison facilities – by private actors according to the logic of the market inevitably collapses socially and legally embedded understandings of the public and private spheres of the economy: private companies are charged with public missions, while public undertakings are forced to compete with private enterprises under market conditions. Also, where markets did not exist before, in many cases regulation is required to create and police them. These processes are accompanied, however, by hybrid mechanisms of indirect control and an explosion of new forms of legal regulation,[60] as the need arises to define public missions – and indeed 'the public interest' – in legal rather than political terms.

In a parallel development, the State has been widely diagnosed with a severely reduced capacity for hierarchical political control under conditions of functional differentiation. The term 'governance' has spread rapidly from political sociology to official discourse to describe the collapse of strict distinctions between the regulator and the regulated and a transformation of the State's action from 'a role based in constitutional powers towards a role based in coordination and fusion of public and private resources'.[61] This results then in various forms of co-optation of private actors in an array of legal arrangements of neo-corporatism, private regulation, co-regulation and self-regulation.[62]

---

[60] Giandomenico Majone's work here has been fundamental. See e.g. Majone, 'The Rise of the Regulatory State in Europe', (1994) 17 *West European Politics* 77; Majone, 'Paradoxes of Privatization and Deregulation', (1994) 1 *Journal of European Public Policy* 54; and Majone, 'From the Positive to the Regulatory State: Causes and Consequences of Changes in the Mode of Governance', (1997) 17 *Journal of Public Policy* 139.

[61] Pierre and Peters, *Governance, Politics and the State* (New York: St Martin's, 2000), p. 25. See further e.g. W. Streeck and Ph. C. Schmitter (eds.), *Private Interest Government – Beyond Market and State* (London: Sage, 1985); J. R. Hollingsworth, Ph. C. Schmitter and W. Streeck (eds.), *Governing Capitalist Economies: Performance and Control of Economic Sectors* (Oxford University Press, 1994); Mayntz, 'Politische Steuerung: Aufstieg, Niedergang und Transformation einer Theorie', (1995) *Politische Vierteljahresschrift* Sonderheft p. 26, 149; and R. Mayntz and F. W. Scharpf (eds.), *Gesellschaftliche Selbstregelung und Politische Steuerung* (Frankfurt a.M.: Campus, 1996). Cf. P. Kenis and V. Schneider (eds.), *Organisation und Netzwerk – Institutionelle Steuerung in Wirtschaft und Politik* (Frankfurt a.M: Campus, 1996).

[62] EU Law itself is no stranger to the phenomenon. See e.g. H. Schepel, *The Constitution of Private Governance – Product Standards in the Regulation of Integrating Markets* (Oxford: Hart, 2005); Chalmers, 'Private Power and Public Authority in European Union Law', (2006) 8 CYELS 59; and Schiek, 'Private Rulemaking and European Governance: Questions of Legitimacy', (2007) 32 ELR 443.

The withdrawal of the State as a collective actor (*Entstaatlichung*) is thus accompanied by the publicisation (*Verstaatlichung*) of private actors.[63] Private law structures are being 'publicised' at the same time as the province of administrative law is extending to private actors, blurring the traditional distinctions between public and private law.[64]

Privatisation may have become a common trend in all Member States, but takes place according to different methods and timetables, and results in different degrees of State withdrawal from the economy.[65] While corporatist arrangements of self-regulation constitute relics of inefficient clientelism in some Member States, they are hailed as the cutting edge of modern governance in others. Even if EU-wide trends can be identified, circumstances are likely to differ sharply not only between Member States, but even more so between different economic sectors – including as a function of European integration – both within individual Member States and across the Community as a whole. As a consequence, the dividing line between the public and private spheres in the economy is not drawn, nor redrawn, uniformly across the EU.

---

[63] Teubner, 'The "State" of Private Networks: The Emerging Legal Regime of Polycorporatism in Germany', [1993] *Brigham Young University Law Review* 553, at p. 569.

[64] See e.g. Black, 'Constitutionalising Self-Regulation', (1996) 59 MLR 24; Teubner, 'After Privatization? The Many Autonomies of Private Law', (1998) 51 *Current Legal Problems* 393; D. Oliver, *Common Values and the Public/Private Divide* (London: Butterworths, 1999); Freeman, 'Private Parties, Public Functions and the New Administrative Law', (2000) 52 *Administrative Law Review* 813; Aman, 'Globalization, Democracy, and the Need for a New Administrative Law', *UCLA Law Review* 49 (2002), 1687; Scott, 'Private Regulation of the Public Sector: A Neglected Facet of Contemporary Governance', (2002) 29 *Journal of Law and Society* 56; and Freeman, 'Extending Public Law Norms Through Privatization', (2003) 116 *Harvard Law Review* 1285. Cf. W. Hoffmann-Riem and E. Schmidt-Aßmann (eds.), *Öffentliches Recht und Privatrecht als wechselseitige Auffangordnungen* (Baden-Baden: Nomos, 1996).

[65] See e.g. J. Vickers and V. Wright (eds.), *The Politics of Privatisation in Europe* (London: Frank Cass, 1989); C. Graham and T. Prosser, *Privatizing Public Enterprises: Constitutions, the State and Regulations in Comparative Perspective* (Oxford: Clarendon, 1991); Organization for Economic Cooperation and Development, *Regulatory Reform, Privatisation and Competition Policy* (Paris: OECD, 1992); V. Wright (ed.), *Privatization in Western Europe: Pressures, Problems, Paradoxes* (London: Pinter Publishers, 1994); M. Moran and T. Prosser (eds.), *Privatization and Regulatory Change in Europe* (Buckingham: Open University Press, 1994); S. K. Vogel, *Freer Markets, More Rules – Regulatory Reform in Advanced Industrial Countries* (Ithaca: Cornell University Press, 1996); D. Geradin, (ed.), *The Liberalization of State Monopolies in the European Union and Beyond* (Deventer: Kluwer, 1999); and D. Coen and A. Héritier (eds.), *Refining Regulatory Regimes: Utilities in Europe* (Cheltenham: Elgar, 2005).

1.4. The public/private distinction before the EU Courts: research questions and approach

It is not the role of the Court of Justice to fashion a comprehensive legal framework to institutionalise 'open markets with free competition' or 'a highly competitive social market economy'. Nevertheless, case by case, the Court inevitably sets the parameters for the nature of the legal framework of the internal market. In developing and applying European economic law, the Court of Justice is now required to spell out the conditions under which private undertakings can be said to exercise public functions; and those under which public undertakings must be subjected to market discipline. It has to define when private, public and mixed decision-making processes infringe the prohibitions of cartels and of dominance abuse, and the conditions under which they may represent the legitimate exercise of regulatory functions. As the State is often no longer the only actor offering public services, and deregulation and privatisation lead private enterprises to compete with public, semi-public or privatised undertakings with various degrees of market power, this exercise is increasingly complex. Moreover, the Court's task is politically delicate, as it affects the national, regional and local political arenas, and thereby the resultant balance of power.

The basic lines of separation between 'State' and 'Market' in EU law are drawn in two main distinct ways.

The first has to do with the question of whether particular activities or institutions fall within the scope of Community law at all. This category, in turn, falls apart in two main mechanisms of exclusion. The first pertains to the scope of specific provisions. The question here would be, for example, whether a particular entity is to be classified as an 'undertaking' for purposes of the competition rules, or whether a particular profession is to be qualified as 'employment in the public service' for purposes of the exemption from the discipline of the free movement of workers.

The second category concerns the substance and power of definition of 'public interest' exceptions of various descriptions that justify derogations from the disciplines of the internal market. The second main battlefield lies within the sphere of Community law and focuses on the relationship between the competition rules – formally exclusively addressed to private parties – and the free movement rules – formally addressed exclusively to the Member States. It is true that limited provision was made for resolving some borderline, or 'interface' issues, such as those concerning state aids, public monopolies, and special and exclusive rights. The present degree of complexity, however, was not anticipated.

To chart its course through this minefield, armed with the doctrines of teleology and *effet utile*, the Court has long held on to 'functional' interpretations that emphasised the need for a uniform effective application of EU law throughout the Community. The logical result of this approach was a disregard for national legal and institutional categories. Notably, in *Höfner*, the Court held a government agency to be an 'undertaking' for purposes of competition law because it engaged in an activity 'that has not always been, and is not *necessarily*, carried out by public entities'.[66] Conversely, in *Calì*, it refused to apply the competition rules to a private undertaking because it exercised powers 'which are *typically* those of a public authority'.[67] The problem with this approach is that it suggests the existence of 'deep' Community-wide concepts of 'public' and 'private', based on an understanding of what constitutes a legitimate 'public interest' and on legal standards for the ways in which these interests can be pursued. At the same time, in the absence of common policies or political agreement on harmonised policies, the Court often struggles to argue its competence to find, let alone impose, such unifying concepts. The ebb and flow of harmonisation is thus relevant to the question of how far the Court is prepared to venture out on any particular course in a given case.

Stating the core problem in this manner suggests that a number of standard explanations may apply to the Court's case law on the public/private distinction. For example, the structure of the Treaty is based on prohibitions of market distortions that are subject to certain limited exceptions and justifications. The Court consistently interprets exceptions restrictively and the prohibitions extensively. Where secondary rules are adopted, the scope for such exceptions is further reduced due to the effects of pre-emption, whereby Member States are foreclosed from taking certain types of action. Further, when the Court is required to resolve legal issues in the absence of clear textual guidance generally, it tends to reach for the objectives of the Treaty; its general principles (e.g. proportionality, non-discrimination); the doctrines that it has developed to fill the gaps (e.g. direct effect, *effet utile* and pre-emption);

---

[66] Case C-41/90 *Höfner and Elsner* v. *Macroton* [1991] ECR I-1979, para. 22. Emphasis added.
[67] Case C-343/95 *Diego Calì & Figli* v. *SEPG* [1996] ECR I-1547, para. 23. Emphasis added.

and standard criteria (e.g. the essential and/or mandatory requirements that fall under the 'rule of reason'). Below, we will attempt to chart whether, and to what extent, these explanations apply, or whether more meaningful principles can be derived from the case law that are specific to the demarcation of the public and private spheres in Community law.

The main questions we wish to address are:

- What, under EU law, are the limits to legitimate governmental interference in market processes in the context of European integration today and why?
- Are there fundamental differences between the ways in which the Court treats this problem under the free movement and competition rules?
- To what extent do these norms complement each other, or are they converging?

The answer is derived based on a review of the case law concerning the free movement and competition rules. It is also based on the case law concerning the exceptions to these rules – in particular the Treaty Articles 31, 86, 86(2) and 87 to 89 EC, that were originally intended to deal with the area where public intervention might come into conflict with the free movement and competition rules.

The problems involved are essentially threefold, although they overlap:

- how (i.e. according to which criteria) does the Court attribute measures to either the public or the private sphere?
- how does the Court establish whether the free movement and competition rules are applicable?
- how does the Court establish (a) whether public interest exceptions and/or justifications apply; and (b) what their scope is?

In all three respects, a further dimension that will be addressed is their dynamic aspect, i.e. how has the law on these issues evolved over time. A main aspect of this is the question of whether there are significant differences between the relevant case law before and after 'the November revolution'.

Our discussion of the Court's case law is organised in two main parts. In the first part (Chapters 2 to 4), we will review cases concerning the fundamental freedoms and the competition regime. There, we will first look at the development of the criteria the Court uses to apply these rules to their addressees as originally intended, i.e. Member States and private undertakings respectively. In the next subsection, we will review cases where the original legal categories are reversed: the conditions under which the competition rules are applied to State measures and the fundamental freedoms are applied to private parties.

The second part (Chapters 5 to 8) concerns the interface between the public and private realms as explicitly provided for by the Treaty: the exceptions for public undertakings and State aid. A first subsection discusses commercial monopolies under Article 31, a second looks at undertakings with special and exclusive rights under Article 86 EC, whereas the last subsection deals with State aid under Articles 87 to 88 EC. Finally, we attempt to pull the various threads together in conclusion.

PART I · ECONOMIC ACTIVITIES V. THE EXERCISE OF PUBLIC AUTHORITY

This first part of our text deals with various boundary issues concerning the public and private spheres under the free movement and competition rules, which were not designed to deal with such issues, but intended to address, for the free movement rules, public authorities and, for the competition rules, private undertakings.

2 Free movement: treaty provisions and secondary rules

2.1. The interplay of prohibitions and justifications under the free movement rules

The fundamental freedoms are the cornerstones of the internal market, which Article 3(c) EC after all defines as 'characterised by the abolition, as between Member States, of obstacles to the free movement of goods, persons, services and capital'. The dimension of free movement law that concerns us most directly here is the way in which the Court defines a body capable of taking a 'State measure' caught by the free movement rules. However, that issue should be seen in the context of the interplay of two other dimensions: the determination of the kinds of measures that are caught by the free movement rules; and, for measures caught, the definition of legitimate public interest justifications. It appears that the development of these two dimensions is related, and is rather less linear than is often presented. The basic narrative is relatively straightforward: in classic trade agreement fashion the Treaty provisions on free movement of goods, services, workers and capital outlaw discrimination on grounds of origin or nationality. For these kinds of measure, the Treaty provides explicitly circumscribed justifications on the classic grounds of public health, public policy, public security and so on, that the Court interprets narrowly. However, as the Court has taken to demanding more from State measures than the mere absence of overt discrimination, it has also widened the scope for Member States to invoke legitimate public interest defences for restrictions to the fundamental freedoms. The ambiguity in the story comes from both the historical and substantive divergences in the development of this case law under the different free movement regimes, and from the distractions of *Keck*.[1a]

[1a] Joined cases C-267 and 268/91 *Keck and Mithouard* [1993] ECR I-6097.

For the free movement of goods, Article 28 EC prohibits quantitative restrictions as well as measures of equivalent effect on trade between the Member States. As such, the provision forms the very core of EC law: this has been underlined further by its expansive interpretation by the Court of Justice. Thus, in *Dassonville*, it famously declared that 'all trading rules enacted by Member States which are capable of hindering, directly or indirectly, actually or potentially, intra-Community trade are to be considered as measures having an effect equivalent to quantitative restrictions'.[1] In its canonical judgment on the German treatment of *Cassis de Dijon*, this scope was explicitly confirmed to cover not only all forms of formal discrimination, but also measures that apply indistinctly to domestic products and products from other Member States but have exclusionary effects on market access across national borders. At the same time, the Court opened the way for an exception concerning 'mandatory requirements' beyond the grounds explicitly listed in Article 30:

Obstacles to movement within the Community resulting from disparities between the national laws relating to the marketing of the products in question must be accepted in so far as those provisions may be recognised as being necessary in order to satisfy mandatory requirements relating in particular to the effectiveness of fiscal supervision, the protection of public health, the fairness of commercial transactions and the defence of the consumer.[2]

This new category of public interest justifications was then subjected to a 'least restrictive means' proportionality test.[3] These 'mandatory requirements' resonate with an earlier judgment of the Court in *Van Binsbergen*, where the Court could be argued to have started a similar approach to justification for restrictions on the free movement of services. In that case, dealing with restrictions on the ability to give legal advice, it was held that:

specific requirements imposed on the person providing the service cannot be considered incompatible with the Treaty where they have as their purpose the application of professional rules justified by the public good – in particular rules relating to organisation, qualifications, professional ethics, supervision and liability – which are binding upon any person established in the State in which

---

[1] Case 8/74 *Dassonville* [1974] ECR 837, para. 5.
[2] Case 120/78 *Cassis de Dijon* [1979] ECR 649, para. 8.
[3] Case 261/81 *Rau* [1982] ECR 3961, para. 12.

the service is provided, where the person providing the service would escape from the ambit of those rules being established in another Member State.[4]

The Court then repeated this rather unhelpful formula ('The Treaty', sic) through the 1980s,[5] fashioning, however, a general public-interest exception to restrictions on the freedom to provide services that discriminated either on the basis of nationality or on the basis of country of establishment. It was not until the summer of 1991 that the Court spelled out an approach to Article 49 EC that was similar to its take on Article 28. In *Sägers*, the Court held:

It should be pointed out that Article 49 of the Treaty requires not only the elimination of all discrimination against a person providing services on the ground of his nationality but also the abolition of any restriction, even if it applies without distinction to national providers of services and to those of other Member States, when it is liable to prohibit or otherwise impede the activities of a provider of services established in another Member State where he lawfully provides similar services.[6]

It then came up with what is now the standard formulation for the justification regime, allowing restrictions for 'imperative reasons relating to the general interest', provided that these apply to all persons or undertakings concerned and provided that the particular interest is not already protected by the rules to which the service provider is subject in his or her Member State of establishment.[7]

Then came *Keck*. There, the Court found it necessary to 're-examine and clarify' its case law 'in view of the increasing tendency of traders to

---

[4] Case 33/74 *Van Binsbergen* [1974] ECR 1299, para. 12. The paragraph is probably best read in the context of the notion of abuse of the internal market rules for the purpose of circumventing restrictive national legislation – *in casu*, a Dutch person providing services in the Netherlands trying to circumvent Dutch legislation by establishing himself in Belgium.

[5] See Joined Cases 110 and 111/78 *Willy van Wesemael* [1979] ECR 35, para. 28; Case 279/80 *Webb* [1981] ECR 3305, para. 17; Case 205/84 *Commission* v. *Germany* [1986] ECR 3755, para. 27; and Case C-154/89 *Commission* v. *France* [1991] ECR I-659, para. 14.

[6] Case 79/90 *Sägers* [1991] ECR I-4221, para. 12. Noted by Roth [1993] CMLR 145. Less emphatic, but no less clear in Case C-288/89 *Goudse Kabel* [1991] ECR I-4007, paras. 11–13; and Case C-353/89 *Commission* v. *Netherlands (Mediawet)* [1991] ECR I-4069, paras. 15–17. The Court was later to add to the formula to cover not just rules that 'prohibit or otherwise impede' the activities of foreign service providers, but also rules that make these activities 'less advantageous' or 'less attractive'. See Case C-55/94 *Gebhard* [1995] ECR I-4565, para. 37; Case C-272/94 *Guiot* [1996] ECR I-1905, para. 10; and Case C-165/98 *Mazzoleni* [2001] ECR I-2189, para. 22.

[7] Case C-79/90 *Sägers* [1991] ECR I-4221, para. 15.

invoke Article 28 as a means of challenging any rules whose effect it is to limit their commercial freedom even where such rules are not aimed at products from other Member States'.[8] And so:

It is established by the case-law beginning with 'Cassis de Dijon' that, in the absence of harmonisation of legislation, obstacles to free movement of goods which are the consequence of applying, to goods coming from other Member States where they are lawfully manufactured and marketed, rules that lay down requirements to be met by such goods (such as those relating to designation, form, size, weight, composition, presentation, labelling, packaging) constitute measures of equivalent effect prohibited by Article 28. This is so even if those rules apply without distinction to all products unless their application can be justified by a public-interest objective taking precedence over the free movement of goods.

By contrast, contrary to what has previously been decided, the application to products from other Member States of national provisions restricting or prohibiting certain selling arrangements is not such as to hinder directly or indirectly, actually or potentially, trade between Member States within the meaning of the *Dassonville* judgment, so long as those provisions apply to all relevant traders operating within the national territory and so long as they affect in the same manner, in law and in fact, the marketing of domestic products and of those from other Member States.

Provided that those conditions are fulfilled, the application of such rules to the sale of products from another Member State meeting the requirements laid down by that State is not by nature such as to prevent their access to the market or to impede access any more than it impedes the access of domestic products. Such rules therefore fall outside the scope of Article 28 of the Treaty.[9]

The judgment caused a storm and drew much well-deserved criticism, especially in light of the tension between the drama of the announcement of a major overhaul on the one hand, and the utter obscurity of the term 'selling arrangements' on the other.[10] With the years,

---

[8] Joined Cases C-267 and 268/91 *Keck and Mithouard* [1993] ECR I-6097, para. 14.

[9] Joined Cases C-267 and 268/91 *Keck and Mithouard* [1993] ECR I-6097, paras. 15–17.

[10] Cf. e.g. Chalmers, 'Repackaging the Internal Market – The Ramifications of the *Keck* Judgment', (1994) 19 ELR 385; Gormley, 'Reasoning Renounced? The Remarkable Judgment in *Keck and Mithouard*', [1994] *European Business Law Review* 63; Mattera, 'De l'Arrêt 'Dassonville' à l'Arrêt 'Keck': l'Obscure Clarté d'une Jurisprudence Riche en Principes Novateurs et en Contradictions', [1994] RMUE 117; Poiares Maduro, '*Keck*: The End? The Beginning of the End? Or Just the End of the Beginning?', (1994) 1 *Irish Journal of European Law* 33; Steindorff, 'Unvollkommener Binnenmarkt', (1994) 158 ZHR 149; Becker, 'Von "Dassonville" über "Cassis" zu "Keck" – Der Begriff der Maßnahmen gleicher Wirkung in Art. 30 EGV', (1994) 29 EuR 162; Matthies, 'Artikel 30 EG-Vertrag nach Keck' in O. Due, M. Lutter and J. Schwarze (eds.), *Festschrift für Ulrich*

however, *Keck* has proven rather less significant than could be contemplated at the time. Still, it remains a useful starting point to discuss subsequent developments.

The scope of Article 28

It is now clear that the category of selling arrangements is limited to measures that do not require any modifications not just of the product itself,[11] but also of labelling and packaging.[12] The Court has also made clear to take the factual discrimination test *within* the category of selling arrangements very seriously indeed. Whether indistinctly applicable marketing rules impede access to the market for imported products usually involves detailed factual analysis that the Court gladly leaves to national courts to sort out.[13] On occasion however, the Court applies the test by itself. In *Gourmet*, for example, it held that a Swedish total ban on alcohol advertising was a discriminatory burden on imported beverages:

Even without its being necessary to carry out a precise analysis of the facts characteristic of the Swedish situation, which it is for the national court to do, the Court is able to conclude that, in the case of products like alcoholic beverages, the consumption of which is linked to traditional social practices and to local habits and customs, the prohibition of all advertising directed at consumers in the form of advertisements in the press, on the radio and on television, the direct mailing of unsolicited material or the placing of posters on the public highway is liable to impede access to the market by products from other Member States more than it impedes access by domestic products, with which consumers are instantly more familiar.[14]

Especially in light of the Court's previous case law on public interest derogations, it seems that *Keck* was largely a symbolic exercise in

---

Everling (Baden-Baden: Nomos, 1995), p. 803; and Everling, 'Der Einfluß des EG-Rechts auf das nationale Wettbewerbsrecht im Bereich des Täuschungsschutzes', (1994) 21 *Zeitschrift für das gesamte Lebensmittelrecht* 221. With cooler heads, Weatherill, 'After *Keck*: Some Thoughts On How To Clarify the Clarification', (1996) 33 CMLR 885; Picod, 'La Nouvelle Approche de la Cour de Justice en Matière d'Entraves aux Échanges', (1998) 34 RTDE 169; and Enchelmaier, 'The Awkward Selling of a Good Idea, or a Traditionalist Interpretation of Keck', (2003) 22 YEL 249.

[11] Case C-390/99 *Canal Satélite Digital* [2002] ECR I-607, para. 30.
[12] Case C-33/97 *Colim* [1999] ECR I-3175, para. 37; Case C-12/00 *Commission* v. *Spain* [2003] ECR I-459, para. 76; and Case C-416/00 *Tommaso Morellato* [2003] ECR I-9343, para. 29.
[13] See e.g. Joined Cases C-34, 35 and 36/95 *De Agostini* [1997] ECR I-3843, paras. 43–4; and Case C-441/04 *A-Punkt Schmuckhandels* [2006] ECR I-2093, para. 25.
[14] Case C-405/98 *Gourmet International* [2001] ECR I-1795, para. 21.

procedural subsidiarity without much material impact.[15] For example, just before the Court decided *Keck*, in *LPO*,[16] it held that a registered optician's monopoly on the sale of contact lenses was caught by Article 28 EC, but justified by the public health exception of Article 30 EC. In *Commission* v. *Greece*,[17] decided not much later, but after *Keck*, a pharmacist's monopoly on the sale of infant milk formula was held to fall outside the scope of Article 28 EC altogether under the 'selling arrangements' rule. In both cases, the privileges concerned were embedded as national legal norms. If these cases had been decided in reverse order, it is likely that the opticians would have benefited from the *Keck* rule, as the pharmacists from Article 30 EC. A similar argument could be made concerning the earlier 'Sunday trading' cases, where the Court found that trade barriers prima facie caught by Article 28 EC could escape if they were objectively justifiable on grounds acceptable under Community law and proportionate to the objective concerned.[18] In *Punto Casa* and *Tankstation 't Heuske*, similar cases have since been held not to fall within Article 28 under *Keck*.[19]

It is important to note that the *Keck* rule on selling arrangements is not alone in limiting the scope of Article 28 EC along de minimis lines. In the 1995 *Peralta* Case, citing *Meng*, the Court first found that Italian State measures prohibiting the discharge into the sea of harmful substances fell outside of the scope of *effet utile* as there was no link with concerted action.[20] Moreover, in line with earlier case law in *Krantz*, the legislation concerned was not precluded by Article 28 EC either, because it:

makes no distinction according to the origin of the substances transported, its purpose is not to regulate trade in goods with other Member States and the restrictive effects which it might have on the free movement of goods are too

---

[15] See for recent assessments Kovar, '*Dassonville, Keck* et les Autres: de la Mesure Avant Toute Chose', (2006) 42 RTDE 213; and Oliver and Enchelmaier, 'Free Movement of Goods: Recent Developments in the Case law', (2007) 44 CMLR 649.

[16] Case C-271/92 *LPO* [1993] ECR I-2899.

[17] Case C-391/92 *Commission* v. *Greece* [1995] ECR I-1621.

[18] Cf. Joined Cases 60 and 61/84 *Cinéthéque* v. *Fédération Nationale des Cinémas Français* [1985] ECR 2605 (encouraging film production); Case 145/88 *Torfaen Borrough Council* v. *B&Q* [1989] ECR 3851; and Joined Cases C-306/88, 304/90 and 169/91 *Stoke on Trent City Council* v. *B&Q* [1992] ECR I-6457 (Sunday trading).

[19] Cf. Joined Cases C-69 ad 258/93 *Punto Casa* v. *Sindaco del Commune di Capena* [1994] ECR I-2355; and Joined Cases C-401 and 402/92 *Tankstation 't Heuske* [1994] ECR I-2199.

[20] Case C-379/92 *Criminal proceedings against Matteo Peralta* [1994] ECR I-3453, para. 22.

uncertain and indirect for the obligation which it lays down to be regarded as being of a nature to hinder trade between Member States.[21]

Not limited to selling arrangements nor linked to a public interest exception, this reasoning in so far as it is effects based (although it takes the purpose of the contested measure into account) comes closer to an appreciability test more familiar from the competition rules. For example, in *Pavlov*, the Court held that the decision by the medical specialists (classified as undertakings) to set up a pension fund entrusted with the management of supplementary pensions fell below the de minimis threshold of appreciability.[22] In the free movement sphere, more clearly so than where the competition rules and therefore in principle restrictions of competition between private parties are concerned, the application of appreciability/de minimis rules can be seen as a manifestation of subsidiarity.

The scope of the other freedoms

Despite being invited to do so repeatedly, the Court has consistently refused to extend whatever retreat *Keck* was thought to imply for the scope of the other fundamental freedoms. On the contrary, the Court has advanced the vertical scope of all three other free movement regimes beyond direct discrimination to include indistinctly applicable measures in so far as these render the exercise of the freedoms 'less attractive'.[23] In *Bosman*, it denied any relevance of *Keck* to UEFA's transfer

---

[21] Case C-379/92 *Peralta* [1994] ECR I-3453, para. 24. This reasoning was first cited in Case C-69/88 *Krantz* v. *Ontvanger der Directe Belastingen* [1990] ECR I-583, para. 11. Cf. Case C-339/89 *Alsthom Atlantique* v. *Sulzer* [1991] ECR I-107, paras. 14–15; and Case C-93/92 *Motorradcenter* v. *Pelin Baskiciogullari* [1993] ECR I-5009, para. 12. It was repeated subsequently in Case C-96/94 *Centro Servizi Spediporto* [1995] ECR I-2883, para. 41; Case C-266/96 *Corsica Ferries France* [1998] ECR I-3949, para. 31; and Case C-12/97 *ED Srl* v. *Italo Fenocchio* [1999] ECR I-3845, para. 11.

[22] Cases C-180/98 to 184/98 *Pavel Pavlov et al.* v. *Stichting Pensioenfonds Medische Specialisten* (*Pavlov*) [2000] ECR I-6451. Formally speaking there is a double test in competition cases, i.e. appreciable effect on competition and (appreciable) effect on trade.

[23] See Case C-55/94 *Gebhard* [1995] ECR I-4565, para. 37. On the convergence of the four freedoms, see Jarass, 'A Unified Approach to the Fundamental Freedoms' in M. Andenas and W.-H. Roth (eds.), *Services and Free Movement in EU Law* (Oxford University Press 2002), p. 141; Kingreen, 'Grundfreiheiten' in A. von Bogdandy (ed.), *Europäisches Verfassungsrecht* (Berlin: Springer, 2003), p. 631; and Oliver and Roth, 'The Internal Market and the Four Freedoms', (2004) 41 CMLR 407. Cf. J. Snell, *Goods and Services in EC Law – A Study of the Relationship between the Freedoms* (Oxford University Press, 2002); and C. Barnard, *The Substantive Law of the EU – The Four Freedoms* (Oxford University Press, 2004). On convergence of the freedoms with competition law, see Waelbroeck, 'Les Rapports Entre les Règles sur la Libre Circulation des Marchandises

rules in the context of the free movement of workers since, even if
the rules at issue applied in similar fashion within as between Member
States, 'they still directly affect players' access to the employment
market in other Member States'.[24] In the regime on services, the Court
pointedly advanced the vertical scope of Article 49 EC just one year
after *Keck*. In classic teleological fashion, it announced:

In the perspective of a single market and in order to permit the realisation of
its objectives, that freedom likewise precludes the application of any national
legislation which has the effect of making the provision of services between
Member States more difficult than the provision of services purely within one
Member State.[25]

In *Alpine Investments*, another year on, it then declined to apply *Keck* by
analogy to the Dutch prohibition of 'cold calling', a non-discriminatory
restriction on the provision of financial services that had no bearing on
the service itself. The Court held, however, that since the rule affected
offers made to potential recipients in other Member States, it 'directly'
affected access to foreign services markets.[26] For the free movement
of capital, finally, the Court held in the British *Golden Share* case that,
even though the restrictions at issue applied without distinction to
residents and non-residents, they still 'affect the position of a person
acquiring a shareholding as such and are thus liable to deter investors
from other Member States from making such investments and, consequently, affect access to the market'.[27] Arguably in defiance of the spirit
of *Keck*, the Court thus proceeded to strike down the golden shares and
in the process elevated the free movement of capital to the status of
protecting investment per se, rather than a norm aimed at prohibiting

---

et les Règles de Concurrence Applicables aux Entreprises dans la CEE' in F. Capotorti
et al. (eds.), *Du droit International au Droit de l'Intégration* (Baden-Baden: Nomos, 1987),
p. 781; and Mortelmans, 'Towards Convergence in the Application of the Rules on
Free Movement and on Competition', (2001) 38 CMLR 613.

[24] Case C-415/93 *Jean-Marc Bosman* [1995] ECR I-4921, para. 103. In Case C-190/98 *Volker
Graf* [2000] ECR I-493, paras. 24–5, the Court devised a *Peralta*-type of de minimis rule
based on Case C-69/88 *Krantz* [1990] ECR I-583 to legislation that denied workers
terminating their employment contract (in order to take up another job abroad, for
example) the same compensation as they would receive upon being terminated by
their employers. This did not affect access to the market, so the Court, since the
entitlement was based on 'an event too uncertain and indirect a possibility for
legislation to be capable of being regarded as liable to hinder freedom of movement of
workers'.

[25] Case C-381/93 *Commission v. France* [1994] ECR I-5145, para. 17.

[26] Case C-483/93 *Alpine Investments* [1995] ECR I-1141, para. 38.

[27] Case C-98/01 *Commission v. UK* [2003] ECR I-4641, para. 47.

unequal treatment of foreign investors. In the Case of KPN and TPG, the Court held Dutch golden shares to constitute restrictions in the meaning of Article 56(1) EC largely because of the possibility of the Dutch authorities asserting themselves in important business decisions to defend the 'general interest'. This potentiality alone, according to the Court, could undermine the economic interests of the companies involved, discourage direct or portfolio investment and depress the stock market value of the normal shares.[28]

The European social model and the fundamental freedoms

The new-found assertiveness under the other freedoms have come to the fore over the last decade in a string of case law dealing with sensitive sectors previously thought to be shielded not just by notions of State sovereignty, but by Community law itself. In 1998, the Court decided two cases dealing with national systems of medical insurance. In carefully choreographed convergence, the Court held in *Decker*, for goods, and *Kohll*, for services, that even if Community law does not detract from the powers of the Member States to organise their social security systems,[29] 'the Member States must nevertheless comply with Community law when exercising those powers', and that the fact that such rules fall within the sphere of social security cannot exclude the application of Articles 28 and 49, respectively, of the Treaty.[30] Consequently, the Court held the refusal to reimburse the cost of a pair of spectacles bought in another Member State and dental treatment received in another Member State to constitute unjustified obstacles to the free movement of goods and the freedom to provide services.[31] More recently, the Court extended the principle to industrial relations

---

[28] Joined Cases C-282 and 283/04 *Commission* v. *Netherlands* [2006] ECR I-9141, paras. 26–31. The Court declined to apply the *Krantz/Peralta/Graf* rule, Case C-69/88 *Krantz* [1990] ECR I-583, of effects that are 'too indirect and too uncertain'.

[29] Case C-120/95 *Nicolas Decker* [1998] ECR I-1831; and Case C-158/96 *Raymond Kohll* [1998] ECR I-1931. In support of the principle that, in the absence of harmonisation, the Member States remain free to organise their social security systems, the Court cited Case 238/82 *Duphar et al.* v. *Netherlands* [1984] ECR 523; Case C-70/95 *Sodemare* [1997] ECR I-3395; Case 110/79 *Coonan* v. *Insurance Officer* [1980] ECR 1445; Case C-349/87 *Paraschi* [1991] ECR I-4501; and Joined Cases C-4 and 5/95 *Stöber* [1997] ECR I-511.

[30] Case C-120/95 *Decker* [1998] ECR I-1831, paras. 23 and 25; Case C-158/96 *Kohll* [1998] ECR I-1931, paras. 19 and 2, respectively.

[31] The decisions in *Kohll* and *Decker* have sparked off a copious amount of case law. See e.g. Case C-157/99 *Smits and Peerbooms* [2001] ECR I-5473; Case C-385/99 *Müller-Fauré* [2003] ECR I-4509; Case C-56/01 *Inizan* [2003] ECR I-12403; Case C-372/04 *Yvonne Watts* [2006] ECR I-4325; and Case C-444/05 *Aikaterina Stamatelaki* [2007] ECR I-3185. For a

in *Laval* and *Viking*. Acknowledging the explicit exclusion from Community competence of the right of association, the right to strike and the right to impose lock-outs in Article 137(5) EC, the Court repeated that, even if the Member States are still free to lay down the conditions governing the existence and the exercise of the rights in question, 'the fact remains that, when exercising those rights, the Member States must nevertheless comply with Community law'.[32] Collective action is, hence, not excluded from the scope of Articles 43 and 49 EC, respectively.

Although the issues are rather more obscure, a similar dynamic can be detected in the *Golden Share* cases in the sphere of industrial policy.[33] In different ways, to varying degrees and even for different reasons, the Member States under attack from the Commission separated control from share ownership regarding certain undertakings, reserving to themselves rather more power of decision than their shareholdings would normally warrant. Especially in case of recently privatised or 'strategic' undertakings, exercising control by way of golden shares could seem a reasonable and market-friendly alternative to public ownership. Advocate General Ruiz-Jarabo Colomer accordingly argued forcefully – and repeatedly – that the Member States involved should benefit from a 'presumption of legality' bestowed by Article 295 EC, which provides that the Treaty 'shall in no way prejudice the rules in Member States governing the system of ownership'.[34] The Court would have none of it, and dismissed the argument in Delphic fashion by holding that the provision 'does not have the effect of exempting the Member States' systems of property ownership from the fundamental rules of the Treaty'.[35]

---

recent assessment, see Hervey, 'The Current Legal Framework on the Right to Seek Healthcare Abroad in the European Union', (2007) 9 CYELS 261.

[32] Case C-438/05 *ITF* v. *Viking* [2007] ECR I-10779, para. 40; and Case C-341/05 *Laval* [2007] ECR I-11767, para. 87.

[33] Case C-367/98 *Commission* v. *Portugal* [2002] ECR I-4731; Case C-483/99 *Commission* v. *France* [2002] ECR I-4781; Case C-503/99 *Commission* v. *Belgium* [2002] ECR I-4809; Case C-463/00 *Commission* v. *Spain* [2003] ECR I-4581; Case C-98/01 *Commission* v. *UK* [2003] ECR I-4641; Case C-174/04 *Commission* v. *Italy* [2005] ECR I-4933; Joined Cases C-282 and 283/04 *Commission* v. *Netherlands* [2006] ECR I-9141; and C-112/05 *Commission* v. *Germany* [2007] ECR I-8995.

[34] See his Opinions in Cases C-367/98 *Commission* v. *Portugal* [2002] ECR I-4731, paras. 39 et seq.; Cases C-463/00 and 98/01 *Commission* v. *Spain and UK* [2003] ECR I-4581, paras. 37 et seq.; and Case C-112/05 *Commission* v. *Germany*, judgment of 23 October 2007, nyr, paras. 47 et seq.

[35] Case C-367/98 *Commission* v. *Portugal* [2002] ECR I-4731, para. 48; and Case C-483/99 *Commision* v. *France* [2002] ECR I-4781, para. 44, under reference to Case C-302/97 *Konle*

The justification regime under the fundamental freedoms

As was the case in *Cassis de Dijon*, the Court has coupled the vertical extension of the scope of the fundamental freedoms with the development of a regime of generic public interest justifications, increasingly rolled into one 'rule of reason' under which the values of market integration are balanced against other values. The *Gebhard* formula is the classic statement:

National measures liable to hinder or make less attractive the exercise of fundamental freedoms guaranteed by the Treaty must fulfill four conditions: they must be applied in a non-discriminatory manner; they must be justified by imperative requirements in the general interest; they must be suitable for securing the attainment of the objective they pursue; and they must not go beyond what is necessary in order to attain it.[36]

The category of imperative public interest requirements is wide open, with the Court being decidedly liberal in allowing Member States the

[1999] ECR I-3099, para. 38 (prior authorisation requirement for the acquisition of land), where the Court, in turn, refers, less convincingly, to Case 182/83 *Fearon* v. *Irish Land Commission* [1984] ECR 3677, para. 7 (regulatory takings of land).

[36] Case C-55/94 *Gebhard* [1995] ECR I-4565, para. 37. The Court does still insist, on occasion, that the new categories of generic public interest derogations can only be invoked to justify indistinctly applicable measures, and that, accordingly, distinctly applicable measures can only find refuge in the express derogations. For goods, see e.g. Case 113/80 *Commission* v. *Ireland* [1981] ECR 1625, paras. 8 and 11; and Joined Cases C-321 to 324/94 *Jacques Pistre* [1997] ECR I-2343, para. 52 ('domestic legislation which is discriminatory in character may be justified only on one of the grounds listed in Article 30'). For services, see Case 352/85 *Bond van Adverteerders* [1988] ECR 2085, para. 32 (holding that 'national rules which are not applicable to services without distinction as regards their origin and which are therefore discriminatory are compatible with Community law only if they can be brought within the scope of an express derogation'); and, more recently and much less plausibly, Case C-224/97 *Erich Ciola* [1999] ECR I-2517, para. 16. This is, however, increasingly untenable both conceptually and in view of the many instances where the Court belies itself, *Kohll* and *Decker* themselves being prominent examples. More serious than the latter cases, where the Court allowed for the possibility of overriding reasons relating to the general interest justifying discriminatory measures, is the reverse. In the French *Golden Share* case, the Court classified the French alleged need to safeguard the petroleum supply under the rubric of 'public security' and applied the narrow test developed for that ground in Case C-54/99 *Eglise de Scientologie* [2000] ECR I-1335 ('public security may be relied on only if there is a genuine and sufficiently serious threat to a fundamental interest of society'). Case C-483/99 *Commission* v. *France* [2002] ECR I-4781, para. 48. The restrictions at issue did not, however, by the Court's own admission, give rise to unequal treatment of foreign investors, something the restrictions in *Scientologie* assuredly did do.

power of definition: it only insists on these interests being 'non-economic'.[37] Apart from the evergreens of public health and consumer protection, the Court has thus allowed everything from environmental protection to road safety to such awkwardly formulated public goods as 'the need to avoid deterioration of the conditions under which goods are delivered at short distance in relatively isolated areas'.[38] It is under the proportionality test that the Court has shown its vigour. Muddled though the concept is in Community law,[39] in this context it usually implies both a means-ends rationality test[40] and least restrictive means test.[41]

Even if the *Cassis de Dijon* framework for public interest justifications remains valid, there is, arguably, a discernable shift taking place in the context of its application. The regime of 'mandatory requirements' was developed, by and large, as a way of smoothing out regulatory differences between Member States in the process of market integration. Indeed, together with the principle of mutual recognition and the pre-emption doctrine, the 'mandatory requirements' formed the blueprint for the Single Market program. The principle of mutual recognition limited the need for harmonisation to those – exceptional – areas where Member States could still legitimately restrict imports, either on grounds of Article 30 EC or on grounds of the 'mandatory requirements'. As restrictions to Article 28 EC, these areas automatically fell within the competence of the Community legislator under Article 95

---

[37] Case C-120/95 *Decker* [1998] ECR I-1831, para. 39; and Case C-158/96 *Kohll* [1998] ECR I-1931, para. 41. The Services Directive limits available justifications for restrictions to public policy, public security, public health and the protection of the environment. Article 16, Directive 206/123/EC of the European Parliament and of the Council on services in the internal market, OJ 2006 L376/36. Given the amount of sectors and services that Articles 1 and 2 exclude from the scope of the Directive, however, the effect of this limitation is rather less dramatic than it may seem.

[38] Case C-254/98 *TK Heimdienst* [2000] ECR I-151, para. 34. See further e.g. Case 302/86 *Commission* v. *Denmark* [1988] ECR 4607 (environmental protection); and Case C-55/93 *Van Schaik* [1994] ECR I-4837, para. 19 (road safety).

[39] See, generally, De Búrca, 'The Principle of Proportionality and its Application in EC Law', (1993) 13 YEL 105; N. Emiliou, *The Principle of Proportionality in European Law: A Comparative Study* (Deventer: Kluwer, 1996); Van Gerven, 'The Effect of Proportionality on the Actions of the Member States of the European Community: National Viewpoints from Continental Europe' in E. Ellis (ed.), *The Principle of Proportionality in the Laws of Europe* (Oxford: Hart, 1999), p. 42; T. Tridimas, *The General Principles of EC Law* (Oxford University Press, 1999), pp. 124 et seq.; and P. Craig, *EU Administrative Law* (Oxford University Press, 2006), pp. 655 et seq.

[40] See e.g. Case C-217/99 *Commission* v. *Belgium* [2000] ECR I-10251.

[41] The classic here is still Case 104/75 *De Peijper* [1976] ECR 613.

EC. Once legislation was in place, the doctrine of pre-emption prevented Member States from invoking justifications for unilateral restrictions.[42]

It could be argued that the 'rule of reason' is now operating more and more in the context of market regulation rather than one of market integration, evolving into a test to balance market disciplines with the very political, civil and social foundations of welfare States. In the process, the balancing act is less a matter of finding ways for Community law to accommodate particular national regulatory idio-syncracies and more a matter of working out the relationships between different values embodied and protected within the province of Com-munity law. This is perhaps clearest in *Schmidberger* and *Omega*, where restrictions on free movement were alleged to be necessary for the pro-tection of fundamental rights. The Court went to great lengths to avoid framing this as a clash between the economic logic of the internal market on the one hand and that of nationally protected human rights on the other. In *Omega*, dealing with a German ban on a particularly gruesome laser game justified on the need to protect human dignity, it held:

[T]he Community legal order undeniably strives to ensure respect for human dignity as a general principle of law. There can be therefore no doubt that the objective of protecting human dignity is compatible with Community law, it being immaterial in that regard that, in Germany, the principle of respect for human dignity has a particular status as an independent fundamental right.

Since both the Community and the Member States are required to respect fundamental rights, the protection of those rights is a legitimate interest which, in principle, justifies a restriction of the obligations imposed by Community law, even under a fundamental freedom guaranteed by the Treaty such as the freedom to provide services.[43]

---

[42] This, in truth, applies only where the Community has fully occupied the field. 'Once rules on the common organisation of the market may be regarded as forming a complete system', exceptions are no longer justified, 'unless Community law expressly provides otherwise'. Case 16/83 *Karl Prantl* [1984] ECR 1299, para. 13. On the various forms of harmonisation and the implications for the scope of legitimate exceptions, see Slot, 'Harmonisation', (1996) 21 ELR 378. On pre-emption, see Cross, 'Pre-emption of Member State Law in the European Economic Community: A Framework for Analysis', (1992) 29 CMLR 44. On how it all fits together, see Weiler, 'The Constitution of the Common Market Place: Text and Context in the Evolution of the Free Movement of Goods' in P. Craig and G. de Búrca (eds.), *The Evolution of EU Law* (Oxford University Press, 1999), p. 349; and Weatherill, 'Pre-emption, Harmonisation and the Distribution of Competence to Regulate the Internal Market' in C. Barnard and J. Scott (eds.), *The Law of the Single Market – Unpacking the Premises* (Oxford: Hart, 2002), p. 41.

[43] Case C-36/02 *Omega Spielhallen* [2004] ECR I-9609, paras. 34 and 35. Cf. Case C-112/00 *Schmidberger* [2003] ECR I-5659, para. 74 (goods).

In *Laval*, the Court took this yet a step further, applying the rule of reason in the relationship between different objectives of the Treaty itself. At issue was action by a trade union designed to impede the posting of Latvian workers in the Swedish construction industry on conditions that fell short of the applicable Swedish collective agreement. The Court held:

[I]t must be pointed out that the right to take collective action for the protection of workers of the host State against possible social dumping may constitute an overriding reason of public interest within the meaning of the case law of the Court which, in principle, justifies a restriction of one of the fundamental freedoms guaranteed by the Treaty.

It should be added that, according to Article 3(1)(c) and (j) EC, the activities of the Community are to include not only an 'internal market characterised by the abolition, as between Member States, of obstacles to the free movement of goods, persons, services and capital', but also 'a policy in the social sphere'. Article 2 EC states that the Community is to have as its task, inter alia, the promotion of 'a harmonious, balanced and sustainable development of economic activities' and 'a high level of employment and social protection'.

Since the Community has thus not only an economic but also a social purpose, the rights under the provisions of the EC treaty on the free movements of goods, persons, services and capital must be balanced against the objectives pursued by social policy, which include, as is clear from the first paragraph of Article 136, inter alia, improved living and working conditions, so as to make possible their harmonisation while improvement is being maintained, proper social protection and dialogue between management and labour.[44]

Arguably, *Kohll* and *Decker* should be read in this key as well. Here, the Court disentangled the *general principle* of social security that remains insulated from Community law, from its *operation* by tackling the financial modalities involved. Moreover, even then, cross-subsidies or restraints on trade involved in the latter could have benefited from the exception available for the legitimate public interest of a social character, if it could be established that these restraints were in fact necessary for the social security system to function. The Court stated in *Decker*:

It must be recalled that aims of a purely economic nature cannot justify a barrier to the fundamental principle of the free movement of goods. However, it cannot be excluded that the risk of seriously undermining the financial

---

[44] Case C-341/05 *Laval*, judgment of 18 December 2007, nyr, paras. 103–105.

balance of the social security system may constitute an overriding reason of general interest capable of justifying a barrier of that kind.[45]

Given that the Luxembourg scheme reimbursed according to flat rates for spectacles and tariffs for dental treatment, reimbursing Kohll and Decker was held to have no effect on the financing of the social security scheme in these cases.[46] The link between the regime on public services of Article 86(2) EC and the justification regime under free movement provisions was made even more explicit in the Dutch *Golden Share* case, where the Court held that 'the guarantee of a service of general interest, such as universal post service' may constitute an overriding reason in the general interest. It struck the arrangement down, however, since the special share at issue went beyond 'what is necessary to safeguard the solvency and continuity of the provider of the universal postal service'.[47] The nature of the motivations required here mirrors not just the reasoning used to determine whether cross-subsidies may be acceptable in the context of ensuring the financial stability of a universal service system,[48] but more generally touches upon the interplay between politically protected 'solidarity' and market disciplines in both its material and institutional dimensions.

2.2. State measures and the concept of 'public bodies' under the free movement provisions

The scope of 'State measures' that are caught by the free movement rules is central to this first part of our examination of the redefinition of the public and private spheres in the Court's case law. Although this issue is related to the contentious subject of horizontal direct effect of the free movement provisions – between individuals or private undertakings – we are not primarily concerned with that issue here.[49]

---

[45] Case C-120/95 *Decker* [1998] ECR I-1831, para. 39. Identical phrasing in Case C-158/96 *Kohll* [1998] ECR I-1931, para. 41, with the added reference to Case C-398/95 *SETTG* v. *Ypourgos Ergasias* [1997] ECR I-3091, para. 23.

[46] Case C-120/95 *Decker* [1998] ECR I-1831, para. 40; and Case C-158/96 *Kohll* [1998] ECR I-1931, para. 42.

[47] Joined Cases C-282 and 283/04 *Commission* v. *Netherlands* [2006] ECR I-9141, paras. 38–9.

[48] Case C-320/91 *Procureur du Roi* v. *Paul Corbeau (Corbeau)* [1993] ECR I-2533. Cf. Case C-475/99 *Firma Ambulanz Glöckner* v. *Landkreis Südwestpfalz (Glöckner)* [2001] ECR I-8089; and Case C-280/00 *Altmark Trans et al.* v. *Nahverkehrsgesellschaft Altmark et al. (Altmark Trans)* [2003] ECR I-7747.

[49] On the obligations on private parties arising from the free movement provisions, see below, Chapter 4. The horizontal direct effect of Directives is tenaciously denied by

Instead, we wish to show that the process of rebalancing the horizontal and vertical reach of the free movement rules as described above is identifiable in relation to the definition of 'public bodies'.

The Court has repeatedly been called on to decide whether semi-public or semi-private organisations are capable of taking 'measures having equivalent effect to quantitative restrictions' as prohibited under Article 28 EC. The case law does not suggest that there is any bright line test for this. In a line of cases concerning publicity campaigns for home-grown fruits, it considered that measures taken by both the *Irish Goods Council*[50] and the *Apple and Pear Development Council*[51] were to be attributed to the State. Rather than defining precise criteria to justify this attribution, the Court's approach was simply to accumulate as much evidence as possible concerning the State's involvement in the creation, financing and regulation of the organisations in question.[52]

Thus, in *Buy Irish*, it emphasised the State's involvement in the Council's finances and the appointments of its directors. In *Apple and Pear Development Council*, it was persuaded by the fact that the Council was set up by the government and financed by a levy imposed on growers.[53] In *Hennen Olie*, on the interpretation of Article 29, the Court emphasised the control exercised by the State by means of binding instructions to the body in question.[54] Advocate General Capotorti in the *Buy Irish* case offered the following definition:

> The Irish Goods Council has the same appearance as a public institution with auxiliary functions in the economic field; more precisely, it constitutes an instrument which: (a) pursues objectives which correspond or are parallel to certain objectives of the Irish Government, with regard to the development of national economic activity, and (b) may be used or influenced by that government.

It repeated this approach in a number of subsequent cases dealing with pharmacists' associations. In 1989, the Court held the *Royal*

---

the Court of Justice. See Case C-91/92 *Faccini Dori* [1994] ECR I-3325, para. 20; and recently e.g. Joined Cases C-397 to 403/01 *Pfeiffer* [2004] ECR I-8835, para. 108. That stance, however, is increasingly untenable in the light of cases such as Case C-44/98 *Unilever* [2000] ECR I-7535 and especially Case C-144/04 *Mangold* [2005] ECR I-9981.

[50] Case 249/81 *Commission* v. *Ireland ('Buy Irish')* [1982] ECR 4005.

[51] Case 222/82 *Apple and Pear Development Council* [1983] ECR 4083.

[52] Case 249/81 *Commission* v. *Ireland ('Buy Irish')* [1982] ECR 4005.

[53] Case 222/82 *Apple and Pear Development Council* [1983] ECR 4083. See also Case C-325/00 *Commission* v. *Germany* [2002] ECR I-9977.

[54] Case C-302/88 *Hennen Olie* [1990] ECR I-4625.

Pharmaceutical Society of Great Britain, a private law body, capable of taking 'measures' in the sense of Article 28 EC, especially by virtue of its broad disciplinary powers.[55] The Court mentioned the following elements:

– the obligatory nature of enrolment in its register;
– its adoption of rules as regards ethics; and especially
– the disciplinary committee within the Society set up by legislation, whose decisions are open for appeal at the High Court.[56]

The *Landesapothekerkammer* in *Hünermund*[57] did not enjoy such disciplinary powers. Yet, without much ado, the Court considered this compensated for by the association's status of public law body.[58]

Hence, in this 'functional' approach, the Court treats self-regulatory associations in exactly the same way as authorities of a 'public' nature in a formal sense: if such associations meet a considerable but not strictly defined threshold of public involvement, this brings them within the scope of Article 28 EC. However, this is Article 28 after *Keck*: therefore, restrictions that appear caught by a widening of the scope of the Article 28 EC prohibition where private organisations are considered to meet the standards for 'public' bodies may escape that prohibition for lack of relevance to Community trade – as concerning mere 'selling arrangements' under the *Keck* formula. Consequently, the net effect in *Hünermund* was that the advertising restrictions imposed by the *Landesapothekerkammer* were not caught.

Again, the Court's horizontal advance is partially compensated by a vertical retreat – and vice versa. As noted in the previous section, on balance, this involves a rationalisation of its case law along the cross-cutting lines of functionalism and subsidiarity.

---

[55] Joined Cases 266 and 267/87 *Royal Pharmaceutical Society of Great Britain* [1989] ECR 1295.
[56] With a different emphasis Advocate General Darmon described the society as 'a professional body having as its task the provision of a public service which it performs in the public interest', endowed with powers 'characteristic of the rights and powers derogating from the generally applicable rules of law' (para. 14 of the Opinion).
[57] Case C-292/92 *Hünermund* [1993] ECR I-6787. Noted by Roth (1994) 31 CMLR 845.
[58] Case C-292/92 *Hünermund* [1993] ECR I-6787, para. 14. Advocate General Tesauro construed the case thus (para. 5): 'The important thing is that the measure in dispute does form part of the rules of conduct adopted by a professional organisation, but by virtue of authority conferred by the State and subject to control by the State. It cannot therefore be denied that the provision in cause is a State measure, particularly when it is considered that the Landesapothekerkammer, unlike the Royal Pharmaceutical Society, is a body governed by public law.'

2.3. 'Public bodies' under secondary law

As was seen above, the case law on the qualification of 'public bodies' shows a functional approach that is limited at the level of its material consequences by the vertical realignment introduced in *Keck* and *Peralta*. It is logical that in the absence of political guidance at Community level by means of secondary legislation, the Court will tend to opt for judicial restraint. Conversely, it should be more sceptical of State measures where secondary law is in place – following harmonisation by European Parliament and Council, or Commission implementation measures.

In line with these expectations, when interpreting secondary Community rules, the Court sees even less reason to pay respect to national legal qualifications than under the free movement provisions themselves, and tends to employ an even bolder functional approach. This leads to a broader application of Community concepts of, for example, public bodies, and hence to broadening of the scope of the relevant norms of EU law. As before, the functional and subsidiarity variables remain in play, but the former is strengthened, whereas the latter is weakened. This relative change can be understood as a logical consequence of the process of 'pre-emption': once the Member States have approved a Community legal framework, not only the scope for exceptions to common norms is reduced, but also that for national legal classifications which may affect the application of both the harmonised rules and the exceptions thereto.

Pre-emption thus adds a third variable alongside *functionalism* and *subsidiarity* – a dynamic one – that explains the Court's approach.

The importance of pre-emption and its effect on the Court's approach comes out strongly, first, in the general case law on direct effect of Directives. Second, it is confirmed in the Court's case law concerning Directives that are intended to address the distinction between the public and private spheres by introducing specific categories such as in the areas of supervision of the transparency of the financial relations between certain categories of undertakings and the Member States, and that of public procurement.

It should be noted that an apparent paradox arises when, sometimes even in the same context, the Court opts for a formal approach. It appears, however, that this can be explained in full consistency with 'pre-emption' by the degree of specificity of the Community legislation concerned and the degree to which the Community has actually occupied the relevant field. Referring to 'pre-emption' thus is another way of saying that, as the degrees and types of harmonisation vary widely, the applicable judicial standard is likewise differentiated, and as the degree of harmonisation increases, so the judicial standard becomes tighter.

(i) The Court's case law on the direct effect of Directives increases the reach of Directives both horizontally and vertically. When ruling on the direct effect of Directives, the Court uses a concept of public bodies that is much broader than that found in the interpretation of free movement itself. It explicitly disregards national legal designations in order 'to prevent the State from taking advantage of its own failure to comply with Community law'.[59] With that rationale, in its 1990 *Foster* judgment, the Court held that:

a body, whatever its legal form, which has been made responsible, pursuant to a measure adopted by the State, for providing a public service under the control of the State and has for that purpose special powers beyond those which result from the normal rules applicable in relations between individuals is included in any event among the bodies against which the provisions of a Directive capable of having direct effect may be relied upon.[60]

Moreover, where secondary rules specifically aim to elaborate Community law norms for the public sphere, the Court does not attribute any importance to the capacity wherein the State is acting, be it as employer or as public authority.[61] That distinction lies at the heart of the controversy surrounding Commission Directive 80/723 ('the Transparency Directive').[62] This Directive imposes on Member States

---

[59] Case 152/84 *Marshall* [1986] ECR 723, para. 49

[60] Case C-188/89 *Foster* [1990] ECR I-3313, para. 20, noted by Szyszcak (1990) 27 CMLR 859. Cf. Case 8/81 *Becker* [1982] ECR 53; Case 152/84 *Marshall* [1986] ECR 723; Case 222/84 *Johnston* [1986] ECR 1651; Case 103/88 *Costanzo* [1989] ECR 1839; Case C-297/03 *Sozialhilfeverband Rohrbach* [2005] ECR I-4305; and Case C-6/05 *Medipac-Kazantzidis* [2007] ECR I-4557. Cf. Curtin, 'The Province of Government: Delimiting the Direct Effect of Directives in the Common Law Context', (1990) 15 ELR 195; and S. Prechal, *Directives in EC Law*, 2nd edn, (Oxford University Press, 2005). In some circumstances, the Court does actually allow private parties to enforce their rights enshrined in Directives against private sector actors. Cf. Case 177/88 *Dekker* v. *VJV* [1990] ECR I-3941; and Case C-180/95 *Nils Draehmpaehl* v. *Urania* [1997] ECR I-2195, noted by Ward (1998) 23 ELR 65.

[61] Case 152/84 *Marshall* [1986] ECR 723, para. 49.

[62] Commission Directive 80/723/EEC on the Transparency of Financial Relations between Member States and Public Undertakings (Transparency Directive) OJ 1980 L195/35, as amended by Directive 85/413/EEC OJ 1985 L229/20. (Following further amendments, the Transparency Directive was codified as Commission Directive 2006/111/EC of 16 November 2006 on the Transparency of Financial Relations between Member States and Public Undertakings as well as on Financial Transparency within certain Undertakings, OJ 2006 L318/17.) The original Transparency Directive, based on

accounting standards for public undertakings, which 'should enable a clear distinction to be made between the role of the State as public authority and its role as proprietor'.[63]

In *Commission v. Italy*, the Court held this distinction 'to flow from the recognition of the fact that the State may act either by exercising public powers or by carrying on economic activities of an industrial or commercial nature by offering goods and services on the market'.[64] The case turned on the concept of 'public undertaking', which the Transparency Directive had defined as 'any undertaking over which the public authorities may exercise directly or indirectly a dominant influence by virtue of their ownership of it, their financial participation therein, or the rules which govern it'.[65] The 'undertaking' in question, however – the *Amministrazione Autonoma dei Monopoli di Stato*, selling cigarettes – did not have legal personality separate from that of the State and should therefore, according to Italy, have been regarded as a 'public authority'. The Court rejected that argument using standard 'functional' (or indeed teleological) reasoning, holding that the purpose of the Directive as well as the unity and effectiveness of Community provisions would be called into question by recourse to domestic law.[66]

Article 90(3) EC, was challenged unsuccessfully in Joined Cases 188 to 190/80 *France, Italy and United Kingdom v. Commission* [1982] ECR 2545. A Commission Communication (1991 OJ C273/2) based on the Directive imposing additional obligations as regards annual financial reports was annulled by the Court in Case C-325/91 *France v. Commission* [1993] I-3283. Noted by Papaioannou (1994) 31 CMLR 155.

[63] Sixth recital of the preamble of the Directive.

[64] Case 118/85 *Commission v. Italy (Transparency Directive)* [1987] ECR 2599, para. 7.

[65] Article 2 of the Directive defines 'public authorities' as 'the State and regional or local undertakings', and, beyond the definition of 'public undertaking' mentioned above, presumes to be 'public' those undertakings in relation to which the public authorities: (i) hold the major part of capital; or (ii) control the majority of votes attached to shares; or (iii) can appoint more than half of the members in the supervisory or managerial bodies. In Joined Cases 188 to 190/80, *France, Italy and United Kingdom v. Commission* [1982] ECR 2545, para. 24, the Court explicitly restricted the definition of 'public undertaking' to the Directive, adding that 'it should be emphasised that the object of those provisions is not to define that concept as it appears in Article 90 of the Treaty'. Evidently, this has not deterred commentators from doing just that. See e.g. D. G. Goyder, *EC Competition Law* 4th edn (Oxford: Oxford University Press, 1993), p. 484; Hochbaum, 'Artikel 90' in Von der Groeben, Thiesing and Ehlermann, *Kommentar zum EWG-Vertrag*, 4th edn (Baden-Baden: Nomos, 1991), Vol. 2, pp. 2540 ff.

[66] Case 118/85 *Transparency Directive* [1987] ECR 2599, paras. 10 and 11. Advocate General Mischo's Opinion is a most eloquent plea for the 'functional' approach, complete with comparative analysis of State involvement in commercial activities. See in particular [1987] ECR 2616–7.

The Court has applied this functional approach perhaps most explicitly in the field of public procurement.[67] Given the relatively large presence of the State in European markets, the public procurement rules were always going to be crucial in establishing the internal market.[68] They serve both to battle discrimination and to prevent distortions of competition,[69] or, as the Court puts it, to avoid the possibility that public bodies 'may choose to be guided by considerations other than economic ones'.[70] The evolution over the years of the relevant legislation has been marked by a constant effort to 'keep up' with processes of privatisation, liberalisation and changing patterns of the relationship between the public sphere and market mechanisms generally.[71] This has been clearest in the inclusion of the so-called utilities sectors from the early 1990s, but has also been reflected in the gradually increased personal scope of the Directives covering the more traditional sectors. The original definition of 'contracting authorities' was simply 'State, local and regional authorities', complemented by an annexed list of other public bodies.[72] The Court has consistently been bullish in casting its net as wide as possible. In the 1988 case of *Beentjes*, it had to deal with a 'local land consolidation committee'. Although this body lacked legal personality, its tasks and the composition of its

---

[67] This section is based on Schepel, 'The Public/Private Divide in Secondary Community Law: a Footnote to the European Economic Constitution', (2006) 8 CYELS 259, pp. 260–6.

[68] See generally C. Bovis, *EC Public Procurement – Case Law and Regulation* (Oxford University Press, 2006). Calling for a major overhaul of the whole edifice, judged to be disproportionately burdensome, Arrowsmith, 'The EC Public Procurement Directives, National Procurement Policies and Better Governance: The Case for a New Approach', (2002) 27 ELR 3.

[69] It should be noted that the Court has held that procurement contracts which are not covered by Community legislation must nevertheless comply with the principles of equal treatment and non-discrimination arising from the Treaty which it interprets as imposing an obligation of transparency. See Case C-275/98 *Unitron Scandinavia* [1999] ECR I-8291, para. 31; and Case C-324/98 *Teleaustria* [2000] ECR I-10745, paras. 60 and 61.

[70] See e.g. Case C-380/98 *University of Cambridge* [2000] ECR I-8035, para. 17. It should be noted that the Court has allowed environmental considerations to be taken into account within the definition of the 'economically most advantageous tender'. See Case C-513/99 *Concordia Bus Finland Oy Ab* [2000] ECR I-7213.

[71] See e.g. Bovis, 'Financing Services of General Interest, Public Procurement and State Aids: The Delineation between Market Forces and Protection in the European Common Market', [2005] *Journal of Business Law* 1. Emblematic is further the Commission's effort to come to terms with so-called PPTs. See its Green Paper on public-private partnerships and Community law on public contracts and concessions, COM(2004) 327.

[72] See Article 1(b), Public Works Directive 71/305, OJ 1971 L85/5.

membership were set out by law, and its members were appointed by the provincial authorities. When considering whether this committee was subject to the requirements of the original Public Works Directive, the Court stated unambiguously:

For the purposes of this provision, the term 'the State' must be interpreted in functional terms. The aim of the directive, which is to ensure the effective attainment of freedom of establishment and freedom to provide services in respect of public works contracts, would be jeopardised if the provisions of the directive were held to be inapplicable solely because a public works contract is awarded by a body which, although it was set up to carry out tasks entrusted to it by legislation, is not formally part of the State administration.[73]

In the current definition, then, the concept of 'contracting authorities' includes the State, regional and local authorities and 'bodies governed by public law'. The latter concept, in turn, is defined as follows:

A 'body governed by public law' means any body:

- established for the specific purpose of meeting needs in the general interest, not having an industrial or commercial character;
- having legal personality; and
- financed, for the most part, by the State, regional or local authorities, or other bodies governed by public law; or subject to management supervision by those bodies; or having an administrative, managerial or supervisory board, more than half of whose members are appointed by the State, regional or local authorities, or by other bodies governed by public law.[74]

---

[73] Case 31/87 *Beentjes* [1988] ECR 4635, para. 11.

[74] Article 1(a), Directive 2004/17/EC of the European Parliament coordinating the procurement procedures of entities operating in the water, energy, transport and postal services sectors, OJ 2004 L143/1 and Article 1(9), Directive 2004/18/EC of the European Parliament and of the Council on the coordination of procedures for the award of public works contracts, public supply contracts and public service contracts, OJ 2004 L134/114. This recent overhaul keeps these provisions stable as compared to the previous legislation. Cf. Council Directive 93/36/EEC coordinating procedures for the award of public supply contracts, (1993) OJ L199/1; Council Directive 93/37/EEC concerning the coordination of procedures for the award of public works contracts, OJ 1993 L199/54; Council Directive 93/38/EEC coordinating the procurement procedures of entities operating in the water, energy, transport and telecommunications sectors, OJ 1993 L199/84. See generally e.g. Marchegiani, 'La nozione di Stato inteso in senso funzionale nelle direttive comunitarie in materia di appalti pubblici e sua rilevanza nel contesto generale del diritto comunitario', (2002) 12 *Rivista Italiana di Diritto Pubblico Comunitario* 1233; and Munanza, 'Privatised Services and the Concept of "Bodies Governed by Public Law" in EC Directives on Public Procurement', (2003) 28 ELR 273.

The Court's general approach to the term is a textbook example of functionalist teleology.[75] Given the public procurement regime's double objective of introducing competition and transparency, the Court holds that the concept must be interpreted 'as having a broad meaning'.[76] That implies a functional approach with utter disregard for national legal classifications: the effectiveness of the directives 'would not be fully preserved if the application of those directives to an entity could be excluded solely on the basis of the fact that, under the national law to which it is subject, its legal form and rules which govern it fall within the scope of private law'.[77] It is hence settled case law that the concept of a 'body governed by public law' is to be defined exclusively on the basis of the three cumulative conditions spelled out in the legislation.[78]

The Court reads public financing, management or supervision as alternative indicators for an overarching condition of 'close dependence' on the State.[79] As regards State expenditures, it held in that light in *University of Cambridge*:

Whilst the way in which a particular body is financed may reveal whether it is closely dependent on another contracting authority, it is clear that that criterion is not an absolute one. Not all payments made by a contracting authority have the effect of creating or reinforcing a specific relationship of subordination or dependency. Only payments which go to finance or support the activities of the body concerned without any specific consideration therefore may be described as 'public financing'.[80]

The full force of this reasoning became clear in the public broadcasting case of *Bayerischer Rundfunk*. Emphasising the need for a functional interpretation, the Court held that the method of financing public broadcasting by levying fees on everyone in possession of a television

---

[75] Explicitly so. See Case C-237/99 *Commission* v. *France* [2001] I-939, para. 43.

[76] Case 373/00 *Adolf Truley* [2003] ECR I-1931, para. 43.

[77] Case C-214/00 *Commission* v. *Spain* [2003] ECR I-4667, para. 56. Cf. Case C-84/03 *Commission* v. *Spain* [2005] ECR I-139.

[78] Case C-214/00 *Commission* v. *Spain* [2003] ECR I-4667, para. 56. That the three elements must be seen as cumulative conditions was established in Case C-44/96 *Mannesmann Anlagenbau* [1998] ECR I-73, para. 21.

[79] Case C-44/96 *Mannesmann Anlagenbau* [1998] ECR I-73, para. 20; and Case C-380/98 *University of Cambridge* [2000] ECR I-8035, para. 20.

[80] Case C-380/98 *University of Cambridge* [2000] ECR I-8035, para. 23. On the issues involved regarding university education, see Lane, 'Public Procurement, Public Bodies and the General Interest: Perspectives from Higher Education', (2005) 11 ELJ 487.

set, regardless of whether they actually use the services provided, was clearly 'not for consideration'.[81] It further attributed the payments of fees to the public authorities, since the system was 'brought into being by the State, is guaranteed by the State and is secured by methods of charging and collection which fall within public authority powers'.[82] A finding of 'public financing', moreover, obliterates the need for any further analysis:

[T]he very existence of the public broadcasting bodies depends on the State. The criterion of the dependence of those bodies on the State is thereby satisfied, and it is not necessary for the public authorities to have any real influence on the various decisions of the bodies in question on the awarding of contracts.[83]

The condition of having been established 'to meet needs in the general interest' seems on the face of it to rest on a fairly familiar distinction between bodies pursuing activities in the 'public interest' and bodies engaged in economic activities. The Court has emphasised that the concept is one of Community law which must be given 'an autonomous and uniform interpretation throughout the Community'.[84] Its best attempt at a definition, however, is simply this:

needs in the general interest, not having an industrial or commercial character, are generally needs which are satisfied otherwise than by the availability of goods and services in the market place and which, for reasons associated with the general interest, the State chooses to provide itself or over which it wishes to retain a decisive influence.[85]

This may seem to imply that public bodies escape the reach of the public procurement regime as soon as they operate in market conditions in competition with private undertakings. The Court will have none of that, however. Indeed, 'the absence of competition is not a condition necessarily to be taken into account in defining a body governed by public law', and the concept of needs in the general interest

---

[81] Case C-337/06 *Bayerischer Rundfunk* [2007] ECR I-11173, para. 45.
[82] Case C-337/06 *Bayerischer Rundfunk* [2007] ECR I-11173, para. 48.
[83] Case C-337/06 *Bayerischer Rundfunk* [2007] ECR I-11173, para. 55.
[84] Case C-373/00 *Adolf Truley* [2003] ECR I-1931, paras. 36 and 40.
[85] See e.g. Case C-360/96 *BFI Holding* [1998] ECR I-6821, paras. 50–1; and Case C-18/01 *Korhonen* [2003] ECR I-5321, para. 47. The Court has also held that explicit legal or statutory conferrals of 'public interest functions are unnecessary'. It suffices that the responsibility for general interest needs can be established 'objectively'. Case C-470/99 *Universale-Bau* [2002] ECR I-11617, para. 62.

'does not exclude needs which are or can be satisfied by private under-takings as well'.[86] It offered two reasons for this in *BFI Holding*:

The fact that there is competition is not sufficient to exclude the possibility that a body financed or controlled by the State, territorial authorities or other bodies governed by public law may choose to be guided by other than economic considerations. Thus, for example, such a body might consider it appropriate to incur financial losses in order to follow a particular purchasing policy of the body upon which it is dependent.

Moreover, since it is hard to imagine any activities that could not in any circumstances be carried out by private undertakings, the requirement that there should be no private undertakings capable of meeting the needs for which the body in question was set up would be liable to render meaningless the term 'body governed by public law'.[87]

Thus equipped, the Court held it to be 'undeniable' that the removal and treatment of household refuse meets a need in the general interest, even if many local authorities choose to entrust this task to private undertakings.[88] In *Adolf Truley*, it found that it 'cannot be disputed' that funeral undertakers may be regarded as meeting needs in the general interest for reasons of public hygiene and health.[89] In *Mannesmann*, it determined that the Austrian State printing office was established to meet a need in the general interest since it was required to produce documents which 'are linked to public order and the institutional operation of the State and require guaranteed supply and production conditions which ensure that standards of confidentiality and security are observed'.[90] It is only in fairly extreme cases, for example, the organisation of trade fairs in *Agorà*,[91] that the Court has managed to exercise some self-restraint in its newly found enthusiasm for the 'general interest'. The problem with this line of reasoning is, of course, that it threatens to introduce more distortions of competition than it eliminates: why should a 'public' garbage collection undertaking be subjected to all the procedural burdens and associated cost of public

---

[86] Case C-360/96 *BFI Holding* [1998] ECR I-6821, paras. 47 and 53.
[87] Case C-360/96 *BFI Holding* [1998] ECR I-6821, paras. 43–4.
[88] Case C-360/96 *BFI Holding* [1998] ECR I-6821, para. 52. It substantiated its finding by reasoning that 'the degree of satisfaction of that need considered necessary for reasons of public health and environmental protection cannot be achieved by using disposal services wholly or partly available to private individuals from private economic operators'.
[89] Case 373/00 *Adolf Truley* [2003] ECR I-1931, paras. 51–3.
[90] Case C-44/96 *Mannesmann Anlagenbau* [1998] ECR I-73, para. 24.
[91] Joined Cases C-23 and 260/99 *Agorà* [2001] ECR I-3605.

contracting when its 'private' competitor doing the exact same job in the neighbouring town is not? The concern is compounded by the 'infection theory' introduced in *Mannesmann*: there, the Court held it to be of no consequence that the 'official' printing business constituted only a small part of the State printing office's activities. Once a body is found to be 'established for the purpose of meeting needs in the general interest', it is subject to the public procurement regime even for the award of contracts that have nothing to do with the public interest task.[92] The stance is, moreover, at odds with the technique employed in the utilities directives: there, the principle has been well established that certain activities, not entities, are subject to the public procurement rules unless and until the activity 'is directly exposed to competition on markets to which access is not restricted'.[93]

In fairness, the Court realised that it could not keep the market question out of the equation already in *BFI Holding* itself. There it remarked that the existence of competition is 'not entirely irrelevant', as it 'may be indicative of the absence of a need in the general interest'.[94] As such, it is to be taken into account as one of 'all the factual and legal circumstances' that courts are to assess in determining whether or not a body is established in the general interest.[95] In *Korhonen*, it seemed to go further than that:

If the body operates in normal market conditions, aims to make a profit, and bears the losses associated with the exercise of its activity, it is unlikely that the needs it aims to meet are not of an industrial or commercial nature. In such a case, the application of the Community directives relating to the coordination of procedures for the award of public contracts would not be necessary, moreover, because a body acting for profit and itself bearing the

---

[92] Case C-44/96 *Mannesmann Anlagenbau* [1998] ECR I-73, para. 26. The principle is defended on the basis of the requirement of legal certainty 'which requires a Community rule to be clear and its application foreseeable by all those concerned'. *Ibid.*, para. 34. It should be noted that infection has a fairly simple remedy: the Court held the commercial subsidiary of the State printing office, in which the latter held a majority ownership and to which it could transfer proceeds from its own public service tasks, to be outside the scope of the Directive. The infection theory itself has been confirmed, e.g. in Case C-373/00 *Adolf Truley* [2003] ECR I-1931, para. 56; and Case C-18/01 *Korhonen* [2003] ECR I-5321, para. 58.

[93] Article 30(1), Directive 2004/17/EC of the European Parliament coordinating the procurement procedures of entities operating in the water, energy, transport and postal services sectors, OJ 2004 L143/1. See further below.

[94] Case C-360/96 *BFI Holding* [1998] ECR I-6821, paras. 48–9.

[95] See Case C-373/00 *Adolf Truley* [2003] ECR I-1931, para. 66.

risks associated with its activity will not normally be involved in an award procedure on conditions which are not economically justified.[96]

The upshot seems to be, then, that the Court mistrusts the motives behind decision-making in 'semi-public' commercial enterprises to such an extent that it will only release bodies from obligations under the public procurement rules when they are fully exposed to the harsh realities of the market: no public financing, no fall-back provisions or public cushions in case of failure. Only in case the entity is fully responsible for, and is to bear the consequences of, economically unsound decisions will the body not be considered to be established 'in the general interest'.

It is from this angle, of the Court's mistrust of messy combinations of political and economic considerations and desire for clarity, that the *Teckal* line of reasoning may be understood. In that case, the Court introduced an exception to the steadfast rule that a public contract is deemed to exist whenever a contracting authority enters into an agreement with a person which is legally distinct from it, even when that other person itself is a contracting authority. That rule, according to the Court, does not apply:

where the authority exercises over the person concerned a control which is similar to that which it exercises over its own departments and, at the same time, that person carries out the essential part of its activities with the controlling authority or authorities.[97]

The Court thus extends the treatment it logically confers on hierarchically controlled and politically supervised 'in-house' administrative, technical and other resources to the situation where, formally, there are two distinct entities involved. In subsequent cases, it has emphasised that the new rule, since it constitutes a derogation from the general rules of Community law, is to be interpreted strictly with the burden of proof on the entity seeking to rely on the 'existence of exceptional circumstances'.[98] The first criterion, then, requires 'a power of decisive influence over both strategic objectives and significant decisions'.[99] The second condition is only met 'if that undertaking's

---

[96] Case C-18/01 *Korhonen* [2003] ECR I-5321, para. 51.
[97] Case C-107/98 *Teckal* v. *Comune di Viano* [1999] ECR-8121, para. 50.
[98] Case C-26/03 *Stadt Halle* [2005] ECR I-1, para. 46; Case C-485/03 *Parking Blixen* [2005] ECR I-8612, para. 64.
[99] Case C-485/03 *Parking Blixen* [2005] ECR I-8612, para. 65.

activities are devoted principally to that authority and any other activities are only of marginal significance'.[100]

The rationale for the exception is not entirely clear. In *Teckal* itself, the Court seemed to be focused on the mere absence of independence of decision-making.[101] That would seem to indicate not much more than a rather fastidious contract lawyer's concern with a meeting of wills. In later cases, however, the Court's efforts to limit the exception tended to coincide with a substantive concern of separating market mechanisms from the 'public interest'. In *Stadt Halle*, it was asked to apply the *Teckal* exception to a contract between a local authority and a semi-public company of which both the local authority concerned and private undertakings were shareholders. The Court declined:

[T]he relationship between a public authority which is a contracting authority and its own departments is governed by considerations and requirements proper to the pursuit of objectives in the public interest. Any private capital investment in an undertaking, on the other hand, follows considerations proper to private interests and pursues objectives of a different kind.[102]

In *Cabotermo*, it spelled out explicitly that the conditions laid down in *Teckal* 'are aimed precisely at preventing distortions of competition'.[103] The implication of this is, of course, that the Court has decided to leave strictly hierarchical 'political' decision-making alone. In the context of the second of *Teckal*'s conditions, the Court said so:

The requirement that the person in question must carry out the essential part of its activities with the controlling authority or authorities is aimed precisely at ensuring that Directive 93/36 remains applicable in the event that an undertaking controlled by one or more authorities is active in the market and therefore likely to be in competition with other undertakings.

An undertaking is not necessarily deprived of freedom of action merely because the decisions concerning it are controlled by the controlling authority, if it can still carry out a large part of its economic activities with other operators.

It is still necessary that that undertaking's services be intended mostly for that authority alone. Within such limits, it appears justified that that undertaking is not subject to the restrictions of Directive 93/36, since they are in

---

[100] Case C-340/04 *Cabotermo* [2006] ECR I-4137, para. 63.

[101] Case C-107/98 *Teckal* v. *Comune di Viano* [1999] ECR-8121, para. 51.

[102] Case C-26/03 *Stadt Halle* [2005] ECR I-1, para. 50. Cf. Case C-29/04 *Commission* v. *Austria* [2005] ECR I-9705; Case C-410/04 *ANAV* v. *Comune di Bari* [2006] ECR I-3303; and Case C-220/05 *Jean Auroux* v. *Commune de Roanne* [2007] ECR I-385, para. 64.

[103] Case C-340/04 *Cabotermo* [2006] ECR I-4137, para. 59.

place to preserve a state of competition which, in that case, no longer has any *raison d'être*.[104]

(ii) As the Court applies the EU law criteria that determine the public/private distinction in secondary legislation strictly, this can lead to divergence between economic sectors, and even within such sectors, depending on the degree of harmonisation attained in respect of specific areas of regulation. This is illustrated cogently by two cases that involve the same telecommunications operator under different Directives, respectively concerning utilities procurement and open network provision.

Within the procurement field, the utilities sector is especially problematic. This is reflected by the fact that – after originally being excluded – the water, energy, transport and telecommunications sectors were caught by the public procurement rules, by means of a series of specific Directives only from 1990 onwards.[105] Because the public and private ownership patterns for utilities vary especially widely between Member States, the Utilities Directives have given rise to novel techniques of distinguishing between the public and private spheres. More remarkably, as competition is progressively introduced in the sectors involved, a threshold can be reached at which the procurement rules cease to apply – even on a case-by-case basis. For example, Utilities Directive 90/531 (updated and replaced in 2004) explicitly excluded certain activities, and not certain bodies, from its scope. The Directive did not only apply to public bodies and public undertakings, but also to undertakings that enjoy special and exclusive rights (for example by means of authorisations, licences or concessions). Yet, it took account of telecommunications liberalisation: the procurement rules applied to telecommunications operators that enjoy special and exclusive rights except as regards those services 'where other entities are free to offer the same services in the same geographical area and under substantially

---

[104] Case C-340/04 *Cabotermo* [2006] ECR I-4137, paras. 60–2. Cf. Case C-220/06 *Asociación Profesional e Empresas de Reparto y Manipulado de Correspondencia* [2007] ECR I-12175, paras. 61–2.

[105] Directive 90/531, OJ 1990 L297/1, since amended by Directive 93/38, OJ 1993 L199/84, and Directive 92/13/EEC, OJ 1991 L76/14, coordinating the applicable laws and procedures (Remedies Directive), and replaced by Directive 2004/17/EC of the European Parliament and of the Council of 31 March 2004 coordinating the procurement procedures of entities operating in the water, energy, transport and postal services sectors, OJ 2004 L134/1. Cf. S. Arrowsmith, *The Law of Public and Utilities Procurement*, 2nd rev. edn (London: Sweet & Maxwell, 2005); and Brown, 'The Extension of the Community Public Procurement Rules to Utilities', (1993) 30 CMLR 721.

the same conditions' – i.e. that 'are directly exposed to competitive forces in markets to which entry is unrestricted'.[106]

Article 8(1) of Directive 90/531 stated that the operators themselves were to notify the services to which the exception applied: a remarkable instance of auto-certification in regard to the applicability of EU legal rules, along the lines of the attestation procedure elaborated in Procurement Remedies Directive 92/13. The Court in its 1996 judgment in *The Queen* v. *Treasury ex parte BT* confirmed that it was indeed for the operators concerned, and not for the Member States, to determine which services were to be excluded.[107] The Court objected, however, to the claim of British Telecom (BT) that all of its activities were to be excluded for sectors where competition was guaranteed as a matter of legal principle. Instead, the Court held that whether or not activities were subject to competitive forces should to be verified as a matter of '*law and of fact*', involving all relevant characteristics of the relevant services, including price factors, the existence of alternative services, and the market position of the entity concerned – for example, dominance.[108] This apparent functionalism was actually firmly grounded in the secondary Community rules in force.

In the final analysis, it was the Commission, exercising its supervisory duties under Article 8(2) of Directive 90/531, that established the definitive list of entities caught by the public procurement regime. It verified the notification by such entities of services as being subject to effective competition: both the liability for undertakings and the Commission enforcement regime are elaborated in Remedies Directive 92/13. Hence, in this case, the interplay between undertakings and the Community level overruled national attempts at classification, with effective competition as the key variable.[109] This demonstrates clearly how harmonisation can pre-empt national legal classifications, even to the extent that certain determinations can be made by the undertakings involved, within the framework of Community sanctions and a

---

[106] Directive 90/531, OJ 1990 L297/1, since amended by Directive 93/38, OJ 1993 L199/84, Article 8(1); and thirteenth recital of the preamble.

[107] Case C-239/93 *The Queen* v. *Treasury ex parte British Telecom* [1996] ECR I-1631, para. 25.

[108] Case C-239/93 *The Queen* v. *Treasury ex parte British Telecom* [1996] ECR I-1631, para. 34.

[109] See generally on the extension of the public procurement regime to the private sphere, Arrowsmith, 'Deregulation of Utilities Procurement in the Changing Economy: Towards a Principled Approach?', (1997) 7 ECLR 420; and Rittner, 'Abschied vom "Öffentliche Auftragswesen" für private Unternehmen', (1997) 8 EuZW 161. Cf. Skouris, 'Der Einfluß des europäischen Gemeinschaftsrecht auf die Unterscheidung zwischen Privatrecht und Öffentlichem Recht', [1998] EuR 111.

harmonised liability regime. It also shows the point where functionalism, formalism and pre-emption converge.

Another 1996 case involving the same telecommunications operator, *Queen* v. *Secretary of State for Trade and Industry ex parte BT*,[110] demonstrates how different Directives introduce different parallel regimes for the same legal subject. More importantly, it highlights the second order problems involved in formulating secondary rules that take into account differences in speed and scope of liberalisation and privatisation between the Member States, and how such rules consequently require adjustment over time. In this Case, BT objected to the decision of the United Kingdom to impose on it supply obligations based on the Open Network Framework Directive 90/387 and the Leased Lines Directive 92/44.[111] At the time of the Court's ruling, these Directives still applied to 'public or private bodies to which a Member State grants special or exclusive rights for the provision of a public telecommunications network'.[112] Clearly, as these Directives were intended for the setting of limited liberalisation then common to most Member States, they jarred with the fully liberalised regime in the UK, where such rights had formally long since been abolished.

Advocate General Tesauro accepted the consequences of this and suggested extending the application of the Directive 92/44, written for *de iure* monopolies, to *de facto* dominant positions.[113] In doing this, the Advocate General anticipated a then pending amendment to the Leased Lines Directive,[114] which replaced the reference to special and exclusive rights, and made the obligations involved contingent on the existence of 'significant market power' (a form of dominance), to be determined by a combination of their market position and other factors (e.g. turnover, access to financial resources and experience).[115] After the

---

[110] Case 302/94 *The Queen* v. *Secratary of State for Trade and Industry ex parte British Telecom* [1996] ECR I-6417.

[111] Directive 90/387/EEC on the establishment of the internal market for telecommunications services through the implementation of open network provision (OJ 1990 L192/1), and Directive 92/44/EEC on the application of open network provision to leased lines (OJ 1992 L165/27).

[112] Article 2(1) of the Open networks Directive, above n. 80.

[113] Case 302/94 *The Queen* v. *Secretary of State for Trade and Industry ex parte British Telecom* [1996] ECR I-6417, para. 44 of the Opinion.

[114] Case 302/94 *The Queen* v. *Secratary of State for Trade and Industry ex parte British Telecom* [1996] ECR I-6417, paras. 24 and 46 of the Opinion.

[115] Eventually, in 2002, a new regime of access regulation squarely based on dominance according to general competition law principles succeeded the ONP regime. Cf. C. Koenig, A. Bartosch and J.-D. Braun (eds.), *EC Competition and Telecommunications*

amendment came into force in 1997, asymmetrical regulation was imposed on all undertakings, public or private, and regardless of their statute, which met such criteria: the dividing line between the public and private spheres was not blurred, but removed, in order to resolve bottleneck issues in the transition to competitive markets.

Given broad support in the Council for the impending reform anticipated by the Advocate General's Opinion, *Queen* v. *Secretary of State for Trade and Industry ex parte BT* presented the Court with an opportunity to make a fundamental point along functionalist lines, anticipating preemption. Instead, the Court reached for a technicality and held that remaining licences to operate *international* lines were sufficient to constitute 'exclusive and special rights' and bring British Telecom into the fold – although international operations were largely irrelevant to BT's obligations under Directive 92/44.[116] Hence, the impending scope for pre-emption was not anticipated, but instead a formal rule was applied, albeit itself one of secondary Community law. This illustrates clearly how the Court's functionalism, in its interaction with pre-emption, remains within the bounds of formal distinctions of Community law – thereby creating a margin of freedom for national policies that are consistent with the distinctions in force. This suggests that the resultant tensions are seen as second order problems, to be resolved, primarily, by political means.

2.4. Public authority exceptions to free movement under primary law

The designation of measures as 'public' in nature, and hence subject to free movement, has its corollary in the limits drawn to the scope of public authority exceptions to those rules. Once measures are caught by the rule, it must be established whether they are released by the exception, which may call for a further evaluation of the nature of public authority. Here, we are not concerned by *public interest* exceptions generally, for example, not the exceptions to the right to subject free movement of workers respectively the freedom of establishment to

---

Law: A Practitioner's Guide (New York: Aspen, 2002); P. Nihoul and P. Rodford, *EU Electronic Communications Law – Competition and Regulation in the European Telecommunications Market* (Oxford University Press, 2004); Coates and Sauter, 'Communications (Telecoms, Media and Internet)' in J. Faull and A. Nikpay (eds.), *The EC Law of Competition*, 2nd edn (Oxford University Press, 2007), p. 1475.

[116] Case 302/94 *The Queen* v. *Secretary of State for Trade and Industry ex parte British Telecom* [1996] ECR I-6417, paras. 44–5.

restrictions based on public policy, public security and public health (as found in Articles 39(3) and 46(1) EC), but with those that specifically refer to *public authority*, for example, related to employment in the public service as found in Article 39(4) EC and the exercise of public authority in Article 45 EC. The question of whether these exceptions apply has given rise to fundamental considerations concerning the nature of public authority. In examining this, the Court employs a teleological approach, geared to guaranteeing strict proportionality and the unity of EU law.

(i) *The Court aims to limit the scope of the exceptions 'to what is strictly necessary for safeguarding the interests which that provision allows the Member States to protect'.* For example, in a controversial line of case law, the Court has stripped both the 'public service' exception to the free movement of workers and the 'exercise of official authority' exception to the freedom of establishment to their core. Article 39(4) EC excludes from the ambit of the free movement of workers in Article 39(1) EC 'employment in the public service'. As the Court pointed out:

as a derogation from the fundamental principle that workers in the Community should enjoy freedom of movement and not suffer discrimination, Article 39(4) EC must be construed in such a way as to limit its scope to what is strictly necessary for safeguarding the interests which that provision allows the Member States to protect.[117]

Consequently, according to the case law of the Court, Article 39(4) EC covers those posts which involve direct or indirect participation in the exercise of powers conferred by public law and duties designed to safeguard the general interests of the State or of other public authorities and which thus presume on the part of those occupying them the existence of a special relationship of allegiance to the State and reciprocity of rights and duties which form the foundation of the bond of nationality. On the other hand, the Article 39(4) EC exception does not cover posts which, whilst coming under the State or other organisations governed by public law, still do not involve any association with tasks belonging to the public service properly so called.[118]

---

[117] Case 225/85 *Commission v. Italy* [1987] ECR 2625, para. 7.
[118] Case C-473/93 *Commission v. Luxembourg* [1997] ECR I-3207, para. 2; Case 149/79 *Commission v. Belgium* [1980] ECR 3881; paras. 10 and 11. Cf. Case 307/84 *Commission v. France* [1986] ECR 1725; Case 66/85 *Deborah Lawrie-Blum v. Land Baden-Württemberg (Lawrie-Blum)* [1986] ECR 2121; Case 225/85 *Commission v. Italy* [1987] ECR 2625; Case 33/88 *Allué and Coonan* [1989] ECR 1591; Case C-41/91 *Bleis* [1991] ECR I-5627; Case

(ii) By employing a functional approach, the Court aims to ensure that the scope of application is the same throughout the Community. Hence, the Court has consistently discarded national legal definitions of concepts such as 'public service' or 'civil servant' in the context of Article 39(4) which states that free movement of workers does not apply 'to employment in the public service'. Already in its 1974 judgment in *Sotgiu*, it explained that 'these legal designations can be varied at the whim of national legislatures and cannot therefore provide a criterion for interpretation appropriate to the requirements of Community law'.[119] In *Lawrie Blum* it stated:

To make the application of Article 39(4) EC dependent on the legal nature of the relationship between the employee and the administration would enable the Member States to determine at will the posts covered by the exception laid down in that provision.[120]

In *Reyners*, in the context of Article 45 EC, it held that the 'Community character' of the provision must be taken into account 'in order to avoid the effectiveness of the Treaty being defeated by unilateral provisions of Member States'.[121] When, in *Commission v. Luxembourg*, Luxembourg argued for an 'institutional' interpretation, the Court dismissed this plea, stating: 'the criterion for determining whether Article 39(4) EC is applicable must be functional and must take account of the tasks and responsibilities inherent in the post'.[122]

In this case, as in *Commission v. Belgium*[123] and *Commission v. Greece*,[124] the Court thus objected to Member States subjecting whole sectors to a nationality condition.[125] This is, however, functionalism *within* the

---

C-173/94 *Commission v. Belgium* [1997] ECR I-3265; and Case C-290/94 *Commission v. Greece* [1997] ECR I-3285. Comment in e.g. O'Keeffe, 'Judicial Interpretation of the Public Service Exception to the Free Movement of Workers' in D. Curtin and D. O'Keeffe (eds.), *Constitutional Adjudication in European Community and National Law* (Dublin: Butterworths, 1992), p. 89; and Badura, 'Die Organisations- und Personalhoheit des Mitgliedstaates in der europäischen Union' in O. Due, M. Lutter and J. Schwarze (eds.), *Festschrift für Ulrich Everling* (Baden-Baden: Nomos, 1995), p. 33.

[119] Case 152/73 *Sotgiu* [1974] ECR 153, para. 5.
[120] Case 66/85 *Lawrie-Blum* [1986] ECR 2121, para. 26.
[121] Case 2/74 *Reyners* [1974] ECR 631, para. 50.
[122] In Case C-473/93 *Commission v. Luxembourg* [1997] ECR I-3207, para. 27.
[123] Case C-173/94 *Commission v. Belgium* [1997] ECR I-3265.
[124] Case C-290/94 *Commission v. Greece* [1997] ECR I-3285.
[125] Similarly in relation to Article 39(3) and 46 EC (then 48(3) and 56), the Court stated: 'The right of Member States to restrict freedom of movement for persons on grounds of public policy, public security or public health is not intended to exclude economic

institutional category of State-employed workers. In *Commission* v. *Italy*, a case concerning the status of private security guards, the Court excluded from the scope of Article 39(4) EC 'employment by a private natural or legal person, whatever the duties of the employee'.[126] However, in subsequent cases involving merchant navy officers in Spain and masters of fishing vessels in Germany, the Court returned to its functionalist approach:

The fact that masters are employed by a private natural or legal person is not, as such, sufficient to exclude the application of Article 39(4) EC since it is established that, in order to perform the public functions which are delegated to them, masters act as representatives of public authority, at the service of the general interests of the flag state.[127]

This functionalism was then limited by a proportionality test, as follows:

However, recourse to the derogation from the freedom of movement of workers provided for by Article 39(4) EC cannot be justified solely on the ground that rights under powers conferred by public law are granted by national law to holders of the posts in question. It is still necessary that such rights are in fact exercised on a regular basis by those holders and do not represent a very minor part of their activities. Indeed, ... the scope of that derogation must be limited to what is strictly necessary for safeguarding the general interests of the Member States concerned, which cannot be imperilled if rights under powers conferred by public law are exercised only sporadically, even exceptionally, by nationals of other Member States.[128]

sectors such as the private security sector from the application of that principle, from the point of view of access to employment, but to allow Member States to refuse access to their territory or residence there to persons whose access or residence would in itself constitute a danger for public policy, public security, or public health.' Case C-114/97 *Commission* v. *Spain* [1998] ECR I-6717, para. 42, with reference, for public health, to Case 131/85 *Gül* [1986] ECR 1573, para. 17.

[126] Case C-283/99 *Commission* v. *Italy* [2001] ECR I-4363, para. 25. In an earlier Spanish case, private security services were found to fall outside the exercise of official authority as they were not 'vested with powers of constraint' as '[M]erely making a contribution to the maintenance of public security, which any individual may be called upon to do, does not constitute exercise of official authority'. Case C-114/97 *Commission* v. *Spain* [1998] ECR I-6717, paras. 35 and 37.

[127] Case C-47/02 *Albert Anker, Klaas Ras and Albertus Snoek* v. *Germany* [2003] ECR I-10447, para. 62; and Case C-405/01 *Colegio de Oficiales de la Marina Merçante Española* v. *Administratión del Estado* [2003] ECR I-10391, para. 43.

[128] Case C-47/02 *Albert Anker, Klaas Ras and Albertus Snoek* v. *Germany* [2003] ECR I-10447, para. 63; and Case C-405/01 *Colegio de Oficiales de la Marina Merçante Española* v. *Administratión del Estado* [2003] ECR I-10391, para. 44.

The Court has taken a similar approach to Article 45 EC, which excludes from the free movement of services and service providers 'activities which are connected, even occasionally, with the exercise of official authority'.[129] Here, the Court has generally focused on the question of whether or not there is the power to take binding decisions,[130] to the exclusion of functions that are 'auxiliary' or 'preparatory' to the 'effective exercise' of official authority such as private inspection bodies.[131]

These two objectives meet in the 'functional' approach adopted by the Court for the construction of 'Community concepts'. This leaves, however, the problem of the actual contents of the Community concept of 'official authority'. Whereas the Court has limited itself to a sober case-by-case approach, its Advocates General have linked public authority under EU law to the national state's monopoly on the legitimate use of force (*Gewaltsmonopol*). The *locus classicus* in Community law is still Advocate General Madras' Opinion in *Reyners*:

Official authority is that which arises from the sovereignty and majesty of the State; for him who exercises it, it implies the power of enjoying the prerogatives outside the general law, privileges of official power and powers of coercion over citizens.

Connexion [sic] with the exercise of this authority can therefore arise only from the State itself, either directly or by delegation to certain persons who may even be unconnected with the public administration.[132]

Then Advocate General Mancini unshelved Montaigne and Hegel in his Opinion in *France* v. *Commission*, in order to arrive at this definition of 'public service':

---

[129] In Case C-465/05 *Commission* v. *Italy* [2007] ECR I-11091, para. 43, the Court made a distinction between 'activities of civil society' and the exercise of official authority.

[130] Cf. Case 2/74 *Reyners* [1974] ECR 631; Case 147/86 *Commission* v. *Greece* [1988] ECR 1637; Case C-306/89 *Commission* v. *Greece* [1991] ECR I-5863; Case C-42/92 *Thijssen* [1993] ECR I-4047; and Case C-272/91 *Commission* v. *Italy* [1994] ECR I-1409. See generally Henssler and Kilian, 'Die Ausübung hoheitlicher Gewalt im Sinne des Art 45 EG', (2005) 40 *Europarecht* 192.

[131] Case C-404/05 *Commission* v. *Germany* [2007] ECR I-10239, para. 38; and Case C-393/05 *Commission* v. *Austria* [2007] ECR I-10195, para. 36. This is linked to the Court's holding that the exception cannot be extended to an entire profession if the activities connected with the exercise of official authority are 'separable' from the professional activity as a whole. Cf. Case C-451/03 *Servizi Ausiliari Dottori Commercialisti* v. *Calafiori* [2006] ECR I-2941, para. 47.

[132] Case 2/74 *Reyners* [1974] ECR 631, paras. 664–5.

Those who occupy it must don full battle dress: in non-metaphorical terms, the duties must involve acts of will which affect private individuals by requiring their obedience or, in the event of disobedience, by compelling them to comply.[133]

Fortunately, these bleak images of institutionalised violence as the portrayal of public authority do not represent the full view of State functions of the European Courts. In the Spanish merchant navy case the Court considered:

first, rights connected to the maintenance of safety and to the exercise of police powers, particularly in case of danger on board, together with, in appropriate cases, powers of investigation, coercion and punishment, which go beyond the requirement merely to contribute to maintaining public safety by which any individual is bound, and secondly, authority in respect of notarial matters and the registration of births, marriages and deaths, which cannot be explained solely by the requirements entailed in commanding the vessel. Such duties constitute participation in the exercise of rights under powers conferred by public law for the purposes of safeguarding the general interests of the flag State.[134]

This indicates that more civil aspects of public authority must also be considered. Closer to the core of the economic sphere, under the competition rules, the Court has found activities as diverse as control and supervision of air space and anti-pollution surveillance functions carried out by a private undertaking which 'by their nature, their aim and the rules to which they are subject are connected with the exercise of powers ... which are typically those of a public authority'[135] to be outside the scope of competition law.

This suggests that a functional understanding is applied: any body exercising public powers, or 'acting as a public authority', regardless of its statute, is not regarded as an undertaking. This is the case, for example, even where public authority functions have been delegated

---

[133] Case 307/84 *Commission* v. *France* [1986] ECR 1725, para. 5 of the Opinion. As examples, Mancini names 'posts which involve the exercise of powers relating to policing, defence of the state, administration of justice and assessment to tax'. See also Mancini, 'The Free Movement of Workers in the Case-Law of the European Court of Justice' in D. Curtin and D. O'Keeffe (eds.), *Constitutional Adjudication in European Community and National Law* (Dublin: Butterworths, 1992), p. 67.

[134] Case C-405/01 *Colegio de Oficiales de la Marina Mercante Española* v. *Administratión del Estado* [2003] ECR I-10391, para. 42; cf. Case C-47/02 *Albert Anker, Klaas Ras and Albertus Snoek* v. *Germany* [2003] ECR I-10447, para. 61.

[135] Thus, in Case C-364/92 *SAT-Fluggesellschaft* [1994] ECR I-43, para. 30. Cf. Case C-343/95 *Diego Calì & Figli* v. *SEPG* [1996] ECR I-1547, para. 23.

to a purely private enterprise.[136] Conversely, but likewise reflecting a functional approach, public authorities or public law bodies themselves are protected only in so far as they are 'acting in their capacity as public authorities'. This indicates that the Court is willing to distinguish between activities that may be closely related as a matter of national law.[137] Before moving on to competition law, we will first examine the scope of public authority exceptions to free movement under secondary law.

2.5. Public authority exceptions to free movement under secondary law

As was observed earlier, the Court is prepared to apply definitions of public bodies in Community secondary law in a functional manner, where this is necessary to ensure their effective application across the legal systems of the different Member States – in particular when ruling on direct effect. Nevertheless, where possible, it sticks to a formal approach – in particular where the language of the Directives involved is clear. It likewise refuses to anticipate pre-emption, taking in its stride the fact that this may lead to discrepancies in the treatment of the same organisation between various Directives. It is therefore difficult to predict whether predictability or effectiveness is likely to carry the balance in a particular case.

Its approach to public authority exceptions under secondary law is more clear-cut. Here, the emphasis is primarily on the general rule that exceptions are interpreted in a restrictive manner: hence, the most stringent interpretation is likely to be applied, even where this could mean relying on designations of national law.

(i) The Court is willing to use a formal approach based on national legal distinctions when applying secondary law exceptions, in particular where this has a restrictive effect.[138] The Sixth VAT Directive defines as a 'taxable person'

---

[136] Case C-343/95 *Diego Calì & Figli v. SEPG* [1996] ECR I-1547, para. 23.
[137] Case 30/87 *Corinne Bodson v. SA Pompes Funèbres des Régions Libérées (Bodson)* [1988] ECR 2479, para. 18. Here, funeral services' concessions granted by communes acting as public authorities were not regarded as agreements between undertakings as the local authorities were carrying out an administrative, not an economic, activity.
[138] The following section is based on Schepel, 'The Public/Private Divide in Secondary Community law: a Footnote to the European Economic Constitution', (2006) 8 CYELS 259, pp. 267–271.

any person who carries out an economic activity, 'whatever the purpose or results of that activity'. Economic activities, in turn, are defined as 'all activities of producers, traders and persons supplying services' and 'all activities of the professions'.[139] The Directive then proceeds to exempt certain 'public' activities from VAT duties. Article 4(5) reads as follows:

> States, regional and local governments and other bodies governed by public law shall not be considered taxable persons in respect of the activities or transactions in which they engage as public authorities, even when they collect dues, fees, contributions or payments in connection with these activities.
>
> However, when they engage in such activities or transactions, they shall be considered taxable persons in respect of these activities or transactions where treatment as non-taxable persons would lead to significant distortions of competition.

The third subparagraph then refers to Annex D for a list of activities in relation to which these bodies are 'in any case' to be treated as taxable persons. That list includes activities such as telecommunications, the supply of water, gas and electricity, port and airport services, and passenger transport. The fourth subparagraph refers to Article 13 for a list of activities of these bodies that Member States may consider 'activities in which they engage as public authorities'. The list for 'certain activities in the public interest' includes services supplied 'by the public postal services', medical care and services 'closely linked to welfare and social security work' or 'closely linked to the protection of children' by bodies governed by public law or by 'other organisations recognised as charitable by the Member State concerned'.

One solution would be to concentrate on the juxtaposition of 'economic activities' and activities engaged in as public authorities, in much the same vein as occurs under the competition rules when defining an 'undertaking'. The Netherlands argued as much in a case dealing with the activities of notaries and bailiffs, but was rebuked decisively. The term 'economic activities', the Court held, has a wide scope and is objective and neutral in nature. Hence, 'the fact that the activities of notaries and bailiffs consist of the performance of duties which are conferred and regulated by law in the public interest is

---

[139] Article 4(1) and (2), Sixth Council Directive 77/388/EEC on the harmonisation of the laws of the Member States relating to turnover taxes – Common system of value added tax: uniform basis of assessment, OJ 1977 L145/1, last amended by Council Directive 2005/92/EC, OJ 2005 L345/19.

irrelevant'.[140] The public authority exceptions, then, will have to be carved out under Article 4(5).

The Court has taken a radical stance under the first subparagraph of that provision. It is now settled case law that the two elements must be understood as cumulative conditions: the body concerned must be a body governed by public law and the activity at issue must be carried out by such a body acting as a public authority.[141] The most obvious consequence of this is to exclude from the scope of the exemption all activities carried out by private parties, regardless of whether they consist in the performance of acts falling 'within the prerogative of the public authority'.[142] The Court seems to take for granted that this is to the detriment of both the uniform application of Community law and the uniform collection of the Community's own resources, as was made spectacularly clear in the 2000 toll road cases: for no better reason than the formal legal status of the respective relevant bodies, toll collection in France and Greece is now exempt from VAT, whereas it is not in the United Kingdom and Ireland.[143]

The next question is how acting 'as a public authority' qualifies the activities of public law bodies. Here, the Court is even more rigidly institutionalist. In *Carpaneto Piacentino*, it held:

An analysis of the first subparagraph of Article 4(5) in the light of the scheme of the directive shows that it is the way in which the activities are carried out that determines the scope of the treatment of public bodies as non-taxable persons. In so far as that provision makes such treatment of bodies governed by public law conditional upon their acting 'as public authorities', it excludes therefrom activities engaged in by them not as bodies governed by public law but as persons subject to private law. Consequently, the only criterion making it possible to distinguish between those two categories of activity is the legal regime applicable to them under national law.[144]

The Court has later refined the public/private law distinction to activities 'under the special legal regime applicable to them' as opposed to

---

[140] Case 235/85 *Commission v. Netherlands* [1987] ECR 1471, para. 10.

[141] Case 235/85 *Commission v. Netherlands* [1987] ECR 1471, para. 21.

[142] Case 235/85 *Commission v. Netherlands* [1987] ECR 1471, para. 21; and Case C-202/90 *Ayuntamiento de Sevilla* [1991] ECR I-4247, para. 19.

[143] See Case C-276/97 *Commission v. France* [2000] ECR I-6251, para. 46; Case C-358/97 *Commission v. Ireland* [2000] ECR I-6301, para. 44; Case C-359/97 *Commission v. United Kingdom* [2000] ECR I-6355, para. 56; and Case C-260/98 *Commission v. Greece* [2000] ECR I-6537, para. 41.

[144] Joined Cases 231/87 and 129/88 *Comune di Carpaneto Piacentino* [1989] ECR 3233, para. 15.

'the same legal conditions that apply to private economic operators'.[145] All the same, the Court sacrifices the uniform application of Community law in its deference to national legal classifications, something it is normally famously allergic to. Unsurprisingly, both the Commission and Advocates General have argued for a more 'functional' approach to the issue. The Commission has consistently argued that the reference to activities engaged in 'as public authorities' limits the exemption to acts relating to 'fundamental powers of public authorities', which it defines, in turn, as activities which can never be delegated to private bodies or which, 'by their nature', simply cannot be carried out by private individuals with a view to making a profit.[146] In the toll road cases, Advocate General Alber followed this thinking through. The planning and construction of roads, bridges and tunnels, so he argued, are 'an essential part and thus the core of public responsibilities' and as such activities in the exercise of public authority. The provision of choice – between the toll-free normal roads and the more convenient and faster toll-road – however, is 'selection' and as such 'alien to State activity'.[147] There are systemic problems with this approach, surely. The main problem with it seems to be that it would seem to make the second subparagraph of Article 4(5) superfluous – after all, if activities engaged in as public authorities are defined by the absence of market conditions, it is hard to imagine how exempting them from VAT would lead to 'significant distortions of competition'. The Court, however, bases its interpretation on another systemic issue. In *Carpaneto Piacentino*, it explained that it could not base a definition of a body acting as a public authority on the subject-matter or purpose of the activity at issue 'since those factors have been taken into account by other provisions of the directive for other purposes',[148] specifically the economic nature of certain activities referred to in the third subparagraph of Article 4(5) and Annex D and the public interest purpose of the activities referred to in the fourth subparagraph and Article 13. In so far as this implies a

---

[145] See e.g. Case C-276/97 *Commission* v. *France* [2000] ECR I-6251, para. 40; and Case C-446/98 *Fazenda Pública* [2000] ECR I-11435, para. 17. In the latter case, it also clarified that the 'special legal regime applicable to bodies governed by public law' involves 'the use of public powers'. *Ibid.*, para. 24.

[146] See, e.g. Case 235/85 *Commission* v. *Netherlands* [1987] ECR 1471, para. 17; and Case C-260/98 *Commission* v. *Greece* [2000] ECR I-6537, para. 23.

[147] Case C-359/97 *Commission* v. *United Kingdom* [2000] ECR I-6355, point 65 of the Opinion.

[148] Joined Cases 231/87 and 129/88 *Comune di Carpaneto Piacentino* [1989] ECR 3233, para. 13.

functional approach to the interpretation of the latter provisions, the Court has generally been consistent in its case law on Article 13.[149] In *Marktgemeinde Welden*, it authorised Member States to 'consider that the activities listed in Article 13 of the directive are carried out by bodies governed by public law as public authorities, even if they are performed in a similar manner to those of a private trader'.[150] In *Kingscrest*, it even went so far as to fit private profit-making institutions into the definition of 'charitable organisations' offering welfare and social services. That case is a textbook example of the Court's reasoning in functional mode. 'Whether a specific transaction is exempt from VAT cannot depend on its classification in national law', the Court held:[151] the exemptions of Article 13 have their own independent meaning in Community law and must be given a Community definition.[152] That, in turn, depends heavily on the objectives pursued by the exemptions of Article 13. In this particular case:

It is clear that those exemptions, by treating certain supplies of services in the general interest in the social sector more favourably for the purposes of VAT, are intended to reduce the cost of those services and to make them more accessible to the individuals who may benefit from them.

In the light of that objective, it must be observed that the commercial nature of an activity does not preclude it from being, in the context of Article 13 of the Sixth Directive, an activity in the general interest.[153]

Yet the contrast between the institutional approach under the first subparagraph of Article 4(5) and this functional approach under Article 13 seems awkward. The Court's interpretation of Article 4(5), it is true,

---

[149] There are exceptions. One is Case 107/84 *Commission v. Germany* [1985] ECR 2655, where the Court held that the expression 'the public postal services' in Article 13 should be understood in 'the organic sense of that expression' and so refused to exempt the activities that the *Bundesbahn* and *Lufthansa* carried out on behalf of the *Bundespost*. Another one is Case C-453/93 *Bulthuis-Griffioen* [1995] ECR I-2341, where the Court refused to extend the exemption for the supply of services and goods 'closely linked to welfare' to a natural person, since the text expressly refers to 'bodies' or 'organisations'.

[150] Case C-245/95 *Finanzamt Augsburg v. Marktgemeinde Welden* [1997] ECR I-779, para. 20.

[151] Case C-498/03 *Kingscrest v. Commissioners of Customs and Excise* [2005] ECR I-4427, para. 25. Cf. Case C-315/00 *Maierhofer* [2003] ECR I-563, para. 26.

[152] Case C-498/03 *Kingscrest v. Commissioners of Customs and Excise* [2005] ECR I-4427, para. 22. Cf. e.g. Case C-358/97 *Commission v. Ireland* [2000] ECR I-6301, para. 51; and Case C-284/03 *Temco Europe* [2004] ECR I-11237, para. 16.

[153] Case C-498/03 *Kingscrest v. Commissioners of Customs and Excise* [2005] ECR I-4427, paras. 30 and 31.

saves the coherence between the first and second subparagraphs of that provision: the institutional definition allows for the possibility of activities engaged in 'as public authorities' to be in competition with activities engaged in by private traders. Hence it makes sense not to make such activities exempt if this leads to significant distortions of competition – as the list in Annex D illustrates well in, say, the case of telecommunications. However, by forcing a complete disconnection between the reference to public authority tasks in Article 4(5) and the reference to 'the general interest' in Article 13, it also bans logic from the relationship between the first and fourth subparagraphs of Article 4(5). The way in which the Court has cast the relationship now is that *because* Article 13 refers to the purpose of activities in the public interest, Article 4(5) cannot be interpreted in that light. However, if the list in Article 13 were really to be severed completely from the definition of 'public authority' in Article 4(5), then surely the easier option for the legislator would have been to constitute the activities listed there as autonomous exemptions rather than as a list of activities which Member States 'may consider as activities they engage in as public authorities'. The more obvious conceptualisation of the relationship, in that light, would seem to be that Article 13 provides a list of examples of the kinds of activities that should be exempted in any case under Article 4(5).

(ii) The terms of explicit public service exceptions to secondary legislation are applied stringently, consistent with the objective of harmonisation. This can be illustrated by two unrelated cases decided in 1998. In *Kainuun Liikenne Oy*, the Court was asked to rule on the right of Member States to revoke public transport service obligations under Regulation 1191/69.[154] It held that although undertakings might request to be relieved from such duties, the Member States were under no obligation to grant such an application to this effect, and were entitled to maintain 'in whole or in part' such an obligation, provided this serves solely to ensure the provision of adequate transport services and that, where several ways of providing equivalent such services existed, the way least costly to the community was selected. Hence, the discretion of the authorities was

---

[154] Case C-412/96 *Kainuun Liikenne Oy and Oy Pohjolan Liikenne Ab* [1998] ECR I-5141, concerning Regulation 1191/69 on action by the Member States concerning the obligations inherent in the concept of a public service in transport by rail, road and inland waterway, OJ English Special Edition 1969 (I) 276.

subject to strict public interest (necessity in relation to an objective defined in Regulation 1191/69) and – in line with the standard set out explicitly in Article 3(1) of the Regulation – a strict proportionality test (i.e. based on the 'least restrictive means' criterion):

> Where there are several ways of ensuring, while satisfying similar conditions, the provision of adequate transport services, the competent autorities must, under Article 3(1) of the Regulation, select the way least costly to the community.[155]

In *Sjöberg*, the Court had to deal with the exemption from the duty to draw up a service timetable and duty roster for transport undertakings granted to 'vehicles used by public authorities to provide public services *which are not in competition* with professional road hauliers' under Regulation 3820/85.[156] Since the undertaking he managed was wholly owned by the Stockholm County Council and Mr Sjöberg had obtained the exclusive right to operate certain transport lines in a tender procedure, he sought to rely on that exception to escape prosecution for infringement of that Regulation and national road safety rules. The Court, however, first construed the absence of competition as a *conditio sine qua non* and then rejected the argument that the monopoly excluded competition:

> It is common ground that until the contract is concluded an undertaking wishing to acquire the operation of a public service must engage in competitive conduct. Nor, once the contract has been signed, is that undertaking immune from competition, since it will operate the service in such a way as to ensure that the contract will be renewed when it comes to an end.[157]

Note that the solution in *Sjöberg* was based specifically on the definition of 'public services which are not in competition' of the Regulation, read in conjunction with the purposes of the Regulation, i.e. to improve road safety and to prevent disruption of competition. It is worth underlining, however, that where no such provision exists the presence or absence of competition as such does not as a rule determine whether public service exceptions apply.

---

[155] Case C-412/96 *Kainuun Liikenne Oy and Oy Pohjolan Liikenne Ab* [1998] ECR I-5141, para. 34.

[156] Council Regulation 3820/85/EEC on the harmonisation of certain social legislation relating to road transport OJ 1985 L379/1.

[157] Case C-387/96 *Criminal proceedings against Anders Sjöberg (Sjöberg)* [1998] ECR I-1225, para. 20.

2.6. Conclusion

Both the vertical and horizontal scope of the free movement rules have shifted over time. The early broadening of the scope of free movement in *Dassonville* and *Cassis* was accompanied by the acceptance of new public interest exceptions. Given the pre-existing case law on exceptions to free movement, the vertical 'withdrawal' on selling arrangements exemplified by *Keck* can also be seen as part of a rationalisation trend – including a de minimis approach in *Peralta* – that often lacks material impact. This vertical realignment has been followed by a trend of horizontal rationalisation in cases such as *Kohll* and *Decker*, with potentially more significant effects. The variables at play can be summarised as functionalism, subsidiarity and (more dynamically) pre-emption.

This is confirmed by the analysis of State measures and the concept of 'public bodies' under the free movement provisions. Here the Court's horizontal advance is partially compensated by a vertical retreat (as in *Hünermund*) – and vice versa. As noted above, on balance, this involves a rationalisation of its case law along the cross-cutting lines of functionalism and subsidiarity.

Next, when looking at 'public bodies' under secondary law, it can be seen that the Court's case law on direct effect of Directives increases the reach of Directives both horizontally and vertically.

At the same time, harmonisation itself sets limits to the functional approach: whenever possible, the Court uses the formal distinctions introduced by the Community Directives themselves as thresholds for the application of these secondary rules. As the Court applies the EU law criteria that determine the public/private distinction in secondary legislation strictly, this can lead to divergence between economic sectors, and even within such sectors, depending on the degree of harmonisation attained in respect of specific areas of regulation.

Concerning public authority exceptions to free movement, the Court aims to limit the scope of the exceptions 'to what is strictly necessary for safeguarding the interests which that provision allows the Member States to protect'. This is simply an application of the general rule of Community law that exceptions are interpreted strictly. At the same time, by employing a functional approach, the Court aims to ensure that the scope of application is the same throughout the Community – protecting the unity of EU law.

A similar line is found concerning public authority exceptions to free movement under secondary law. The Court is willing to use a formal approach based on national legal distinctions when applying secondary law exceptions, in particular where this has a restrictive effect. The terms of explicit public service exceptions to secondary legislation are applied stringently, consistent with the objective of harmonisation and consistent with the rule of limited exceptions. Neither functionalism nor formalism affect the ground rules concerning the public interest exceptions to free movement provided by the Treaty and the mandatory requirements that may be invoked by the Member States.

3   The competition rules

3.1. Introduction

This chapter will discuss how the Court decides whether the competition rules are applicable. That is: under which circumstances the competition rules apply in spite of involvement of public authorities and/or claims that restrictions of competition are in the public interest and in which cases public interest considerations prevail.

First the concepts of 'undertaking', 'economic activity', 'public authority' and 'activities with an exclusively social function' are explored. This charts the main standards applied to decide whether activities are in principle subject to the competition rules.

Next, a number of cases are discussed in which undertakings are involved, and which are therefore subject to the competition rules, and where restrictive agreements were found to be present, and no specific public interest exception existed but where the Court nevertheless concluded that Article 81 EC did not apply. The objective is to identify according to which criteria the court decides such cases, and to establish whether those criteria have general validity beyond the particular case at hand.

3.2. The concept of 'undertaking' under the competition rules

In principle, the competition rules of Articles 81 and 82 EC apply exclusively to undertakings. The place of these Articles in the structure of the Treaty already indicates this: Articles 81 and 82 EC are found under Title VI (common rules on competition, taxation and approximation of laws), Chapter 1 (rules on competition) section 1, headed: 'rules applying to *undertakings*'. Moreover, they are explicitly drafted to address undertakings. Thus, Article 81 EC concerns 'all agreements between *undertakings*, decisions by *associations of undertakings* and concerted practices' and Article 82 EC concerns 'any abuse by one or more *undertakings* of a dominant position'.

This is worth highlighting, because in general the Treaty rules are addressed directly and exclusively to the Member States in their role as contracting parties – which is logical given the historic origins of the Treaty as an international agreement between nation States. The exception provided by the competition rules is explained by the fact that the contracting parties by way of exception added competition rules applicable to private parties to the Treaty in order to prevent the state barriers to free movement, levelled by Article 28 EC, from being re-introduced by means of private anti-competitive agreements. The Court spelled this argument out in its landmark 1966 *Consten* Case:

[A]n agreement between producer and distributor which might tend to restore the national divisions in trade between Member States might be such as to frustrate the most fundamental objectives of the Community. The Treaty, whose preamble and content aim at abolishing the barriers between states, and which in several provisions gives evidence of a stern attitude with regard to their reappearance, could not allow undertakings to reconstruct such barriers. Article 81(1) is designed to pursue this aim, even in the case of undertakings placed at different levels in the economic process.[1]

As a result, it might appear that the Member States and their constituent bodies are exempt from these competition rules. Yet, although the scope of the concept of 'undertaking' ultimately determines whether or not the competition rules are applicable to a given entity, the Treaty does not define this concept. Consequently, there is room for a more nuanced approach, as a result of which Community competition law as currently applied cuts across the public sphere.

(i) *The concept of 'undertaking' is applied in functional terms to ensure the uniform application of competition law.* Given the absence of a definition in

---

[1] Cf. Comité Intergouvernemental Creé par la Conférence de Messine, *Rapport des Chefs de Délégation aux Ministres des Affaires Étrangères* (Brussels: 1956), p. 16; discussed in D.G. Goyder, *EC Competition Law*, 4th edn (Oxford: Oxford University Press, 2003). Accordingly, the Court famously adopted market integration as the primary rationale of its approach to the competition rules in Joined Cases 56 and 58/64 *Consten and Grundig v. Commission (Consten)* [1966] ECR 299, p. 340; cf. Case 22/78 *Hugin Kassaregister AB v. Commission* [1979] ECR 1869.

the Treaty itself, the European Courts have developed the concept of undertaking in their case law.[2] On the whole, this case law is clearly functional in nature: the legal status of the entity in question is entirely irrelevant and the courts ignore any formal distinctions made as a matter of national law. This is necessary in order to avoid that certain activities, merely due to their legal form, would be held illegal in one Member State and not in another. Thus, in the context of ruling on the application of the Transparency Directive, the Court stated:

[H]aving recourse to Member States' domestic law in order to limit the scope of provisions of Community law undermines the unity and effectiveness of that law and cannot, therefore, be accepted. Consequently, the fact that a body has or has not, under national law, legal personality separate from that of the State is irrelevant in deciding whether it may be regarded as a public undertaking within the meaning of the Directive.[3]

As is clearly spelled out by the Court here, its functional interpretation of the concept of undertaking serves to guarantee the uniform application of Community law across all Member States and economic sectors.

This approach was pioneered in the Court's ECSC case law of the early 1960s in *Mannesman* v. *High Authority* and *Klöckner and Hoecht* v. *High Authority*: 'An undertaking is constituted by a single organisation of personal, tangible and intangible elements, attached to an autonomous legal entity and pursuing a given long term economic aim.'[4] Under the EC competition rules, the Commission expressed a similar view in its *Polypropylene* Decision.[5]

(ii) The concept of 'undertaking' is based on the definition of 'economic activity'.
In spite of the early lead provided by the ECSC case law, the European

---

[2] See generally e.g. Slot, 'The Concept of Undertaking in EC Competition Law' in O. Due, M. Lutter and J. Schwarze (eds.), *Festschrift für Ulrich Everling*, Vol. 2 (Baden-Baden: Nomos, 1995), p. 1413; and Odudu, 'The Meaning of Undertaking Within Article 81', (2005) 7 CYELS 211.

[3] Case 118/85 *Commission* v. *Italy* [1987] ECR 2599, para. 11. Cf. the Opinion of AG Cruz Vilaca in Case 30/87 *Bodson* [1988] ECR 2479, point 32. It is nevertheless used as a 'sanity check' in clear cases. Cf. the Opinion of AG Jacobs, Case C-41/90 *Höfner and Elsner* v. *Macroton* [1991] ECR I-1979, points 22–3.

[4] Case 19/61 *Mannesman* v. *High Authority* [1962] ECR 357, para. 371; and Joined Cases 17 and 20/61 *Klöckner Werke and Hoecht* v. *High Authority* [1962] ECR 325, para. 341.

[5] OJ 1986 L230/1. For an early Commission view, see its *Christiani and Nielsen* Decision, OJ 1969 L165/12.

Court of Justice first gave a clear statement of its functional definition only as late as 1991 in its *Höfner* Case:

[I]n the context of competition law . . . the concept of an undertaking encompasses every entity engaged in an economic activity regardless of the legal status of the entity and the way in which it is financed.[6]

As the legal status of the entity concerned is immaterial for the applicability of the competition rules, not merely public undertakings and public bodies, but 'the State' itself may constitute an undertaking in this sense. In fact, '[i]ndividuals too may be classified as undertakings, if they are independent actors in the market for goods or services'.[7]

The courts have further elaborated the concept of undertaking in relation to attributing responsibility in competition affairs, concerning issues such as principal-agent relations and conglomerate structures. We will not go into this. Instead, our focus will be limited to the distinction between the public and private spheres: first, based on the concept of 'economic activities'; and second, by looking at 'the public authority task'.

---

[6] Case C-41/90 *Höfner and Elsner* v. *Macroton* [1991] ECR I-1979, para. 21. Cf. Joined Cases C-159 and 160/91 *Poucet and Pistre* [1993] ECR I-637, para. 17; Case C-244/94 *Fédération Française des Sociétés d'Assurance (FFSA)* [1995] ECR I-4013, para. 14; Case C-67/96 *Albany International BV* v. *Stichting Bedrijfspensioenfonds Textielindustrie (Albany)* [1999] ECR I-5751, para. 77; Joined Cases C-115, 116, 117 and 119/97 *Brentjens Handelsonderneming BV* v. *Stichting Bedrijfspensioenfonds voor de Handel in Bouwmaterialen (Brentjens)* [1999] ECR I-6025, para. 77; Case C-219/97 *BV Maatschappij Drijvende Bokken* v. *Stichting Bedrijfspensioenfonds vioor de Vervoer- en Havenbedrijven (Drijvende Bokken)* [1999] ECR I-6121, para. 67; Joined Cases C-180 to 184/98 *Pavel Pavlov et al.* v. *Stichting Pensioenfonds Medische Specialisten (Pavlov)* [2000] ECR I-6451, para. 74; Case C-218/00 *Cisal di Battistello Venziano & C. Sas* v. *INAIL (Cisal)* [2002] ECR I-691, para. 22; and Joined Cases C-264, 306, 354 and 355/01 *AOK Bundesverband et al.* v. *Ichthyol-Gesellschaft Cordes, Hermani & Co, Mundipharma GmnH, Gödeke GmnH and Intersan, Institut für pharmazeutische und klinische Forschung GmbH (AOK)* [2004] ECR I-2493, para. 46.

[7] As noted by Advocate General Jacobs in his Opinion on Case C-67/96 *Albany*; Joined Cases C-115, 116, 117 and 119/97 *Brentjens*; and Case C-219/97 *Drijvende Bokken* [1999] ECR I-6121, citing Case C-35/96 *Italian Customs Agents* [1998] ECR I-3851, para. 36. Individual workers who are not self-employed, however, are not caught. Cf. Case C-22/98 *Jean Claude Becu et al. (Becu)* [1999] ECR I-5665, paras. 24 ff. 'The concept of "worker" within the meaning of Article 48 [now Article 39] of the Treaty pre-supposes that for a certain period of time a person performs services for and under the direction of another person in return for which he receives remuneration.' Case C-179/90 *Merci Convenzionali Porto di Genova* v. *Siderurgica Gabrielli (Merci)* [1991] ECR I-5889, para. 13; and Case 66/85 *Lawrie-Blum* [1986] ECR 2121, para. 17.

3.3. Economic activities of an industrial or a commercial nature

According to the European Court of Justice, the activities of the Member States can be distinguished between 'true' public authority functions and economic activities. As stated in the *Transparency Directive* Case:

[T]he State may act either by exercising public powers or by carrying on economic activities of an industrial or commercial nature by offering goods and services on the market.[8]

This distinction is crucial as activities involving the exercise of public powers are not caught by the competition rules. Activities of an industrial or commercial nature, on the other hand, are.[9] Bringing the functional approach to its extreme, the courts have started to extend the distinction to *within* single entities by unpacking the different activities they are engaged in. This started with the Advocate General's Opinion in *SAT*, where he noted that:

[T]he performance of duties involving the exercise of public authority by a body may prevent the range of activities carried on by it from being subject to the rules of competition only where those duties form an inseparable part of the activity in question.[10]

It was taken further in *Aéroports de Paris* by the Court of First Instance,[11] confirmed on appeal,[12] and elaborated by the Court of First Instance in *SELEX*:

Since the Treaty provisions on competition are applicable to the activities of an entity which can be severed from those in which it engages as a public authority, the various activities of an entity must be considered individually and the treatment of some of them as powers of a public authority does not mean that it must be concluded that the other activities are not economic.[13]

---

[8] *Transparency Directive*, para. 7.
[9] The Opinion of AG Tesauro in Case C-364/92 *SAT-Fluggesellschaft (SAT)* [1994] ECR I-43, point 9; with reference to Case 118/85 *Commission* v. *Italy* [1987] ECR 2599; and Case 30/87 *Bodson* [1988] ECR 2479. Cf. Case C-92/91 *Taillandier* [1993] ECR I-5383, para. 14.
[10] The Opinion of AG Tesauro in Case C-364/92 *SAT-Fluggesellschaft* [1994] ECR I-43, para. 13.
[11] Case T-128/98 *Aéroports de Paris* [2000] ECR II-3929, para. 108, with reference to Case 107/84 *Commission* v. *Germany* [1985] ECR 2655. That reference is misleading at best, given that the case dealt with the VAT Directive's definition of 'bodies governed by public law' for the activities they engage in 'as public authorities', as discussed above.
[12] See Case C-82/01 P *Aéroports de Paris* [2002] ECR I-9297, paras. 75 et seq.
[13] Case T-155/04 *SELEX Sistemi Integrati* [2006] ECR II-4797, para. 54.

The key question is therefore not just whether a given entity is gene-rally engaged in 'economic activity', but whether the entity's specific and individual activity at issue is to be considered 'economic'.

(i) Offering goods or services in a market, in particular doing so for payment, and while assuming the financial risks involved, means engaging in an economic activity as an undertaking. According to one line of case law, starting with *Transparency Directive,* 'any activity consisting in offering goods and services on a given market is an economic activity'.[14] In *SELEX,* the Court of First Instance held Eurocontrol's activity of giving advice to national administrations in the drafting of contracts and specifications in tendering procedures to be 'precisely a case of an offer of services on the market for advice, a market on which private undertakings specialised in this area could also very well offer their services'.[15] The criterion has further been applied and fleshed out in relation to the activities of professionals. Thus in *Italian Customs Agents,* the activity of Italian customs agents was found to have an economic character as they offered services for payment, and assumed the financial risks involved in the exercise of that activity.[16] In *Pavlov,* medical specialists were found to provide services in the market for specialist medical services, as they are paid for the services they provide and assume the financial risks involved.[17] Likewise in *Wouters,* the fact that they charged a fee for their services and bore the financial risks of their activities determined that members of the bar (lawyers engaged in representing individual clients before courts and tribunals) carried on an economic activity, and were therefore undertakings for the purposes of Articles 81, 82 and 86 EC.[18] Moreover, in both *Pavlov* and *Wouters,* the Court held that '[t]he complexity and technical nature of the services they provide and the

---

[14] Case C-35/96 *Italian Customs Agents* [1998] ECR I-3851, para. 36; paraphrasing Case 118/85 *Commission v. Italy* [1987] ECR 2599, para. 7. Cf. Joined Cases C-180 to 184/98 *Pavlov* [2000] ECR I-6451, para. 75; Case C-475/99 *Glöckner* [2001] ECR I-8089, para. 19; Case 218/00 *Cisal* [2002] ECR I-691, para. 23; and Case C-82/01 P *Aéroports de Paris v. Commission (Aéroports de Paris)* [2002] ECR I-9297, para. 79.

[15] Case T-155/04 *SELEX Sistemi Integrati* [2006] ECR II-4797, para. 87.

[16] Case C-35/96 *Italian Customs Agents* [1998] ECR I-3851, para. 37; with reference to Joined Cases 40 to 48, 50, 54 to 56, 111, 113 and 114/73 *Coöperatieve Vereniging 'Suiker Unie' UA and others v. Commission (Suiker Unie)* [1975] ECR 1663, para. 541, where the assumption of financial risks is used to assess whether there is sufficient independence to find restrictive agreements in principal-agent relationships.

[17] Joined Cases C-180 to 184/98 *Pavlov* [2000] ECR I-6451, para. 76.

[18] Case C-309/99 *J. C. J. Wouters, W. W. Savelberg and Price Waterhouse Belastingadviseurs BV v. Algemene Raad van de Nederlandse Orde van Advocaten (Wouters)* [2002] ECR I-1577, paras. 48–9.

fact that the practice of their profession is regulated cannot alter this conclusion'.[19]

(ii) Offering goods or services in competition, or that could be subject to competition, means engaging in an economic activity as an undertaking. It is not always clear whether a market is involved. Nor, to determine whether an economic activity is involved, is it decisive whether an activity is carried on in pursuit of financial gain, as the Court of Justice made clear in its 1995 *Féderation Française des Sociétés d'Assurances (FFSA)* Case:

[T]he mere fact that the CCMSA is a non-profit-making body does not deprive the activity which it carries on of its economic character, since . . . that activity may give rise to conduct which the competition rules are intended to penalise.[20]

Instead, the issue is whether an entity is involved in competition, or, alternatively, enjoys a monopoly concerning an activity which could potentially be subject to competition. It is relatively straightforward to determine whether or not an entity carries on 'an economic activity in competition',[21] as this evidently concerns situations where some residual competition is present in the market, or those cases where, at a minimum, there is periodic competition 'for' the market instead of 'on' the market (as in the case of time-limited concessions to operate particular facilities or transportation networks).[22]

It is much more problematic to decide whether, as the Court stated in *FFSA*, an activity is 'capable of being carried on, at least in principle, by a private undertaking with a view to profit',[23] in which case the entity

---

[19] Joined Cases C-180 to 184/98 *Pavlov* [2000] ECR I-6451, para. 77; Case C-309/99 *Wouters* [2002] ECR I-1577, para. 49.

[20] Case C-244/94 *Féderation Française des Sociétés d'Assurances* v. *Ministère de l'Agriculture et de la Pêche (FFSA)* [1995] ECR I-4013, para. 21. Noted by Blaise and Idot (1996) 32 RTDE 567. Cf. Case C-382/92 *Commission* v. *United Kingdom* [1994] ECR I-2435, para. 44. Cf. Case C-67/96 *Albany* [1999] ECR I-5751, para. 85; Joined Cases C-115, 116, 117 and 219/97 *Brentjens* [1999] ECR I-6025, para. 85; and Case C-219/97 *Drijvende Bokken* [1999] ECR I-6121, para. 75.

[21] Case C-244/94 *FFSA* [1995] ECR I-4013, para. 17. Case C-67/96 *Albany* [1999] ECR I-5751, para. 84; Joined Cases C-115, 116, 117 and 119/97 *Brentjens* [1999] ECR I-6025, para. 84; and Case C-219/97 *Drijvende Bokken* [1999] ECR I-6121, para. 74.

[22] Case C-387/96 *Sjöberg* [1998] ECR I-1225, para. 20. A point missed by AG Tesauro in Case C-364–92 *SAT-Fluggesellschaft mbH* v. *Eurocontrol (SAT)* [1994] ECR I-43, para. 13, where he concluded as regards air traffic control that in this field, 'competition between two bodies not only is not desirable but would not even be possible in practice'. Noted by Drijber, (1995) 32 CMLR 1039.

[23] As opposed to 'a public service to which any idea of commercial exploitation with a view to profit is alien'. The Opinion of AG Tesauro in, *SAT*, points 9 and 13. As in Case C-343/95 *Cali* [1996] ECR I-1547, with reference to charges approved by public

concerned is likewise held capable of restricting competition in the sense of Articles 81 and 82 EC. In this case it is not actual competition or even potential competition that is relevant, but hypothetical competition. This category covers situations where competition may have been deliberately excluded by State measures, for example where a Member State has awarded exclusive rights. In such cases, the competition rules apply, albeit possibly subject to public interest exceptions. Thus, in the 1991 *Höfner* Case, the Court held that:

> The fact that employment procurement activities are normally entrusted to public agencies cannot affect the economic nature of such activities. Employment procurement has not always been, and is not necessarily, carried out by public entities.[24]

Similarly, concerning ambulance services in its 2001 *Glöckner* Case, the Court held that:

> Such activities have not always been, and are not necessarily, carried on by such [private non-profit] organisations or by public authorities.[25]

The main problem with this approach is that, in principle, almost every imaginable activity could be carried out by a private undertaking for profit and could for that reason be subject to the competition rules. Due to market failures the good or service concerned may however in this case be provided – or may be expected to be provided – in a manner which is suboptimal from a public policy perspective, for example in terms of costs, prices, quality and/or accessibility (coverage), and for that reason be subject to intervention. Paradoxically, the problem came to the fore in *SELEX*, that most functional of judgments. In relation to Eurocontrol's standardisation activities, the Court of First Instance made a distinction between the preparation and the adoption of standards. While the latter was considered 'clearly a legislative activity' falling within Eurocontrol's public tasks, the Court seemed to suggest

---

authorities, in *SAT* the Court held that the levying of charges which were set by the contracting Member States was inseparable from the public service activities concerned (and hence implicitly not for profit).

[24] Case C-41/90 *Höfner* [1991] ECR I-1979, paras. 22–3. Cf. Case C-55/96 *Job Centre Coop* [1997] ECR I-7119; Case C-258/98 *Giovanni Carra et al.* [2000] ECR I-4217; Case T-155/04 *SELEX Sistemi Integrati* [2006] ECR II-4797, para. 89. In Case C-82/01 P *Aéroports de Paris* [2002] ECR I-9297, para. 82, the Court confirmed that 'the fact that an activity may be exercised by a private undertaking amounts to further evidence that the activity in question may be described as a business activity'.

[25] Case C-475/99 *Glöckner* [2001] ECR I-8089, para. 20.

that the former could well be seen as offering a service on a market. By the very next paragraph, however, the Court indicated that political choice on the part of public authorities to exclude activities from the market may be enough to exclude classification as an 'economic activity':

In this case, the applicant has not shown that there is a market for 'technical standardisation services in the sector of ATM equipment'. The only purchasers of such services can be States in their capacity as air traffic control authorities. However, they chose to develop those standards themselves in the context of international cooperation through Eurocontrol. Since the standards developed are subsequently adopted by the Council of Eurocontrol, the results of the development activity stay within the organisation itself and are not offered on a given market. In the field of standardisation, Eurocontrol, for its Member States, is therefore only a forum for concerted action which those States established in order to coordinate the technical standards of their ATM systems. It cannot therefore be considered that, in this area, Eurocontrol 'offers them goods and services'.[26]

(iii) Legitimate exclusion from competition for public policy reasons. Hence, it appears that the real test is not whether an economic activity is involved, but whether, from time to time, the Court considers that in accordance with Community law certain activities can be excluded from competition for legitimate reasons of public policy. For this reason we will now approach the problem of demarcating the public sphere from the marketplace (where the competition rules apply) from the opposite perspective, i.e. by looking not at which goods or services could be provided in competition, but at what activities might constitute a public authority task.

3.4. The public authority task

Whether public authority is exercised directly by a public body, or under delegation to a private body or undertaking, is not the key issue. In order to establish immunity from the competition rules for an undertaking, the decisive criterion remains that a public task, or a policy in the general public interest, should be concerned. In the absence of a clear definition, the Court has described this in the 1997 Case *Calì* as 'a task in the public interest which forms part of the essential functions of the State'.[27] Again, there is no exhaustive list of such state functions.

---

[26] Case T-155/04 *SELEX Sistemi Integrati* [2006] ECR II-4797, para. 61.
[27] Case C-343/95 *Diego Calì & Figli* v. *SEPG (Calì)* [1996] ECR I-1547, para. 22.

Although Advocate General Tesauro, in his 1994 Opinion on *SAT*, has identified a hard core of 'fundamental powers in areas such as general and fiscal administration, justice, security and national defence',[28] the Court has taken a broader view of matters falling within the exercise of public interest tasks and not constituting economic activities in the sense of the competition rules. For example, it has not only included the control and supervision of air space (*SAT*), but also the management of the public social security system (*Poucet and Pistre, Cisal, AOK*),[29] and the protection of the environment in marine areas (*Calì*).

The most elaborate statement of the considerations involved was set out by Advocate General Cosmas in his Opinion in *Calì*:

> It is clear from the case law of the Court of Justice, and more especially the judgments in *SAT Fluggesellschaft* and *Poucet*, that certain bodies that are the instruments of a public policy in the (general) public interest and enjoy prerogatives of the public authority, that is to say bodies that exercise an *activity typical of a public authority* or have an *exclusively social function*, do not constitute undertakings and are not therefore subject to the Community rules on competition.
>
> In reaching those conclusions, the Court of Justice has focused on the *nature of the activity* exercised, that is to say whether or not it is of an economic nature and whether it could, in principle, be performed by a private profit-making undertaking. It has also considered the *aim of the activity* and the *rules to which it is subject*. In addition, the Court has looked at a number, or bundle, of indicators that on their own are not sufficient to rule out that an activity is of an economic nature and establish that it falls outside the scope of competition law. Basically, the Court has assessed the extent to which the entity whose activities are under review operates in compliance with the rules laid down by the administrative authorities and whether, more particularly, it has the power to influence the level of consideration demanded in return for the services provided to users, and the extent to which it is profit-making.[30]

The Court followed the Advocate General in his approach to this case, as follows:

> The anti-pollution surveillance for which the SEPG was responsible in the oil port of Genoa is a task in the public interest which forms part of the essential

---

[28] The Opinion of AG Tesauro in Case C-364/92 *SAT* [1994] ECR I-43, para. 9.

[29] Joined Cases C-159 and 160/91 *Christian Poucet v. Assurances Générales de France and Caisse Mutuelle Régionale du Languedoc-Roussillon (Poucet and Pistre)* [1993] ECR I-637; Case C-218/00 *Cisal* [2002] ECR I-691; and Joined Cases C-264, 306, 354 and 355/01 *AOK* [2004] ECR I-2493.

[30] Opinion in Case C-343/95 *Calì* [1996] ECR I-1547, paras. 41–2. Emphases added.

functions of the State as regards protection of the environment in maritime areas.

Such surveillance is connected *by its nature, its aim and the rules to which it is subject* with the exercise of powers relating to the protection of the environment which are *typically those of a public authority*. It is not of an economic nature justifying the application of the Treaty rules on competition.[31]

This means that the question of which activities are 'typically those of a public authority' is determined by analysing their nature, aim and the rules to which they are subject. These criteria are of course relatively indistinct, and the disparity between the areas where this exception has been applied suggests that a wide range of public interest tasks would be eligible and, evidently, undertakings will be tempted to claim that they are acting in the public interest. Presumably, therefore, the Member States themselves remain competent to decide whether public interest tasks are involved, subject to limited judicial review concerning the effects on the internal market, and the exceptions to the market freedoms.[32]

As regards the second category identified by the Advocate General, however, concerning bodies that exercise an exclusively social function, the Court has identified a relatively clear set of criteria that will be discussed in the next section.

3.5. An exclusively social function: solidarity

Unsurprisingly, it is in the field of social security that the Court has come most under fire for eroding Member States' socio-economic policies. Nevertheless, it has made a concerted effort to distinguish between activities of an economic nature, hence by undertakings, and subject to competition and those of bodies fulfilling an exclusively social function, that remain outside the scope of the competition rules. It started out with the recognition of the value of the principle of solidarity in the 1993 *Poucet and Pistre* Case:

Sickness funds, and the organisations involved in the management of the public social security system, fulfil *an exclusively social function*. That activity is based on the principle of national solidarity and is entirely non-profit-making. The benefits paid are statutory benefits bearing no relation to the amount of contributions.

---

[31] Case C-343/95 *Calì* [1996] ECR I-1547, paras. 22–3.
[32] This, in any event, appears to be the approach advocated by the Commission in COM(96) 443, *Services of General Interest in Europe*.

Accordingly, that activity is not an economic activity and therefore, the organisations to which it is entrusted are not undertakings within the meaning of Articles 81 and 82 (sic) of the Treaty.[33]

Although at the time of this judgment it was widely hailed as a recognition of the economic sovereignty of the Member States, it has meanwhile been recognised that among the elements listed there the importance of the solidarity principle is key and limited in scope.

In *FFSA*, another social security case, two years after *Poucet and Pistre*, the Court came to the opposite conclusion in relation to a supplementary old-age insurance scheme because it was optional instead of compulsory, operated on the basis of voluntary participation, and with benefits determined by the amount of contributions paid plus returns on investment. The Court held that an economic activity carried on in competition was concerned:[34] although certain elements of solidarity might make such a scheme less competitive, 'such elements do not prevent the activity carried on . . . from being regarded as an economic activity'.[35] Whether the activity was for profit or non-profit was (as already cited earlier) immaterial.[36] Thus the requirements of compulsory participation and benefits determined irrespective of the amount of contributions were central to classifying an activity as fulfilling an exclusively social function.

Likewise in *Albany*, *Brentjens* and *Drijvende Bokken*, the Court found that sectoral pension funds that themselves determined the level of contributions and benefits operated in accordance with the principle of

---

[33] Joined Cases C-159 and 160/91 *Poucet and Pistre* [1993] ECR I-637, paras. 18–19. Cf. Case 218/00 *Cisal* [2002] ECR I-691. For Laigre, 'Les Organismes de Sécurité Sociale sont-ils des Entreprises?', [1993] *Droit Social* 488, even the *Poucet and Pistre* Case went too far for establishing the principle that social security could be subject to the concept of 'undertaking'. The Court had already ruled in Case 238/82 *Duphar* v. *Netherlands* [1984] ECR 523, para. 16 that Community law does not affect the Member States' powers to organise their social security systems. In Case C-70/95 *Sodemare et al.* v. *Regione Lombardia* [1997] ECR I-3395, the Court upheld, on similar grounds, a non-profit making requirement for private operators wishing to benefit from social benefit system reimbursements for the provision of care for the elderly.

[34] Case C-244/94 *FFSA* [1995] ECR I-4013, paras. 17–19. Cf. Case C-67/96 *Albany* [1999] ECR I-5751; Joined Cases C-115, 116, 117 and 119/97 *Brentjens* [1999] ECR I-6025; and Case C-219/97 *Drijvende Bokken* [1999] ECR I-6121.

[35] Case C-244/94 *FFSA* [1995] ECR I-4013, para. 20. Positively disgusted with what he regards as confusion over the distinction between insurance and social security, Laigre, 'L'Intrusion du Droit Communautaire de la Concurrence dans le Champ de la Protection Sociale', [1996] *Droit Social* 82.

[36] Case C-244/94 *FFSA* [1995] ECR I-4013, para. 21.

capitalisation and were subject to exemptions from affiliation, engaged in competition with insurance companies and were therefore carrying on an economic activity:

In those circumstances, the fact that the fund is non-profit-making and the manifestations of solidarity referred to . . . are not sufficient to deprive the sectoral pension fund of its status as an undertaking within the meaning of the competition rules of the Treaty.[37]

More recently in *Cisal*,[38] concerning compulsory insurance against accident and occupational diseases, and *AOK*,[39] concerning sickness funds, the same result was reached as in *Poucet and Pistre*: the bodies concerned were found to fulfil 'an exclusively social function'. This was because the necessary elements of solidarity were found, notably in the absence of a direct link between the contributions paid and the benefits granted, and the fact that the State in the final instance determined by law the amount of benefits and of contributions concerned.[40]

In *AOK*, the Court classified the activity of the sickness funds as non-economic in nature in particular given the absence of competition as regards the grant of obligatory statutory benefits in relation to the medical treatment and medicinal products which formed the main function of the sickness funds. In this context, the existence of a degree of competition at the level of contribution rates was held to be immaterial. Joint determination by the fund associations of maximum amounts of reimbursement was likewise found not to constitute an economic activity because this task was imposed on them by legislation and took place according to criteria (such as quality and profitability) laid down by law, while the remaining discretion of the funds concerned an area where they do not compete (reimbursement of medicinal products).[41]

---

[37] Case C-67/96 *Albany* [1999] ECR I-5751, para. 85; Joined Cases C-115, 116, 117 and 119/97 *Brentjens* [1999] ECR I-6025, para. 85; and Case C-219/97 *Drijvende Bokken* [1999] ECR I-6121, para. 75. An identical result was reached in relation to occupational pension funds in Joined Cases C-180 to 184/98 *Pavlov* [2000] ECR I-6451, paras. 113–119.

[38] Case C-218/00 *Cisal* [2002] ECR I-691. Noted by Denman, (2002) 23 ECLR 73.

[39] Joined Cases C-264, 306, 354 and 355/01 *AOK* [2004] ECR I-2493.

[40] Case C-218/00 *Cisal* [2002] ECR I-691, paras. 38–45; and Joined Cases C-264, 306, 354 and 355/01 *AOK* [2004] ECR I-2493, para. 52.

[41] Joined Cases C-264, 306, 354 and 355/01 *AOK* [2004] ECR I-2493, paras. 51–64. Noted by Krajewski and Farley, (2004) 29 ELR 842; Lasok, (2004) 25 ECLR 383; and Drijber, (2005) 42 CMLR 523.

As summarised by Advocate General Poiares Maduro, the 'solidarity' exception is an acknowledgement of the enduring legacy of embedded liberalism. In *FENIN*, he noted that introducing a requirement of competition in sectors 'which have no market characteristics' would 'represent an unlimited extension of the scope of competition law':

> Above all, the State does not primarily act as an operator on the market, since one of its main roles is to put in place systems of redistribution. In that context, since action by the State is governed only by an objective of solidarity, it bears no relation to the market. . . . The State is nonetheless under a duty to act consistently: it is free to withdraw certain activities from the market only on the condition that it effectively implements the principle of solidarity and gives effect to redistribution policies. In effect, the State assumes two distinct roles, depending on whether it is acting as an operator on the market or whether it is acting for political purposes, inspired by considerations of solidarity. But it cannot shelter behind the pretext of solidarity in order to avoid economic operators being subject to competition law.[42]

Remarkably, in some ways this 'solidarity' exception seems more robust than the 'public authority' exception. On the theory that 'economic activity' consists in *offering* goods and services on a given market and not the business of purchasing goods and services, the Court in *FENIN* itself refused to dissociate the Spanish health system's activity in purchasing goods from the use these goods were put to:

> [A]n organisation which purchases goods – even in great quantity – not for the purpose of offering goods and services as part of an economic activity, but in order to use them in the context of a different activity, such as one of a purely social nature, does not act as an undertaking simply because it is a purchaser in a given market. Whilst an entity may wield considerable economic power, even giving rise to a monopsony, it nevertheless remains the case that, if the activity for which that entity purchases goods is not an economic activity, it is not acting as an undertaking for the purposes of Community competition law.[43]

---

[42] Case C-205/03 P *FENIN* v. *Commission* [2006] ECR I-6295, para. 27 of the Opinion. Attaching rather more importance to the concept, Boeger, 'Solidarity and EC Competition Law', (2007) 32 ELR 319; and Ross, 'Promoting Solidarity: From Public Services to a European Model of Competition?', (2007) 44 CMLR 1057.

[43] Case T-319/99 *FENIN* v. *Commission* [2003] ECR II-357, para. 37; confirmed in Case C-205/03 P *FENIN* v. *Commission* [2006] ECR I-6295, para. 26. See Krajewski and Farley, 'Non-economic Activities in Upstream and Downstream Markets and the Scope of Competition Law after *Fenin*', (2007) 32 ELR 111; and the disgruntled note by Roth, (2007) 44 CMLR 1131.

(i) Financial solidarity and exclusion from competitive provision are required for classification as a scheme having an exclusively social function. Thus, the social aim of an insurance scheme clearly is not in itself sufficient to preclude the activity in question from being classified as an economic activity. Solidarity in financial terms and exclusion of competitive provision by law are required. Nevertheless, in each case cited above, starting from *FFSA*, where the activities concerned were found to be economic in nature and therefore subject to the competition rules, the Court did not exclude that the elements of solidarity that were found might still be sufficient to justify an exclusive right. Hence, once the activities concerned were found to be within the scope of Community law as an 'undertaking', there were still the exceptions to the competition rules to examine. Thus, in *Albany*:

Undoubtedly, the pursuit of a social objective, the abovementioned manifestations of solidarity and restrictions or controls on investments made by the sectoral pension fund may render the service provided by the fund less competitive than comparable services rendered by insurance companies. Although such constraints do not prevent the activity engaged in by the fund from being regarded as an economic activity, they might justify the exclusive right of such a body to manage a supplementary pension scheme.[44]

Clearly then, a public interest exception is available if the competition rules are found to apply, albeit subject to a proportionality test.

(ii) Convergence with the free movement rules: proportionate exception to safeguard financial stability. It is worth noting that the same rationale can be detected in the Court's free movement decisions in *Kohll* and *Decker*,[45] where it subjected social security to the free movement rules as well – holding that, in this context, measures with a discriminatory effect could be saved only if covered by 'an overriding reason of general interest' – for example, the need to safeguard the financial stability of

---

[44] Case C-67/96 *Albany* [1999] ECR I-5751, para. 85; Joined Cases C-115, 116, 117 and 119/97 *Brentjens* [1999] ECR I-6025, para. 85; and Case C-219/97 *Drijvende Bokken* [1999] ECR I-6121, para. 75.

[45] Finally, in the *Kohll* and *Decker* line of case law, the Court is walking a tightrope distinguishing between social security and insurance, a distinction bound to become more fluid with the diversification of financial services and the emergence of, for example, pension investment funds. Cf. Case C-120/95 *Decker* [1998] ECR I-1831; and Case C-158/96 *Kohll* [1998] ECR I-1931, paras. 23 and 19, respectively. Even if Community law does not detract from the powers of the Member States to organise their social security systems, 'they must nevertheless comply with Community law when exercising those powers'.

the social security system.[46] Clearly, this mirrors the reasoning concerning the conditions under which cross-subsidies may be acceptable in the context of the financial stability of a universal service system for postal services in the Article 86(2) EC *Corbeau* Case of 1993[47] – suggesting convergence between the applicable criteria in free movement and competition cases.

When determining the proper scope of the public authority task, therefore, in effect the Court demands the same respect of the principles of necessity and proportionality that apply in respect of certain restraints of competition which are considered acceptable under Articles 81(3) and 86(2) EC. That is, their perceived legitimate benefits must outweigh their perceived cost.

3.6. Restrictive agreements between undertakings falling outside the scope of the competition rules

In the case of economic activities subject to competition, the requirements for finding an illegal agreement between undertakings, the existence of restrictions of competition in the sense of Article 81(1) EC and the appreciable nature of the effects of these restrictions evidently continue to apply. In this context, it should be noted, however, that even agreements between undertakings that are restrictive of competition may not infringe Article 81 EC. Where public interest issues are at stake, the Court has been more creative in contriving unusual exceptions, albeit with reference to the familiar grounds of teleology, de minimis rules and proportionality.

(i) Teleology: Thus in *Albany, Brentjens* and *Drijvende Bokken,* and subsequently in *Van der Woude,*[48] the Court found a new exception to the competition rules for collective bargaining agreements relating to affiliation to sectoral pension funds, based on a teleological reading of

---

[46] In Case C-238/94 *Jose Garcia and Others* v. *Mutuelle de Prévoyance Sociale d'Aquitaine and Others* [1996] ECR I-1673, the Court excluded social security systems from the non-life insurance Directive (OJ 1973 L228/3). Slightly upbeat, Laigre, 'Régimes de Sécurité Sociale et Entreprises d'Assurance', [1996] *Droit Social* 705. See generally Binon, 'Solidarité et Assurance: Mariage de Coeur ou de Raison?', [1997] RMUE 87; and Mavridis, 'Régimes Complémentaires: Droit de la Concurrence ou Droit Social Communautaire?', [1998] *Droit Social* 239.

[47] Case C-320/91 *Corbeau* [1993] ECR I-2533.

[48] Case C-222/98 *Hendrik van der Woude* v. *Stichting Beatrixoord (Van der Woude)* [2000] ECR I-7111.

the Treaty as a whole. Essentially, it held that because Treaty provisions on social policy stood on equal footing with those on competition and, given the role assigned to 'social dialogue' in this context (where 'it is beyond question that certain restrictions of competition are inherent'), that agreements concluded in the context of collective bargaining fell outside the scope of the prohibition in Article 81(1) EC.[49]

(ii) De minimis: In *Pavlov*, the Court held that the decision by the medical specialists (classified as undertakings) to set up a pension fund entrusted with the management of supplementary pensions did not appreciably restrict competition because 'the costs of the supplementary pension scheme has only a marginal and indirect influence on the final cost of the services offered by self-employed medical specialists'.[50] Hence it was found to fall below the de minimis threshold of appreciability.

(iii) Proportional restrictions on public interest grounds (in the absence of pre-emption): In *Wouters*, the Court went one step further to hold that 'not every agreement between undertakings or every decision of an association of undertakings which restricts the freedom of action of the parties or of one of them necessarily falls within the prohibition laid down in Article 81(1) of the Treaty', and eventually, that 'it does not appear that the effects restrictive of competition such as those resulting for members of the Bar practising in the Netherlands from a regulation such as the 1993 Regulation go beyond what is necessary in order to ensure the proper practice of the legal profession', and hence was found not to infringe Article 81(1) EC.[51] This is in line with the judgements in cases such as *Pronuptia*[52] and *Gøttrup-Klim*,[53] which have been variously described as based on 'ancillary restraints' (i.e. necessary in relation to a lawful agreement), dating back to the 1977 *Metro* Case,[54]

---

[49] Case C-67/96 *Albany* [1999] ECR I-5751, paras. 59–60; Joined Cases C-115, 116, 117 and 119/97 *Brentjens* [1999] ECR I-6025, paras. 59–60; and Case C-219/97 *Drijvende Bokken* [1999] ECR I-6121, paras. 49–50.

[50] Joined Cases C-180 to 184/98 *Pavlov* [2000] ECR I-6451, para. 97. The roots of appreciability are traditionally traced back to Case 56/65 *Société Technique Minière* v. *Maschinenbau Ulm GmbH* [1966] ECR 337; and Case 5/69 *Franz Völk* v. *Ets J. Vervaecke* [1969] ECR 295.

[51] Case C-309/99 *Wouters* [2002] ECR I-1577, paras. 97 and 109.

[52] Case 161/84 *Pronuptia de Paris GmbH* v. *Pronuptia de Paris Irmgard Schillgallis (Pronuptia)* [1986] ECR 353, para. 27.

[53] Case C-250/92 *Gøttrup-Klim et al.* v. *Dansk Landbrugs Grovvareselskab AmbA (Gøttrup-Klim)* [1994] ECR I-5641, paras. 35 and 45.

[54] Case 26/76 *Metro SB-Grossmarkte GmbH & Co* v. *Commission* [1977] ECR 1875, paras. 21–2.

and as based on a 'rule of reason' or a 'new economic approach' which allows the pro- and anti-competitive aspects of an agreement to be weighed under Article 81(1) EC instead of Article 81(3) EC, generally exemplified by the *Nungesser* Case.[55]

The contested Bar Regulation in *Wouters* was enabled by a national law that entrusted the Bar with responsibility for ensuring the 'proper practice' of the legal profession, without however specifying what this might entail. In this context, the Court formulated the relevant test under Article 81 EC:

> For the purposes of application of that provision to a particular case, account must first of all be taken of the overall context in which the decision of the association of undertakings was taken or produces its effects, and more particularly of its objectives ... It has then to be considered whether the consequential effects restrictive of competition are inherent in the pursuit of those objectives.

Apart from the objectives of the agreement, referring to its case law on 'the need to make rules relating to organisation, qualifications, professional ethics, supervision and liability, in order to ensure that the ultimate consumers of legal services and the sound administration of justice are provided with the necessary guarantees in relation to integrity and experience', the Court referred to its consistent position that 'in the absence of specific Community rules in the field, each Member State is in principle free to regulate the exercise of the legal profession it its territory'.[56] It therefore pointed both to a public interest justification, albeit not in those terms, and to the absence of pre-emption on account of the Community.

In *Medina*, on restrictions imposed by the International Olympic Committee (IOC) for anti-doping purposes, the Court elaborated further on the new public interest test, which is now spelled out in three stages,

---

[55] Case 258/78 *L.C. Nungesser KG and Kurt Eisele* v. *Commission (Nungesser)* [1982] ECR 2015. In Joined Cases T-374, 375 and 388/94 *European Nightservices Ltd et al.* v. *Commission* [1998] ECR II-3141, the Court of First Instance opted for a cautious approach which would allow an assessment of pro- and anti-competitive effects of an agreement under Article 81(1) EC only if it is an agreement that does not involve serious or per se restrictions of competition, which should be assessed under Article 81(3) EC. *Ibid.*, para. 136. Cf. J. Faull and A. Nikpay (eds.), *The EC Law of Competition* (Oxford University Press, 1999), pp. 90–6.

[56] Case C-309/99 *Wouters* [2002] ECR I-1577, paras. 97 and 99; with reference to Case C-3/95 *Reisebüro Broede* v. *Gerd Sandker* [1996] ECR I-6511; and Case 107/83 *Klopp* [1984] ECR 2971.

complete with the familiar proportionality test. First, the agreement or decision at issue must pursue a 'legitimate objective'. Second, the limitation of competition resulting from the decision must be 'inherent' in the pursuit of these objectives. Third, the limitation must not go beyond what is necessary to ensure the safeguarding of these objectives. In other words, a balancing test is required to determine whether constraints on competition are proportionate to a legitimate objective, a test that is carried out under Article 81(1) EC in a true 'rule of reason' approach, long before the derogation of Article 81(3) EC is in the picture. In the matter before it, the Court had relatively little trouble under the first two tests, holding that banning athletes who have tested positive to doping tests is 'inherent' in the IOC's legitimate pursuit of the integrity of competitive sport and ethical values in sport. It was under the proportionality test that the Court seemed to have more difficulties with the IOC's rules, noting that these could well prove 'excessive' both in terms of establishing the thresholds above which the presence of prohibited substances constitute doping and in terms of the penalties involved. Since the appellants in *Medina*, presumably unaware of the Court's new test, had failed to plead excess – concentrating rather on the IOC's economic interests in protecting the marketing value of the Games – they lost.[57]

3.7. Delegation of public authority

A final issue concerning the public authority criterion is that of delegation. Clearly, the exercise of public powers includes the rule-making function. However, having regulatory powers as such does not exempt an entity from application of the competition rules. Indeed, in a constellation where the entity involved combines certain regulatory powers with the offering of related goods and services in the market, the exercise of such regulatory powers may in itself constitute a business activity.

In the 1985 *British Telecom* Case, the Court found that a public law body attributed autonomous regulatory powers concerning the fixing of tariffs and the conditions under which services are provided for users (such as British Telecom) could be considered an undertaking in the sense of the competition rules, as:

---

[57] Case C-519/04 P *David Meca-Medina, Igor Macjen* v. *Commission (Medina)* [2006] ECR I-6991, paras. 42 ff. See Szyszczak, 'Competition and Sport', (2007) 32 ELR 95.

[T]he management . . . of public telecommunication equipment and its placing of such equipment at the disposal of users on payment of a fee amounts to a business activity which as such is subject to the obligations imposed by Article 86 of the Treaty.[58]

In other words: even a regulatory task can have a commercial dimension and therefore be subject to anti-trust scrutiny.

Moreover, delegation that leads the undertakings involved to infringe the competition rules is itself illegal. In particular, in its Article 86 EC case law the Court has insisted that undertakings enjoying special and exclusive rights be relieved of any regulatory duties that place such an undertaking 'at an obvious advantage over its competitors'.[59] Similarly, by certain illegal forms of delegation of public powers, the Member States themselves may infringe the *effet utile* of the competition rules, as discussed below. These two aspects of the subject of delegation are discussed at greater length below in section 4.3. on *The application of competition rules to state measures* (on *effet utile*) and again in section 6.8 on *Delegation of regulatory functions under Article 86 EC*.

3.8. Conclusion

This chapter has focused, first, on a number of concepts, notably 'undertaking', 'economic activity', 'activity typical of a public authority' and 'social function', which the Court uses to determine whether particular entities and/or their activities are to be subjected to the competition rules. Next, we have looked at how the Court has, in addition, created a number of exceptions in cases such as *Albany* and *Wouters* to deal with cases where there could be no doubt that economic activities and agreements between private parties were involved, but

---

[58] Case C-41/83 *Italy* v. *Commission ('British Telecom')* [1985] ECR 873. Noted by Ross, (1985) 10 ELR 457.

[59] Cf. Case C-18/88 *Régie des Télégraphes et des Téléphones* v. *SA GB-INNO-BM (RTT* v. *GB-INNO-BM)* [1991] ECR I-5941, paras. 25–6, noted by Gyselen (1992) 29 CMLR 1229; Case C-202/88 *France* v. *Commission (Terminal Directive)* [1991] ECR I-1223, paras. 51–2, noted by Slot (1991) 28 CMLR 964; and Wheeler (1992) 17 ELR 67. More recently, see Commission Decision 2002/344/EC *La Poste*, OJ 2002 L120/19. With origins in secondary law to this effect, cf. Case C-92/91 *Ministère Public* v. *Taillandier* [1993] ECR I-5383; Case C-69/91 *Ministère Public* v. *Decoster* [1993] ECR I-5335; and Joined Cases C-46/90 and 93/91 *Lagauche et al.* [1993] ECR I-5267. Cf. AG Jacobs in his Opinion on Case C-67/96 *Albany*; Joined Cases C-115, 116, 117 and 119/97 *Brentjens*; and Case C-219/97 *Drijvende Bokken* [1999] ECR I-6121, paras. 451–68.

where it nevertheless saw grounds to leave the measures concerned unaffected on public policy grounds.

As has been seen, the Court applies a functional approach when deciding whether a body should be considered an 'undertaking' subject to the competition rules. The concept of 'undertaking' in turn is based on the question of whether economic activities are carried out, meaning offering goods or services in the marketplace, for payment and while assuming the financial risks involved, as well as offering goods or services in competition, or, in its weakest form, that *could* be subject to competition.

Especially in the latter case the question of whether an activity is 'typical of a public authority' or has an exclusively social function is relevant. The Court has held that the nature and aim of an activity and the rules to which it is subject determine whether it is typical of a public authority. In practice, it appears that this leaves the Member States significant freedom in defining such activities.

The relevant case law is more precise on the definition of what constitutes an exclusively social function. Compulsory participation and definition of benefits based on solidarity rather than contributions or returns on investment are required. Where a lesser extent of solidarity exists, the arrangements concerned may fall under the competition rules, but may for example be subject to the exceptions for exclusive rights.

The exercise of public authority is subject to a proportionality requirement, as are the exceptions to free movement and the Article 86 exceptions. This means a similar (if not identical) standard prevails in all three cases. It may, therefore, be justified to claim a degree of convergence.

Short of applying formal exceptions, the Court has been creative in finding ways of letting agreements with a public interest dimension off the hook even if they have a restrictive effect on competition. In doing so, it has not only applied the more standard de minimis approach, but has found an unwritten exception in the system of the Treaty as a whole for collective bargaining agreements (*Albany*) and has stretched the ancillary restraints doctrine, respectively the new economic approach (or 'rule of reason'), to accommodate private restrictions in the legal profession (*Wouters*). It appears here that the Court is willing to limit the scope of the competition rules based on de minimis, respectively preemption or subsidiarity, much more drastically than under the free movement rules. It is interesting to note that in this case a teleological approach (*Albany*) can lead to a more restrictive rather than a more expansive approach to the competition rules' scope.

Finally, if public authority is delegated to an entity active in the market that combines or mixes regulatory and commercial activities, the competition rules may be applied even to the regulatory activities involved. This subject will be developed further below.

4 Public constraints on private parties and private constraints on public measures

4.1. Introduction

Above, we have discussed the free movement and competition rules separately, focusing on how the scope of these respective rules is determined in relation to the addressees for which they were originally intended – i.e. free movement for Member States and competition rules for undertakings. This showed that the Court tends to apply a functional approach to formal categories of public bodies and undertakings. As illustrated by the functional approach to the concepts of 'public bodies' and 'undertaking', the net result is that the competition rules can be applied to 'public authorities' and the free movement rules to private parties. More recently, however, the Court's functionalism is increasingly qualified by subsidiarity and pre-emption. The nature of the constraints that follow from this development, and their limits, will now be elaborated.

The focus of this chapter is on the cross-cutting application of the free movement and competition rules. This discussion is organised in four main parts dealing with the following topics:

- the application of the free movement rules to private parties;
- the application of the competition rules to State measures;
- when behaviour should be attributed to the State, and when to undertakings;
- the relationship between the free movement and the competition rules directly.

As before, the main questions remain: how (i.e. according to which criteria) the Court attributes measures to either the public or private sphere; how it establishes whether the free movement and competition rules are applicable; and how it decides whether public interest exceptions and/or justifications apply, and what their scope is.

4.2. The application of the free movement rules to private parties

(i) The Court takes a limited functionalist approach to measures restricting the free movement of goods. In principle, of course, private parties can restrict the free movement of goods as effectively as Member States can. The Court surely recognises this and, as discussed above, it has shown some willingness to extend the personal scope of the regime by means of an extensive interpretation of 'the State' for these purposes. There are other signs as well. For example, the Court holds Member States responsible for any obstacles to the free movement of goods arising out of 'charges having equivalent effect to customs duties' within the meaning of Articles 23 and 25 EC, even if these obstacles do not have their origin in State measures. This clearly is a functionalist approach. In *Commission* v. *Italy*, the Court defined a charge having equivalent effect as:

[A]ny pecuniary charge, however small and whatever its designation and mode of application, which is imposed unilaterally on goods by reason that they cross a frontier, even if it is not levied by the State.[1]

In *Dubois*, it went further and held it to be 'immaterial' whether the charge was imposed on an economic agent by virtue of a unilateral measure adopted by the authorities or as a result of a series of private contracts.[2] In *Commission* v. *France*, the Court went yet another step further and was prepared to read the good faith requirement of Article 10 EC into Article 28 EC to hold a Member State responsible for not adopting measures that were required to remove barriers to the free movement of goods that were caused by private individuals.[3] It seems

---

[1] Case C-119/92 *Commission* v. *Italy* [1992] ECR I-393, para. 44. The Commission objected to tariffs of customs forwarding agents. The Commission's claim was dismissed because there was no obligation on the importer to have recourse to a forwarding agent in all circumstances. The Commission then started Regulation No. 17 proceedings against the customs agents themselves (Commission Decision 93/438/EEC OJ 1993 L203/27) and went on to attack the arrangement successfully under Articles 10 and 81 in Case C-35/96 *Italian Customs Agents* [1998] ECR I-3851.

[2] Case C-16/94 *Edouard Dubois* v. *Garonor* [1995] ECR I-2421, para. 20.

[3] Case C-265/95 *Commission* v. *France* [1997] ECR I-6959, para. 31. The case dealt with blockades set up by French farmers on the Franco-Spanish border making it impossible

clear, however, that this obligation is limited to the 'core' public authority tasks of keeping law and order – and removing physical obstacles to free movement of goods erected by protesting farmers and environmentalists.[4] In that vain, it is worth noting that, in *Schmidberger*, the Court of Justice was prepared to balance the obligations of Member States under the free movement of goods against their obligations of guaranteeing protesters' rights of assembly and free expression.[5]

In the end, of course, these cases result in not a great deal more than some tinkering at the margins. On the matter of principle, the Court maintains that Articles 28 and 29 of the Treaty 'concern only public measures and not the conduct of undertakings'.[6] In its 2002 judgment in *Sapod Audic*, the Court confirmed that an obligation arising from private contracts 'cannot be regarded as a barrier to trade for the purpose of Article 28 of the Treaty since it was not imposed by a Member State but agreed between individuals'.[7] On the evidence of wording of the provison and of its place in the Treaty, this refusal to grant horizontal direct effect to Article 28 EC is perfectly uneventful. Still, the Court's stance is remarkable for two reasons. First, the Court is still haunted by its isolated *obiter dictum* in *Dansk Supermarked*, where it stated that:

it is impossible in any circumstances for agreements between individuals to derogate from the mandatory provisions of the Treaty on the free movement of goods.[8]

---

[4] for Spanish fruit to be imported into France. See also Case C-112/00 *Schmidberger* [2003] ECR I-5659, para. 54. This case dealt with an environmental manifestation blocking transit through the Brenner tunnel.

[4] However, see AG Cosmas's Opinion in Case C-411/98 *Angelo Ferlini* [1999] ECR I-8081, paras. 76 et seq. The case dealt with discriminatory medical and maternity fees set by a private hospital association. The Advocate General proposed to hold Luxembourg responsible under the new norm since, *in casu*, 'discrimination begins at the level of the legal and regulatory framework not as a result of positive action, but as a result of the failure to protect a category of persons or, at least, of acquiescence in the fact that different treatment may be accorded to them'. *Ibid.*, para. 77.

[5] Case C-112/00 *Schmidberger* [2003] ECR I-5659, paras. 77 et seq.

[6] See e.g. Case 311/85 *Vlaamse Reisbureaus* [1987] ECR 3801, para. 30.

[7] Case C-159/00 *Sapod Audic* v. *Eco-Emballages* [2002] ECR I-5031, para. 74.

[8] Case 58/80 *Dansk Supermarked* v. *Imerco* [1981] ECR 181, para. 17. The case is scrupulously ignored by the Court in later case law. The exception is AG Geelhoed's Opinion in Case C-253/00 *Muñoz* [2002] ECR I-7289, para. 44 ('By means of this case law, the Court has established that, even where provisions of competition law are not involved, EC law directly impinges on private legal relations.') There is quite some support for the general idea. Earliest, Van Gerven, 'The recent case-law of the Court of Justice concerning Articles 30 and 36 of the EEC Treaty', (1977) 14 CMLR 5, p. 22

Second, it is hard to think of any particularly good reason why the Court would treat private parties under the regime on the free movement of goods differently from the way it treats them under the free movement of workers and services.[9]

(ii) The court recognises horizontal direct effect under the free movement of workers and services. As far back as 1974, the Court applied its functional reasoning to the horizontal application of the prohibitions on restrictions to the free movement of workers and services. Noting the fundamental importance of the prohibition of discrimination on grounds of nationality, it held in *Walrave*:

Prohibition of such discrimination does not only apply to the action of public authorities but extends likewise to rules of any other nature aimed at regulating in a collective manner gainful employment and the provision of services.

The abolition as between Member States of obstacles to freedom of movement for persons and to freedom to provide services, which are fundamental objectives of the Community contained in Article 3(c) of the Treaty, would be compromised if the abolition of barriers of national origin could be neutralised by obstacles resulting from the exercise of their legal autonomy by associations or organisations which do not come under public law.

Since, moreover, working conditions in the various Member States are governed sometimes by means of provisions laid down by law or regulation and sometimes by agreements and other acts concluded or adopted by private persons, to limit the prohibitions in question to acts of a public authority would risk creating inequality in their application.[10]

('private enterprises are obliged to respect the obligations contained therein, at least as a matter of principle'). See further Waelbroeck, 'Les Rapports entre les Règles sur la Libre Circulation des Marchandises et les Règles de Concurrence Applicables aux Entreprises dans la CEE', in F. Capotorti *et al.* (eds.), *Du Droit International au Droit de l'Intégration* (Baden-Baden: Nomos, 1987), p. 781; Schaefer, *Die unmittelbare Wirkung des verbots der nichttarifären Handelshemnisse (Art. 30 EWGV) in den Rechtsbeziehungen zwischen Privaten* (Frankfurt a.M.: Lang, 1987); Steindorff, 'Drittwirkung der Grundfreiheiten im europäischen Geeinshaftsrecht' in P. Badura and R. Scholz (eds.), *Festschrift für Peter Lerche* (Munich: Beck, 1993), p. 576; and E. Steindorff, *EG-Vertrag und Privatrecht* (Baden-Baden: Nomos, 1996), pp. 277 ff. *Contra,* Roth, 'Drittwirkung der Grundfreiheiten?' in O. Due, M. Lutter and J. Schwarze (eds.), *Festschrift für Ulrich Everling* (Baden-Baden: Nomos, 1995), p. 1231. Cf. T.O. Ganten, *Die Drittwirkung der Grundfreiheiten* (Berlin: Duncker & Humblot, 2000).

[9] See Snell, 'Private Parties and the Free Movement of Goods and Services' in M. Andenas and W.-H. Roth (eds.), *Services and Free Movement in EU Law* (Oxford University Press, 2002), p. 211.

[10] Case 36/74 *Walrave and Koch* v. *Association Union Cycliste Internationale and Others* [1974] ECR 1405, paras. 17–19. See also Case 13/76 *Gaetano Donà* v. *Mario Mantero (Donà)* [1976] ECR 1333, para. 17.

The judgment remained strangely isolated for two decades until it was notoriously resurrected in *Bosman* to bring UEFA's transfer system within the scope of Article 39 EC concerning the freedom of movement for workers.[11] In *Wouters*, moreover, the Dutch Bar association was held accountable under the provisions on the free provision of services.[12]

Walrave's rationale is a highly explosive mix of functionalism, *effet utile* and teleology. On the one hand, the Court seems concerned with private collective regulation being capable of restrictions to fundamental freedoms equivalent to those imposed by Member State measures. This, then, plays out both as a desire of uniformity of application of Community law in the face of differences in regulatory structures across Member States and as a concern with the effectiveness of the free movement provisions with a view to market integration in the face of the possibility of private restrictions being substituting for public ones within Member States. It seems clear, however, that functional equivalence to public authority in terms of regulatory competence is by no means the only, or even the dominant, rationale. For example, in *Ferlini*, the Court used *Walrave* as authority for the proposition that Article 12 EC applies to a group or organisation that 'exercises a certain power over individuals and is in a position to impose on them conditions which adversely affect the exercise of the fundamental freedoms guaranteed under the Treaty'.[13] The most obvious evidence for this, however, is the Court's judgment in *Angonese*, where it held a single undertaking to be liable under the free movement of workers for imposing burdensome language tests on prospective employees.[14] The recent trade union cases of *Laval* and *Viking* bring out the point less clearly, but perhaps more profoundly.[15] In *Laval*, a Swedish trade union

---

[11] Cf. Case C-415/93 *Bosman* [1995] ECR I-4921, para. 83. Noted by Weatherill, (1996) 33 CMLR 991; and Jans, (1996) 7 EuZW 91. For further applications of the principle to sporting federations, see Joined Cases C-51/96 and 191/97 *Christelle Deliège* v. *Ligue Francophone de Judo et Disciplines Associées ASBL* [2000] ECR I-2549; Case C-176/96 *Jyri Lehtonen and Castors Canada Dry Namur-Braine SBL* v. *Fédératon Royale Belde des Sociétés de Basket-ball ASBL* [2000] ECR I-2681; and Case C-438/00 *Deutscher Handballbund eV* v. *Maros Kolpak* [2003] ECR I-4135.

[12] Case C-309/99 *Wouters* [2002] ECR I-1577, para. 120.

[13] Case C-411/98 *Angelo Ferlini* [1999] ECR I-8081, para. 50.

[14] Case C-281/98 *Roman Angonese* v. *Cassa di Risparmio di Bolzano SpA (Angonese)* [2000] ECR I-4139, paras. 31–3. Noted by Lane and Shuibhne, (2000) 37 CMLR 1237. Cf. Van den Bogaert, 'Horizontality: The Court Attacks?' in C. Barnard and J. Scott (eds.), *The Law of the Single Market – Unpacking the Premises* (Oxford: Hart, 2002), p. 23.

[15] For general background on the importance of these cases, see Bercusson, 'The Trade Union Movement and the European Union: Judgment Day', (2007) 13 ELJ 279.

took collective action against a Latvian construction company when the latter refused to sign a collective agreement for its workers posted in Sweden.[16] In *Viking*, plans to reflag a Finnish ship to Estonia were frustrated by the International Transport Workers' Federation, which, in an effort to force the shipping company to enter into a collective agreement with the Finnish Seamen's Union, imposed on its affiliates – among them the relevant Estonian trade union – the prohibition to enter into negotiations with the company.[17] In both of these cases, the Court relied on *Walrave* and *Bosman* to hold the trade unions liable under the free movement provisions. The paradox is, of course, that in both cases the restrictions on free movement resulted from the trade unions' very lack of ability to achieve collective regulation. The conclusion to be drawn from *Angonese*, *Laval* and *Viking*, then, seems to be that the horizontal direct effect of the free movement of workers and the freedom to provide services is not based on functional equivalence to public authority, but on functional equivalence to public power: the test is the mere ability, whether it stems from regulatory, economic or physical power, to impose restrictions on the fundamental freedoms. This collapse of personal into material scope is perhaps clearest from *Laval*:

It must be pointed out that the right of trade unions of a Member State to take collective action by which undertakings established in other Member States may be forced to sign the collective agreement for the building sector is liable to make it less attractive, or more difficult, for such undertakings to carry out construction work in Sweden, and therefore constitutes a restriction on the freedom to provide services within the meaning of Article 49 EC.[18]

Be that as it may, the familiar pattern of horizontal widening of the scope of free movement combined with a vertical withdrawal (or subsidiarity) is repeated here again. In *Bosman*, the Court ruled that not just Member States could rely on public interest exceptions to the free movement of workers, but private parties as well:

There is nothing to preclude individuals from relying on justifications on grounds of public policy, public security or public health. Neither the scope nor the content of those grounds of justification is in any way affected by the public or private nature of the rules in question.[19]

---

[16] Case C-314/05 *Laval* [2007] ECR I-11767.
[17] Case C-438/05 *ITF* v. *Viking* [2007] ECR I-10779.
[18] Case C-314/05 *Laval*, judgment of 18 December 2007, nyr, para. 99.
[19] Case C-415/93 *Bosman* [1995] ECR I-4921, para. 86.

In *Laval*, the Court even held that:

the right to take collective action for the protection of the workers of the host State against possible social duping may constitute an overriding reason of public interest within the meaning of the case-law of the Court which, in principle, justifies a restriction of one of the fundamental freedoms guaranteed by the Treaty.[20]

In *Viking*, however, the Court did reject the argument that the *Albany* exclusion of collective bargaining agreements from the competition rules should be applied in analogy to the fundamental freedoms. Its reasoning is thin at best. It held, without any elaboration, that 'it cannot be considered that it is inherent in the very exercise of trade union rights and the right to take collective action that the fundamental freedoms will be prejudiced to a certain degree'.[21] Even more cloudily, it opined that the fact that an agreement or an activity is excluded from the scope of the competition rules does not mean that it is excluded from the scope of the free movement provisions 'since these two sets of provisons are to be applied in different circumstances'.[22]

For *Ordo*liberals, this *Verstaatlichung* – or application of the free movement rules to private law arrangements – is wild-eyed heresy. Kluth paints a bleak scenario where the Court's 'preoccupation with social equilibrium' could herald the end of the *Privatrechtgesellschaft* and thereby of the liberal concept of the internal market.[23] Although the Court never did subscribe to private freedom in the *Ordo*liberal sense, there appears to be little justification for such fears. While the Court has gone much further in its application of the competition rules to state measures, even this possibility is interpreted in a manner that appears to allow private agreements that restrict competition, provided they meet basic procedural guarantees of the public interest.

---

[20] Case C-314/05 *Laval*, judgment of 18 December 2007, nyr, para. 103. Cf. Case C-438/05 *ITF* v. *Viking*, judgment of 11 December 2007, nyr, para. 77.

[21] Case C-438/05 *ITF* v. *Viking*, judgment of 11 December 2007, nyr, para. 52.

[22] Case C-438/05 *ITF* v. *Viking*, judgment of 11 December 2007, nyr, para. 53.

[23] Kluth, 'Die Bindung privater Wirtschaftsteilnehmer und die Grundfreiheiten des EG-Vertrages', (1997) 122 *Archiv des öffentlichen Rechts* 227. Cf. S. Wernicke, *Die Privatwirkung im europäischen Gemeinschaftsrecht* (Baden-Baden: Nomos, 2002); and Lohse, 'Fundamental Freedoms and Private Actors – Towards an "Incidental Horizontal Effect"', (2007) 13 EPL 159.

4.3. The application of competition rules to State measures

The '*effet utile*' doctrine was developed in the Court's case law in the course of the 1980s, when it held that the good faith clause of the Treaty barred Member States from acts that deprived the competition rules applicable to undertakings from their useful effect. Just as the competition rules were added to the Treaty to prevent the four freedoms from being circumvented by market parties, so the *effet utile* doctrine was developed by the Court to prevent the Member States from stripping the competition rules of their effect by imposing anti-competitive behaviour on private parties. In its advance and equally spectacular retreat, the doctrine's development is perhaps the starkest example available of the rise and decline of *Ordo*liberal economic constitutionalism.

(i) *Functionalism and teleology:* Originally, in a famous line of functionalist case law, the Court appeared to be developing its *effet utile* doctrine to the point of imposing severe constraints on national economic policy. Although, as was discussed above, the competition rules of the Treaty are aimed at undertakings, not public authorities, the *effet utile* doctrine holds that the Member States can infringe the good faith provision of Article 10 of the Treaty if they frustrate the functioning of the internal market indirectly, by favouring or even imposing infringements of the competition rules. Because the basis for the *effet utile* is the notion that the Member States are bound by good faith, in the spirit of the Treaty, it is evidently a teleological as much as a functional approach.

In the 1977 *INNO* v. *ATAB* Case, the Court stated:

The second paragraph of Article 10 of the Treaty provides that Member States shall abstain from any measure which could jeopardise the attainment of the objectives of the Treaty.

Accordingly, whilst it is true that Article 82 is directed at undertakings, nonetheless it is also true that the Treaty imposed a duty on Member States not to adopt or maintain in force *any measure which could deprive that provision of its effectiveness*.

Thus Article 86 provides that, in the case of public undertakings and undertakings to which Member States grant special or exclusive rights, Member States shall neither enact nor maintain in force any measure contrary inter alia to the rules provided for in Articles 81 to 89.

Likewise, Member States may not enact measures enabling private undertakings to escape from the constraints imposed by Articles 81 to 89 of the Treaty.[24]

Thus it established the judicial doctrine of the *effet utile* of the Treaty itself by analogy (and in combination) with the prohibition in Article 86(1) EC to enact or maintain in force measures contrary to the competition rules in the case of public or privileged undertakings. The reference to Article 86 was dropped in subsequent cases.

The doctrine then developed to encompass two distinct types of objectionable State measures. The first sees to classic rubber stamping of corporatist arrangements. In the mid-1980s, the Court summarily dismissed the *Bureau National Interprofessionnel du Cognac (BNIC)* as a cartel.[25] Even though the BNIC was financed by para-fiscal levies, all of its members were appointed by the Minister for Agriculture, it was entrusted by law with a public-service mission and its decisions were made binding by ministerial decree, the Court was unimpressed. In familiar 'functional' language, in *BNIC* v. *Clair* it made the sweeping statement that:

the legal framework within which agreements between undertakings are made and decisions by associations of undertakings are taken and the classification given to that framework by the various national legal systems are irrelevant as far as the applicability of the Community rules on competition and in particular Article 81 of the Treaty are concerned.[26]

In *BNIC* v. *Aubert*, two years later, the Court took the consequences, holding a ministerial order that made such an illegal agreement binding on all traders to be an infringement of Articles 10 and 81 EC read together.[27] The conclusion from these cases seemed fairly straightforward: the demands of uniformity of application and effectiveness of the competition rules override institutional deference to Member States to the extent that no amount of State involvement could save an

---

[24] Case 13/77 *SA GB-INNO-BM* v. *Association des détaillants en tabac (INNO* v. *ATAB* [1977] ECR 2115, paras. 30–3.

[25] Case 123/83 *BNIC* v. *Clair* [1985] ECR 391, dealing with price fixing; and Case 136/86 *BNIC* v. *Aubert* [1987] ECR 4789, which dealt with fixing production quotas.

[26] Case 123/83 *BNIC* v. *Clair* [1985] ECR 391, para. 17. The case was decided solely on Article 81, condemning only the price-fixing agreement of the trade organisation without going into the merits of the State measure making the agreement binding on all traders.

[27] Case 136/86 *BNIC* v. *Aubert* [1987] ECR 4789, paras. 22–4 See also Joined Cases 209 to 213/84 *Ministère Public* v. *Asjes et al. (Nouvelles Frontieres)* [1986] ECR 1425; and Case 311/85 *Vlaamse Reisbureaus* [1987] ECR 3801.

anti-competitive agreement. This, of course, was radical enough.[28] The second strand, however, went even further. This type of State measure featured in *INNO* v. *ATAB* itself, but is perhaps best exemplified by *Au Blé Vert*: here, French legislation required price fixing by publishers and importers of books and prohibited retailers from undercutting the established price by more than 5 per cent.[29] The Court noted in frustration that no infringement of Article 81 EC by private parties was necessary in order for them to achieve the same results as the ones a cartel would aspire to, and added:

> Accordingly, the question arises as to whether national legislation which renders corporate behaviour of the type prohibited by Article 81(1) superfluous, by making the book publisher or importer responsible for freely fixing binding retail prices, detracts from the effectiveness of Article 81 and is therefore contrary to the second paragraph of Article 10 of the Treaty.[30]

Had this line of case law been developed further, the *effet utile* doctrine might have amounted to a general norm of EU law whereby state measures per se would have been subject to scrutiny on the basis of the substantive requirements of undistorted competition. The Court was clearly hesitant to pursue this. In *INNO* v. *ATAB*, it took refuge in Article 28 EC, holding that, 'in any case', the measures at issue would generally be incompatible with the regime on the free movement of goods.[31] In *Au Blé Vert*, it decided that, 'as Community law stands', the norm resulting from the combined application of Articles 10 and 81 'was not specific enough' to preclude Member States from enacting legislation of the kind at issue.[32] In its famous *Van Eycke* 'restatement' of *effet utile*, the

---

[28] And welcome in some circles. Van der Esch, 'Die Artikel 5, 3f, 85/86 und 90 EWGV als Grundlage der Wettbewerbsrechtlichen Verpflichtungen der Mitgliedstaaten', (1991) 155 ZHR 274, p. 299 hopefully spoke of 'Entkorporatisierung' as not just a possible aim of *Ordnungspolitik*, but as directly effective Community law. Reich, 'Die Bedeutung der Binnemarktkonzeption für die Anwendung der EWG-Wettbewerbsregeln' in J. F. Baur, K. J. Hopt and K. P. Mailänder (eds.), *Festschrift für Ernst Steindorff* (Berlin: De Gruyter, 1990), pp. 1065 and 1080, bluntly concluded: 'für die romanischen EG-Staaten sind Formen kooperativer Wirtschaftslenkung nicht mehr durchsetzbar'.

[29] Case 13/77 *SA GB-INNO-BM* v. *Association des détaillants en tabac (INNO* v. *ATAB)* [1977] ECR 2115 dealt with legislation making prices unilaterally set by tobacco manufacturers and importers generally binding.

[30] Case 229/83 *Leclerc* v. '*Au Blé Vert*' *et al.(Au Blé Vert)* [1985] ECR 1, para. 15.

[31] Case 13/77 *SA GB-INNO-BM* v. *Association des détaillants en tabac (INNO* v. *ATAB)* [1977] ECR 2115, para. 35.

[32] Case 229/83 *Leclerc* v. '*Au Blé Vert*' *et al.(Au Blé Vert)* [1985] ECR 1, para. 20. See also Case 254/87 *Syndicat des Librairies de Normandie* v. *l'Aigle Distribution* [1988] ECR 4457, para. 15. There are of course considerable similarities here with the outcome of the 1997

Court left the door ajar when it spelled out those instances in which Member States could render the competition rules ineffective:

It must be pointed out ... that Articles 81 and 82 of the Treaty per se are concerned only with the conduct of undertakings and not with national legislation. The Court has consistently held, however, that Articles 81 and 82 of the Treaty, in conjunction with Article 10 require the Member States not to introduce or maintain in force measures, even of a legislative nature, which may render ineffective the competition rules applicable to undertakings.

Such *would be* the case if a Member State were to require or favour the adoption of agreements, decisions or concerted practices contrary to Article 81 or to reinforce their effects, or to deprive its own legislation of its official character by delegating to private traders responsibility for taking decisions affecting the economic sphere.[33]

(ii) Subsidiarity. In its 1993 'November revolution', the Court put an end to hopes, fears and voluminous academic debate about the reach of the *effet utile* doctrine.[34] First, in *OHRA* and *Meng*, it retreated from its

Electricity cases. Cf. Case C-157/94 *Commission* v. *Netherlands (Dutch Electricity Monopoly)* [1997] ECR I-5699; Case C-158/94 *Commission* v. *Italy (Italian Electricty Monopoly)* [1997] ECR I-5789; Case C-159/94 *Commission* v. *France (French Electricity and Gas Monopoly)* [1997] ECR I-5815; and Case C-160/94 *Commission* v. *Spain (Spanish Electricity Monopoly)* [1997] ECR I-5851.

[33] Case 267/86 *Pascal Van Eycke* v. *ASPA NV (Van Eycke)* [1988] ECR 4769, para. 16. Emphasis added.

[34] Cf. Galmot and Biancarelli, 'Les Réglementations Nationales en Matière de Prix au Regard du Droit Communautaire', (1985) 21 RTDE 267; Paulis, 'Les Etats peuvent-ils Enfreindre les Article 85 et 86 du Traité CEE?', (1985) 104 *Journal des Tribunaux – Droit Européen* 209; Marenco, 'Le Traité CEE Interdit-il aux Etats Membres de Restreindre la Concurrence?', (1986) 22 CDE 285; Pappalardo, 'Die europäische Gerichtshof auf der Suche nach einem Kriterium für die Anwendung der Wettbewerbsregeln auf staatliche Maßnahmen' in E.-J. Mestmäcker, H. Möller and H.-P. Schwarz (eds.), *Eine Ordnungspolitik für Europa* (Baden-Baden: Nomos, 1987), p. 303; Pescatore, 'Public and Private Aspects of European Community Competition Law', (1987) 10 *Fordham IL Journal* 373; Slot, 'The Application of Articles 3(f), 5 and 85 to 94 EEC' (1987) 12 ELR 179; D. Waelbroeck, 'Application des Règles de Concurrence du Traité de Rome à l'Autorité Publique', (1987) 30 RMC 25; Joliet, 'Réglementations Étatiques Anticoncurrentielles et Droit Communautaire', (1988) 24 CDE 363; Gyselen, 'State Action and the Effectiveness of the EEC Treaty's Competition Provisions', (1989) 26 CMLR 33; Monopolkommission, *Hauptgutachten 1988/1989: Wettbewerbspolitk vor neuen Herausforderungen* (Baden-Baden: Nomos, 1990); Van der Esch, 'Dérégulation, Autorégulation et le Régime de Concurrence non Faussée dans la CEE', (1990) 26 CDE 499; Van der Esch, 'Die Artikel 5, 3f, 85/86 und 90 EWGV als Grundlage der wettbewerbsrechtlichen Verpflichtungen der Mitgliedstaaten', (1991) 155 ZHR 274; A. Bach, *Wettbewerbsrechtliche Schranken für staatliche Maßnahmen nach europäischem Gemeinschaftsrecht* (Tübingen: Mohr, 1992); Möschel, 'Hoheitliche Maßnahmen und die Wettbewerbsvorschriften des Gemeinschaftsrechts' in FIW, *Weiterentwicklung der*

threat to strike down anti-competitive legislation in the absence of any private behaviour of the kind prohibited by Article 81 EC. These cases involved German and Dutch legislation restricting price competition in the insurance industry. At issue in *Meng* was legislation prohibiting insurance agents from passing on commission from insurance companies to their clients; at issue in *OHRA* were measures prohibiting insurance companies from offering rebates and other financial advantages directly to clients, rather than to intermediaries.[35] Similar rules had been held to infringe Articles 10 and 81 EC in *Vlaamse Reisbureaus*, where tour operators sought to limit commission sharing between travel agents and their customers. In this case, however, the relevant legal provisions formed 'part of a structure involving agreements at various levels intended to oblige travel agents to observe the prices of tours fixed by tour operators'. Hence, they were found to reinforce the effects of Article 81 infringements.[36]

In neither *Meng* nor *OHRA*, however, was there evidence of conduct of the type prohibited to Article 81 EC on the part of undertakings. After considerable soul-searching and an extensive comparative fact-finding effort in *Meng*,[37] the Court settled once and for all that the *effet utile* doctrine only applies where there is a link between Member State action and anti-competitive agreements:

Article 3(g), the second paragraph of Article 10 and Article 81 of the EEC Treaty do not, *in the absence of any link with conduct on the part of undertakings* of the kind referred to in Article 81(1) of the Treaty, preclude State rules which prohibit insurance intermediaries from transferring to their clients all or part of the commission paid by insurance companies.[38]

---

europäischen Gemeinschaften und der Marktwirtschaft (Cologne: Heymann, 1992), p. 94; and Mestmäcker, 'Zur Anwendbarkeit der Wettbewerbsregeln auf die Mitgliedstaaten und die europäischen Gemeinschaften' in J. Baur, P.-C. Müller-Graf and M. Zuleeg (eds.), *Europarecht, Energierecht, Wirtschaftsrecht: Festschrift für Bodo Börner zum 70. Geburtstag* (Cologne: Heymann, 1992).

[35] Case C-2/91 *Meng* [1993] ECR I-5751; and Case C-245/91 *OHRA* [1993] ECR I-5851. Noted by Bach [1994] 31 CMLR 1357; Hancher (1994) 5 *Utilities Law Review* 22; Möschel, 'Wird die effet utile Rechtssprechung des EuGH inutile?', (1994) 47 NJW 1709; and Van der Esch, 'Loyauté Fédérale et Subsidiarité', (1994) 30 CDE 523.

[36] Case 311/85 *Vlaamse Reisbureaus* [1987] ECR 3801, para. 12.

[37] Report of the hearing in Case C-2/91 *Meng* [1993] ECR I-5751, para. 5759.

[38] Case C-2/91 *Meng* [1993] ECR I-5751, para. 22. In the English text, 'such *would be* the case' (Case 267/86 *Pascal Van Eycke* v. *ASPA NV (Van Eycke)* [1988] ECR 4769, para. 16) has been changed to 'such *is* the case' (Case C-2/91 *Meng* [1993] ECR I-5751, para. 14; Case C-245/91 *OHRA* [1993] ECR I-5851, para. 10); in the French text, the shift from list of examples to exhaustive list of categories is much clearer by the omission of the word

This means that the Court will declare restrictions of competition by private parties illegal, whereas legislative or regulatory solutions of the same content are acceptable in so far as they respect the principles of non-discrimination and proportionality. A legal rule adopted by a public authority or a regulatory instrument infringes the *effet utile* only if it is based directly on a pre-existing agreement that infringes the competition rules. This appears to be a formal approach that could lead to a different assessment of restraints on competition that are identical in content, based on their legal form, i.e. the exact opposite of functionalism.[39] Thus Advocate General Lenz's nightmare scenario, painted in *Vlaamse Reisbureaus*, regained its relevance:

if Member States were permitted to restrict the sphere of application of the competition provisions of the EEC Treaty by means of legislative measures, they would be able to determine unilaterally the scope of Community law.[40]

It should also be noted that *Meng* sits uneasily with the Court's tougher stance in its combined reading of Articles 82 and 86(1) EC, where it has struck down legislation creating exclusive rights even without proof that the dominant position thus created was actually abused.[41] The Court here finds that:

although merely granting a dominant position by granting exclusive rights within the meaning of Article 86(1) of the Treaty is not in itself incompatible with Article 82, a Member State is in breach of the prohibitions contained in those two provisions if the undertaking in question, merely by exercising the

'notamment'. Later, the Court took to the formula 'Articles 5 and 85 are infringed where'. Cf. Joined Cases C-140 to 142/94 *DIP SpA and Others* v. *Commune di Bassano del Grappa and Commune di Chioggia (DIP)* [1995] ECR I- 3257, para. 15. Later still, the Court has returned to 'Such *would* be the case': Case C-35/96 *Italian Customs Agents* [1998] ECR I-3851, para. 54.

[39] Cf. Gyselen, 'Anti-Competitive State Measures under the EC Treaty: Towards a Substantive Legality Standard', (1994) 19 ELR Competition Checklist 55, p. 61. Judge Ole Due admits as much in Due, 'Pourquoi cette Solution? (De Certains Problèmes Concernant la Motivation des Arrêts de la Cour de Justice des Communautés Européennes)' in *Festschrift Everling* (Baden-Baden: Nomos, 1995), p. 273. Cf. Chan-Mo, 'The Relationship Between State Regulation and EC Competition Law: Two Proposals for a Coherent Approach', (1995) ECLR 87.

[40] Opinion in Case 311/85 *Vlaamse Reisbureaus* [1987] ECR 3801, point 3815. Advocates General Jacobs and Léger have expressed their dissatisfaction with *Meng's* requirement of a 'link' in their respective Opinions in Joined Cases C-180 to 184/98 *Pavel Pavlov* [2000] ECR I-6451, para. 161; and Case C-35/99 *Arduino* [2002] ECR I-1529, para. 88.

[41] See generally Bacon, 'State Regulation of the Market and EC Competition Rules: Articles 85 and 86 Compared', (1997) 18 ECLR 283.

exclusive rights granted to it, is led to abuse its dominant position, or when such rights are liable to create a situation in which that undertaking is led to commit such abuses.[42]

In these cases the Court considers it 'immaterial' whether an actual instance of abuse has been identified or not.[43] The strongest formulations are found in *Bodson*, where it found that abuse was 'imposed' by legislation[44] and *Höfner*, where it held the legislation to create a situation in which the undertaking in question 'cannot avoid infringing Article 82'.[45] Abuse was found to be 'induced' (in various wordings) in *ERT* and a number of subsequent cases.[46] In *La Crespelle*, the Court suggested that the crucial distinction is whether the (alleged) abuse 'is the direct consequence of the national Law'.[47] If this is not the case, it is for the national court to examine whether there actually was an abusive practice, for example, the charging of excessive ('exorbitant') prices.[48] These issues will be discussed further below in the chapters on Article 86.

Second, in *Reiff*,[49] the Court retreated from its stance that no measure of public involvement could render an anti-competitive agreement a legitimate instrument of economic policy. Dealing with corporatist

---

[42] Case C-136/96 *Ministero Pubblico* v. *Silvano Raso et al. (Raso)* [1998] ECR I-533, para. 27. Cf. C-451/03 *Servizi Ausiliari Dottori Commercialisti* v. *Calafiori* [2006] ECR I-2941, para. 27.

[43] Case C-136/96 *Raso* [1998] ECR I-533, para. 31.

[44] Case 30/87 *Bodson* [1988] ECR 2479, para. 34.

[45] Case C-41/90 *Höfner* [1991] ECR I-1979, para. 27.

[46] Case C-260/89 *Elliniki Radiophonia Tileorassi* v. *Dimotiki Etairia Pliroforissis and Sotirios Kouvelas (ERT)* [1991] ECR I-2925. Cf. Case C-179/90 *Merci Convenzionali Porto di Genova* v. *Siderurgica Gabrielli (Merci)* [1991] ECR I-5889; Case C-18/88 *RTT* v. *GB-INNO-BM* [1991] ECR I-5941; and Case C-18/93 *Corsica Ferries Italia* v. *Corpo di Piloti di Genova (Corsica Ferries Italia)* [1994] ECR I-1783. This solution is advocated by Pais Antunes, 'L'Article 90 du Traité CEE', (1991) RTDE 187, pp. 198 ff; and A. Bach, *Wettbewerbsrechtliche Schranken für staatliche Maßnahmen nach europäischem Gemeinschaftsrecht* (Tübingen: Mohr, 1992), pp. 41 ff; cf. Mestmäcker, 'Staat und Unternehmen im europäischen Gemeinschaftsrecht', (1988) *Rabels Zeitschrift* 527, pp. 551 ff; cf. Advocate General van Gerven's Opinion in Joined Cases C-48 and 66/90 *The Netherlands and Others* v. *Commission* [1992] ECR I-565, paras. 33 ff.

[47] Case C-323/93 *Société Civile Agricole d'Insémination la Crespelle Coopérative d'Elévage et d'Insémination Artificielle du Département de la Mayenne (La Crespelle)* [1994] ECR I-5080, para. 20. In this case insemination centres with regional monopolies were allowed to charge the 'additional costs' for the use of semen from other centres; 'although it leaves the insemination centres the task of calculating those costs, such a provision does not leave the centres to charge disproportionate costs and thereby abuse their dominant position' (para. 21).

[48] Case C-323/93 *La Crespelle* [1994] ECR I-5080, paras. 20 and 27. Cf. Case C-242/95 *GT-Link A/S* v. *De Danske Statsbaner* [1997] ECR I-4449.

[49] Case C-185/91 *Reiff* [1993] ECR I-4769.

price fixing mechanisms for the road haulage industry, the judgment presents itself as an exercise in distinguishing the arrangement from the one in the *BNIC* cases on the facts. In *BNIC* v. *Clair*, the Court had held that the 'experts' were:

persons who, although appointed by the public authorities, were proposed for appointment by the trade organisations directly concerned and who consequently must be regarded as in fact representing those organisations in the negotiation and conclusion of the agreement.[50]

The tariff board for road haulage, by contrast, was found to be above board:

The Tariff Boards provided for by the *Güterkraftverkehrsgesetz* are made up of tariff experts from the relevant sectors of the road haulage industry who are not bound by orders or instructions from the undertakings or associations which proposed them to the Federal Minister of Transport for appointment. Those boards cannot therefore be regarded as meetings of representatives of the undertakings in the industry concerned.

Moreover, these experts were 'called on to fix the tariffs on the basis of considerations of public interest', and the relevant tariffs were fixed only after compulsory consultation of an advisory committee made up of representatives of the users of the services concerned.[51] Finally, in *Reiff*, the decision rendering the agreement binding on all traders did not constitute 'delegation' as the public authorities were able (at least in principle) to ensure that public interest considerations were actually taken into account, and had formally reserved the right to overrule the decisions of the tariff boards.[52]

The Court's findings on the facts are implausible at best. The BNIC, after all, was established by public law and endowed with a *mission de service public*, had its decision-making procedures approved by law, had

---

[50] Case 123/83 *BNIC* v. *Clair* [1985] ECR 391, para. 19.

[51] Case C-185/91 *Reiff* [1993] ECR I-4769, paras. 17–18; noted in disbelief by Bach (1994) 31 CMLR 1357. The Court's reasoning also failed to convince the referring court in *Delta*, a case dealing with almost identical price fixing arrangements for inland waterway transport. Given the similarities between the cases, it had been invited to withdraw its questions after the Court had decided *Reiff*. AG Darmon reports that it declined to do so 'not by reason of the differences which might exist between the problems raised by the two procedures, but because, since it disagreed with the solution adopted by the Court, it concluded, for its part, that there was a cartel'. Opinion, Case C-153/93 *Delta* [1994] ECR I-2517, point 5.

[52] Case C-185/91 *Reiff* [1993] ECR I-4769, para. 22. Cf. Case C-153/93 *Delta* [1994] ECR I-2517, para. 21.

its meetings attended by a *Commissaire du gouvernement*, and had its decisions open to judicial review by administrative courts. The competent Minister, moreover, had every right to refuse to extend the agreements reached by the *Bureau*. More importantly, however, the judgment in *Reiff* overturned the BNIC cases on principle. In *BNIC* v. *Clair*, the Court had held that:

> *by its very nature*, an agreement fixing a minimum price for a product which is submitted to the public authorities with a view to obtaining approval for that minimum price so that it becomes binding on all traders on the market in question is intended to distort competition on that market.[53]

Even if, on a most optimistic assessment of the procedural and institutional guarantees in place, one would conclude that the price-fixing arrangement in *Reiff* could conceivably further the public interests that the legislation sought to protect, it is much harder to see how the arrangement would not still, 'by its very nature', have as its objective the restriction of competition. Furthermore, in that case, as noted above, the arrangement could not escape the cardinal lesson of *BNIC* v. *Clair* that public involvement in and approval of anti-competitive agreements are 'irrelevant' for the applicability of Article 81 EC.[54]

(iii) The demise of functionalism: Reiff and progeny not only depart from previous case law, they also pose a problem in relation to *Meng* itself. The issue here is the fate of the delegation test. The *Van Eycke* restatement, it will be remembered, holds Member States to fall foul of *effet utile* if they require, favour or reinforce anti-competitive agreements *or* where they deprive legislation of its official character by delegating to private traders responsibility for taking decisions affecting the economic sphere. That restatement has never been modified, and the Court scrupulously applies both tests. As part of a doctrine of competition law, however, the delegation test has ceased to make any sense after *Meng*: if the delegation involves the granting of regulatory powers to private parties involved in anti-competitive behaviour, the test is wholly superfluous since the legislation will inevitably fall foul of the first test as favouring, requiring or reinforcing that behaviour. If, on the other hand, the State measure has no link with private collusion, *Meng*

---

[53] Case 123/83 *BNIC* v. *Clair* [1985] ECR 391, para. 22. Emphasis added.
[54] Implausibly, the Court maintains that Case 123/83 *BNIC* v. *Clair* [1985] ECR 391, para. 17, quoted above, is still good law, repeating it in e.g.: Case C-35/96 *Italian Customs Agents* [1998] ECR I-3851, para. 40; and Case C-309/99 *Wouters* [2002] ECR I-1577, para. 66.

teaches that the legislation, however anti-competitive, is safe from anti-trust scrutiny. Logically, then, this would seem to suggest that the delegation test is an autonomous norm prohibiting Member States from depriving legislation of its 'official character' *regardless* of its substantive anti-competitive effects and *regardless* of whether the private parties involved take decisions affecting the economic sphere in a manner that infringes Article 81 EC.[55] The delegation test would then effectively be turned into a constitutional norm, far removed from its origins in competition law. Such an understanding of the delegation test would make the Court of First Instance's remarkable outburst in *Piau* seem less of a loose cannon. In that case, dealing with FIFA's regulation of the murky world of football players' agents, the Court noted in *dictum*:

With regard to FIFA's legitimacy, contested by the applicant, to enact such rules, which do not have a sport-related object, but regulated an economic activity that is peripheral to the sporting activity in question and touch on fundamental freedoms, the rule-making power claimed by a private organisation like FIFA, whose main statutory purpose is the promotion of football, is indeed open to question, in the light of the principles common to the Member States on which the European Union is founded.

The very principle of regulation of an economic activity concerning neither the specific nature of sport nor the freedom of internal organisation of sports associations by a private-law body, like FIFA, which has not been delegated any such power by a public authority, cannot from the outset be regarded as compatible with Community law, in particular with regard to respect for civil and economic liberties.

In principle, such regulation, which constitutes policing of an economic activity and touches upon fundamental freedoms, falls within the competence of the public authorities.[56]

It would be, though, a most paradoxical outcome of the Court's 'subsidiarity revolution' to introduce a highly intrusive constitutional anti-delegation doctrine as the price to pay for deference on the substantive anti-competitive test. The Court has, accordingly, never used the test autonomously. Where it has found no infringement of Article 81 EC,

---

[55] AG Tesauro's Opinion in *Meng* suggests such a reading where he denies the need for a 'link' under the delegation test 'precisely because, and to the extent to which, the Member State *deprives its own legisation of its official character*'. Case C-2/91 *Meng* [1993] ECR I-5751, point 18 of the Opinion. Emphasis in original.

[56] Case T-193/02 *Laurent Piau* v. *FIFA* [2005] ECR II-209, paras. 76–8. See the puzzled note by Waelbroeck and Ibañez Colomo, (2006) 43 CMLR 1743.

it has never found delegation either. Furthermore, in the one case where it did find that the State had 'wholly relinquished to private economic operators the powers of the public authorities as regards the setting of tariffs',[57] it also found that the association involved, the *Consiglio Nazionale degli Spedizionari Doganali* (CNSD), had infringed Article 81 EC.[58]

Instead, *Reiff* started a string of case law which seemed to roll the entire *Van Eycke* restatement, including the delegation norm, into one rather diffuse public interest test.[59] To be sure, for a while this happened in a clearly separated two-stage process by which the Article 81 analysis was distinct from the delegation analysis. Under that first test, the Court looks first at the composition of the committee involved. If, as in *Spediporto*, it finds a majority of public officials,[60] or, as in *Reiff* and *Delta*, of 'experts',[61] or, as in *DIP*, at least a minority of interested traders,[62] this goes a long way towards excluding the body from the scope of Article 81 EC. In *Librandi*, however, it made clear that this was not a necessary condition and that no infringement of Article 81 EC takes place as long as the committee involved, in adopting its decisions, 'must observe public interest criteria defined by law'.[63] It also defined the term for these purposes as requiring 'that the interests of the collectivity had to prevail over the private interests of indivual operators'.[64] In all of these cases, the delegation test was applied

---

[57] Case C-35/96 *Italian Customs Agents* [1998] ECR I-3851, para. 57.

[58] Case C-35/96 *Italian Customs Agents* [1998] ECR I-3851, para. 51. Cf. Case T-513/93 *CNSD* v. *Commission* [2000] ECR II-1807.

[59] See Schepel, 'Delegation of Regulatory Powers to Private Parties under EC Competition Law: Towards a Procedural Public Interest Test', (2002) 39 CMLR 31. Cf. Triantafyllou, 'Les Règles de la Concurrence et l'Activité Étatique y Compris les Marchés Publics', (1996) 32 RTDE 57.

[60] Case C-96/94 *Centro Servizi Spediporto* [1995] ECR I-2883, para. 23.

[61] Case C-185/91 *Reiff* [1993] ECR I-4769; and Case C-153/93 *Delta* [1994] ECR I-2517.

[62] Joined Cases C-140 to 142/94 *DIP* v. *Comune di Bassano del Grappa* [1995] ECR I-3257, para. 17. A majority was composed of workers' representatives, representatives of public authorities and experts appointed by the latter.

[63] Case C-38/97 *Librandi* v. *Cuttica Spedizioni* [1998] ECR I-5955, para. 34. Noted by Leroy, (2001) 37 RTDE 49. The case dealt with the same piece of legislation at issue in Case C-96/94 *Centro Servizi Spediporto* [1995] ECR I-2883, amended to reverse the minority-majority relationship.

[64] Case C-38/97 *Librandi* v. *Cuttica Spedizioni* [1998] ECR I-5955, para. 40. At issue, specifically, was the question as to whether there was a difference between the Court's use of the terms 'general' or 'public interest'. There wasn't. See generally Boutayeb, 'Une Recherche sur la Place et les Functions de l'Intérêt General en Droit Communautaire', (2003) 39 RTDE 587. However normatively attractive the requirement of legislatively defined procedural public interest criteria may be, it is entirely unclear how it relates to the different prongs of the *effet utile* test – if indeed

independently as a sanity check of sorts, looking for the power of the Minister involved to reject, amend or approve the proposed tariffs.[65] That changed radically, however, in a number of decisions involving the governing body of the Italian legal profession, the *Consiglio nazionale forense* (CNF). In *Arduino* and *Cipolla*, the Court had to conclude that the legislation at issue did not contain 'either procedural arrangements or substantive requirements capable of ensuring with reasonable probability that, when producing the draft scale, the CNF conducts itself like an arm of the State working in the public interest'.[66] Under the delegation test, however, it found that the Italian State had not 'waived its power to make decisions of last resort or to review implementation of that scale', since the draft tariffs were not binding unless approved by the Minister and since courts had some residual autonomy in settling fees. Astonishingly, the Court then went on to claim that, *for those exact same reasons*, the Italian state was not 'open to the criticism that it requires or encourages the adoption of agreements, decisions or concerted practices contrary to Article 81 of the Treaty or reinforces their effects'.[67]

we accept that they are different. In Joined Cases C-180 to 184/98 *Pavlov* [2000] ECR I-6451, paras. 87–9, the Court drew it into the ambit of the first test, arguing 'that where a body is composed of a majority of representatives of the public authorities and where, on taking a decision, it must observe various public interest criteria', it cannot be considered an 'association of undertakings'. In Case C-309/99 *Wouters* [2002] ECR I-1577, para. 68, it classified it as part of the delegation test, noting that 'when a Member State grants regulatory powers to a professional association, is careful to define the public interest criteria and the essential principles with which its rules must comply and also retains its power to adopt decisions in the last resort', the rules at issue 'remain State measures'. The sad fact is, of course, that procedural interest criteria are neither particularly effective impediments to substantive restrictions of competition nor very useful in the institutional test of divesting legislation of its 'official authority'.

[65] The power to reject, amend or approve was found in Case C-96/94 *Centro Servizi Spediporto* [1995] ECR I-2883, para. 27. The most implausible finding of non-delegation was in Joined Cases C-140 to 142/94 *DIP* v. *Comune di Bassano del Grappa* [1995] ECR I-3257, paras. 21–3. The case dealt with municipal retail licences, to be issued by the mayor according to criteria laid down in a commercial development plan. In the absence of such a plan, however, no licences could be issued without a favourable opinion of the relevant committee.

[66] Case C-35/99 *Criminal Proceedings against Manuele Arduino* [2002] ECR I-1529, para. 39; and Joined Cases C-94 and 202/04 *Cipolla* v. *Meloni* [2006] ECR I-11421, para. 49.

[67] Case C-35/99 *Criminal Proceedings against Manuele Arduino* [2002] ECR I-1529, para. 43; and Joined Cases C-94 and 202/04 *Cipolla* v. *Meloni* [2006] ECR I-11421, para. 53. Cf. the Order in Case C-250/03 *Mauri* v. *Ministero della Giustizia* [2005] ECR I-1267, dealing with the regulation of access to the legal profession via examination. In this desolate Order,

Illegal delegation thus becomes a very literal concept. Logically this decision would have to remain the low point in the standards to which public authorities will be held in *effet utile* cases for some time to come, unless the Court decides to abandon this doctrine completely. As it stands, the *effet utile* doctrine now excludes State measures in the absence of a link with private collusion and immunises private collusion on the feeblest showing of a link with the State.

On the other hand, in the *CIF* case, the Court has stated that national authorities (such as competition authorities) have a duty to disapply (i.e. ignore) provisions of national law that are at odds with EU legal norms, especially the *effet utile*:[68]

where undertakings engage in conduct contrary to Article 81(1) EC and where that conduct is required or facilitated by national legislation which legitimises or reinforces the effects of the conduct, specifically with regard to price-fixing or market-sharing arrangements, a national competition authority, one of whose responsibilities is to ensure that Article 81 EC is observed, has a duty to disapply the national legislation.[69]

The logic of *CIF* is something like *effet utile* squared – in order to render *effet utile* effective, the national rules that infringe *effet utile* must be disapplied: a challenging proposition.[70]

(iv) The revival of teleology: In a remarkable development already briefly mentioned in the previous chapter, the Court has established in a number of cases concerning collective agreements between employers and workers that such agreements, if they concern measures to

---

the Court was reduced to claiming that 'supervision' in each stage of the examination kept the arrangement safe from both the Article 81 test and the delegation norm.

[68] Case C-198/01 *Consorzio Industrie Fiammiferi* v. *Autorità Garante della Concorrenza e del Mercato (CIF)* [2003] ECR I-8055.

[69] Case C-198/01 *Consorzio Industrie Fiammiferi* v. *Autorità Garante della Concorrenza e del Mercato (CIF)* [2003] ECR I-8055, para. 58.

[70] At first sight, the prospects of this case law are dazzling. It does suggest, however, at a minimum, that *effet utile* cases are at least sometimes clear-cut enough to allow national competition authorities to step in on this basis and cast aside national legal rules which, it is assumed, are likely to have at least some modicum of democratic legitimacy underpinning them. It is respectfully submitted here that an abundance or even the existence of such clear-cut cases is not always suggested by the Court's own track record on *effet utile* case law. In particular, cases concerning the legal profession form a slippery slope. One example is Case C-309/99 *Wouters* [2002] ECR I-1577. Another case in point is Case C-35/99 *Criminal Proceedings against Manuele Arduino* [2002] ECR I-1529.

improve the conditions of work and employment, do not fall within the scope of Article 81 EC.[71]

In *Albany*, *Brentjens* and *Drijvende Bokken*, the Court was asked whether state measures that created a framework for employers' and workers' organisations to make affiliation to sectoral pension funds compulsory infringed the *effet utile* of the competition rules. In addressing this issue, the Court adopted a pure teleological approach (albeit, in this instance, not in pursuit of integration and market oriented solutions).

It pointed, first, to the fact that under the Treaty the provisions that require establishing a social policy are on an equal footing with the requirement of a system ensuring undistorted competition. Second, it recalled the fundamental Treaty objective of promoting 'a harmonious and balanced development of economic activities' and a 'high level of employment and of social protection'. Third, it recalled the provision in the body of the Treaty and the agreement on social policy, which require the promotion of collective bargaining in the interest of the objectives of 'improving living and working conditions, proper social protection, dialogue between management and labour, the development of human resources with a view to lasting high employment, and the combating of social exclusion'. Based on these considerations, it stated:

It is beyond question that certain restrictions of competition are inherent in collective agreements between organisations representing employers and workers. However, the social policy objectives pursued by such agreements would be seriously undermined if management and labour were subject to Article 81(1) of the Treaty when seeking jointly to adopt measures to improve conditions of work and employment.

Furthermore, to complete its teleological approach:

It therefore follows from an interpretation of the provisions of the Treaty as a whole which is both effective and consistent that agreements concluded in the context of collective negotiations between management and labour in pursuit of such objectives must, by virtue of their nature and purpose, be regarded as not falling within the scope of Article 81(1) of the Treaty.[72]

---

[71] Case C-67/96 *Albany* [1999] ECR I-5751; Joined Cases C-115, 116, 117 and 119/97 *Brentjens* [1999] ECR I-6025; and Case C-219/97 *Drijvende Bokken* [1999] ECR I-6121.

[72] Case C-67/96 *Albany* [1999] ECR I-5751, paras. 59–60; Joined Cases C-115, 116, 117 and 119/97 *Brentjens* [1999] ECR I-6025, paras. 56–7; and Case C-219/97 *Drijvende Bokken* [1999] ECR I-6121, paras. 46–7.

Because the agreement at issue did not fall under Article 81 EC, the state measures concerned, making affiliation compulsory as 'part of a regime established under a number of social laws, designed to exercise regulatory authority in the social sphere' did not infringe the *effet utile* rule. The logic applied is the same as that of the delegation cases discussed above. Provided that the private agreements involved are consistent with a legitimate public policy objective – *in casu* with a clear legal basis in the Treaty itself[73]– state measures enforcing this agreement are not capable of infringing the *effet utile* of the competition rules either.

In a comparable case concerning compulsory affiliation to a professional pension scheme (*Pavlov*), Advocate General Jacobs instead argued in favour of accepting 'a prima facie infringement justifiable on public interest grounds'. This would mean that:

measures taken by Member States comply with Article 10 where, although they reinforce the restrictive effects of a concertation between undertakings, they are taken in pursuit of a legitimate and clearly defined public interest objective and where Member States actively supervise that concertation.

And that:

even where concertation between private actors (for example in social or environmental matters) analysed in isolation restricts competition within the meaning of Article 81(1), the State might have legitimate reasons to reinforce and officialise on public interest grounds the effects of that concertation.[74]

However, it is questionable whether the teleological approach will work in all cases where there is a legitimate public interest at stake. It is equally questionable that making the legitimacy of State measures dependent on the legality of private agreements – rather than *vice versa* – is tenable. Today, the Court has to find either that private restrictions on competition do not exist (as in *Meng*) or are outside the scope of

---

[73] It could be argued that the *Albany* exception is limited to public interest objectives explicitly mentioned in the Treaty. The Court of First Instance seems to indicate this in Case T-144/99 *Institute of Professional Representatives before the European Patent Office* [2001] ECR II-1087, para. 67 (dismissing claims that rules of professional conduct fall outside the scope of Article 81 EC on the grounds that, 'where those drafting the EC Treaty intended to remove certain activities from the ambit of the competition rules or apply a specific regime to them, they did so expressly').

[74] In his Opinion on Joined Cases C-180 to 184/98 *Pavlov* [2000] ECR I-6451, paras. 163–4. Cf. the Opinion of Advocate General Fennelly in Case C-222/98 *Van der Woude* [2000] ECR I-7111.

Article 81(1) EC (as in *Albany*) to avoid finding an infringement of the *effet utile* by the State measures involved (as in *Commission* v. *Italy*).[75] The real question is evidently whether the public interest objective involved is acceptable and pursued in a proportionate manner.

The substantive outcome in individual cases is likely to be the same, whether the link test is applied or public policy exceptions are allowed under Articles 10, 81(3) or 86(2) EC. Instead, what is at issue here is a point of principle: ultimately, it concerns the question of who decides what public policy exceptions may justify restrictions of competition between private parties. In the absence of pre-emption, this would appear to be determined by the Member States. The approach taken by the Court in *Albany* suggests that such exceptions can also be identified at Community level, within the constitutional framework of the Treaty, albeit that the effects of this federalism are mitigated by pre-emption and subsidiarity, as mentioned.

The approach supported by Advocate General Jacobs would go one step further to examine formally the legitimacy of the public policy objectives established at State level based on this standard. The Court, however, typically avoids getting involved in the merits of public interest claims. Rather it tries to settle such issues based on other jurisdictional thresholds. Thus, in *Pavlov*, the Court found that the restrictions concerned were not appreciable and consequently the public authorities were not precluded, by Article 10 EC and the *effet utile* rule, from making membership in the contested occupational pension funds compulsory.

Likewise, the Advocate General in *Pavlov* may also have overestimated the degree to which the Court in fact requires public interest to be set out in national legislation. *Arduino* is a clear illustration of this point. Likewise, in *Wouters*, where *effet utile* was not at issue, restrictive effects of the Bar Regulation were found not to 'go beyond what was necessary' in order to ensure the proper practice of the legal profession – according to a standard not set out in public legislation, but in a Regulation adopted by the Bar association itself.[76] Here, in the absence of pre-emption at Community level, the Court accepted that restrictive self-regulation could be justified in the public interest, even where this interest was not specified in the enabling national legislation.

---

[75] Case C-35/96 *Italian Customs Agents* [1998] ECR I-3851.

[76] Case C-309/99 *Wouters* [2002] ECR I-1577. Apart from proportionality, this wording is suggestive of the concept of 'ancillary restraint' familiar from both otherwise pro-competitive agreements and Merger control.

4.4. Attribution to the State or to undertakings

If a link between State regulation and concerted action is established, the question arises whether the conduct involved can still be attributed to the undertakings involved, or whether they are protected from the application of the competition rules.[77]

Already in its 1975 *Suiker Unie* Case, the Court ruled that although regulation may limit the autonomy of an undertaking to the point where Article 81(1) EC becomes inapplicable (in this case resulting in the contested conduct being capable of an appreciable restriction), this does not mean that if some room for competition is left practices which reduce the scope for that competition still further are acceptable.[78] In spite of this early guidance, the Court of First Instance has continued to wrestle with this issue. It has variously suggested that the existence of State measures is irrelevant and that the legality of the arrangements between undertakings depended on whether or not the State measure that sanctioned them was acceptable on public interest grounds.

Initially, it held that 'it is settled law that the fact that conduct on the part of undertakings was known, authorised or even encouraged by national authorities has no bearing, in any event, on the applicability of Article 81 of the Treaty or, where appropriate, Article 82'.[79] A number of authors concluded from the doctrine of supremacy that if undertakings can rely on Community law to invalidate (illegal) national law, they cannot rely on (illegal) national law to protect themselves from Community law.[80] A more subtle approach was adopted by the Court of First Instance in *Asia Motors France III*, when it held that:

if a State measure encompasses the elements of an agreement concluded between traders in a given sector or is adopted after consulting with the

---

[77] See generally Castillo de la Torre, 'State Action Defence in EC Competition Law', (2005) 28 *World Competition* 407.

[78] Joined Cases 40 to 48, 50, 54 to 56, 111, 113 and 114/73 *Suiker Unie* [1975] ECR 1663, paras. 71–2 and 619–620.

[79] Case T-148/89 *Tréfilunion* v. *Commission* [1995] ECR II-1063, para. 118; and Case T-7/92 *Asia Motor France et al.* [1993] ECR II-669, para. 71. With reference to Case 229/83 *Au Blé Vert* [1985] ECR 1; and Case 231/83 *Cullet* v. *Leclerc* [1985] ECR 305. Cf. Case 30/87 *Bodson* [1988] ECR 2479, para. 26 ('the application of Article 82 is not precluded by the fact that the absence or restriction of competition is facilitated by laws or regulations').

[80] Marenco, 'Le Traité CEE Interdit-il aux Etats Membres de Restreindre la Concurrence?', (1986) 22 CDE 285, p. 306; and A. Bach, *Wettbewerbsrechtliche Schranken für staatliche Maßnahmen nach europäischem Gemeinschaftsrecht* (Tübingen: Mohr, 1992), p. 172.

traders concerned and with their agreement, those traders cannot rely on the binding nature of the rules to escape the application of Article 81(1).[81]

This means that participants in an illegal agreement cannot escape anti-trust liability if this agreement is subsequently adopted in the form of a public measure. Furthermore:

In contrast, where a binding regulatory provision capable of affecting the free play of competition within the common market and of affecting trade between Member States has no link with conduct on the part of undertakings of the kind referred to in Article 81(1) of the Treaty, mere compliance by undertakings with such a regulatory provision falls outside the scope of Article 81(1). . . . In such a case, the margin of autonomy on the part of economic operators implied by Article 81(1) of the Treaty is absent.[82]

This view is in line with the now familiar requirement of a link established in *Meng*, discussed above. In subsequent cases, the Court of First Instance appeared to be taking the view that the legality of the conduct of the undertakings involved depends on whether the national law involved infringes Community law. In this context, the Court of First Instance dealt as follows with the Commission's refusal to make such an assessment for Dutch electricity law in *Rendo*:

the Commission cannot, with a view to terminating an infringement of Article 85, require undertakings to adopt conduct which is contrary to a national law without assessing that law in the light of Community law.[83]

Similarly, in *Ladbroke*, the Court of First Instance held that the legality of the national law in question must be investigated before it could be decided whether the undertakings involved infringe the competition rules.[84] The Court of Justice, however, on appeal, overturned this ruling on the following grounds:

---

[81] Case T-387/94 *Asia Motors France et al.* v. *Commission* [1996] ECR II-961, para. 60. With reference to Case 123/83 *BNIC* v. *Clair* [1985] ECR 391, para. 19–23, Joined Cases 209 to 213/84 *Asjes et al.* [1986] ECR 1425, para. 77; and Case 311/85 *VVR* v. *Sociale Dienst van de Plaatselijke en Gewestelijke Overheidsdiensten* [1987] ECR 3801, para. 24.

[82] Case T-387/94 *Asia Motors France et al* v. *Commission* [1996] ECR II-961, para. 61. With reference to Case C-2/91 *Meng* [1993] ECR I-5751, para. 22; and Case C-245/91 *OHRA* [1993] ECR I-5851, para. 15.

[83] Case T-16/91 *Rendo and Others* v. *Commission* [1992] ECR II-2417, paras. 106–7. The Court of Justice upheld this point in appeal. Case C-19/93 P *Rendo and Others* v. *Commission* [1995] ECR I-3319, para. 23.

[84] Case T-548/93 *Ladbroke Racing* v. *Commission* [1995] ECR II-2565, paras. 48–9.

the compatibility of national legislation with the Treaty rules on competition cannot be regarded as decisive in the context of an examination of the applicability of Articles 81 and 82 of the Treaty to the conduct of undertakings which are complying with that legislation.

Moreover:

When the Commission is considering the applicability of Articles 81 and 82 of the Treaty to the conduct of undertakings, a prior evaluation of national legislation affecting such conduct should therefore be directed solely to ascertaining whether that legislation prevents undertakings from engaging in autonomous conduct which prevents, restricts or distorts competition.[85]

Subsequently, referring back to earlier case law (albeit to cases primarily intended to demonstrate that Article 82 could not in itself be applied against Member States), the Court of Justice in *Ladbroke* ruled that:

Articles 81 and 82 apply only to anti-competitive conduct engaged in by undertakings on their own initiative. If anti-competitive conduct is required of undertakings by national legislation or if the latter creates a legal framework which in itself eliminates any possibility of competitive activity on their part, Articles 81 and 82 do not apply. In such a situation, the restriction of competition is not attributable, as those provisions implicitly require, to the autonomous conduct of undertakings.

Articles 81 and 82 may apply, however, if it is found that the national legislation does not preclude undertakings from engaging in autonomous conduct which prevents, restricts or distorts competition.[86]

Accordingly, as was already indicated in *Suiker Unie*, where State measures exist, the essential criterion is whether or not State action limited the freedom of the undertakings involved to the point where they

---

[85] Joined Cases C-359 and 379/95 P *Commission* v. *Ladbroke Racing Ltd (Ladbroke)* [1997] ECR I-6265, para. 35.

[86] Joined Cases C-359 and 379/95 P *Ladbroke* [1997] ECR I-6265, paras. 33–4; with references to Case 41/83 *Italy* v. *Commission* [1985] ECR 873, paras. 18–20; Case C-202/88 *France* v. *Commission* [1991] ECR I-1223, para. 55; and Case C-18/88 *GB-Inno-BM* [1991] ECR I-5941, para. 20; Joined Cases 40 to 48, 50, 54, 55, 56, 111, 113 and 114/73 *Suiker Unie* [1975] ECR 1663, paras. 65, 66, 71 and 72; Joined Cases 209 to 215/78 and 218/78 *Van Landewijck et al.* v. *Commission* [1980] ECR 3125; Joined Cases 240 to 242, 261, 262, 268 and 269/82 *Stichting Sigarettenindustrie et al.* v. *Commission* [1985] ECR 3831; and Case C-219/95 P *Ferriere Nord* v. *Commission* [1997] ECR I-4411. This reasoning is consistent with the Court's approach to exclusive rights under Article 86, where it holds illegal such award of exclusive rights that make an infringment of Article 82 EC unavoidable. See the discussion at section 4.3 above.

could not act other than to restrict competition in accordance with a mandatory State measure. This means that undertakings can be found to infringe the competition rules where they retain a margin of freedom, even where national legislation exists that condones – or even requires – behaviour that restricts competition. This should be the case if they partake in an agreement that by itself would amount to an infringement of EC law or if they in some way autonomously limit the remaining scope for competition, i.e. 'on top of' the restrictions already imposed by the applicable State measures.

In its more recent cases, the Court of First Instance follows this approach.[87] The Court of Justice has gone even further to provide national competition authorities with specific instructions. Thus, in *CIF*, it ruled:

if the general Community-law principle of legal certainty is not to be violated, the duty of a national competition authority to disapply such an anti-competitive law cannot expose the undertakings concerned to any penalties, either criminal or administrative, in respect of past conduct where the conduct was required by the law concerned. It follows that that authority may not impose penalties on the undertakings concerned in respect of past conduct when the conduct was required by the national legislation; it may impose penalties on them in respect of their conduct after the decision declaring there to be a breach of Article 81 EC, once the decision has become definitive in their regard. In any event, the national competition authority may impose penalties in respect of past conduct where the conduct was merely facilitated or promoted by the national legislation.[88]

Moreover, if there is a link between a regulatory measure and an agreement infringing Article 81 EC, the Member State may infringe the *effet utile*, and the undertakings involved may simultaneously be guilty

---

[87] Cf. Case T-228/97 *Irish Sugar PLC* v. *Commission (Irish Sugar)* [1999] ECR II-2969, para. 130; Case T-513/93 *CNSD* [2000] ECR II-1807, paras. 58–9; Case T-66/99 *Minoan Lines SA* v. *Commission* [2003] ECR II-5515, paras. 177–8; Case T-65/99 *Strintzis Lines Shipping SA* v. *Commission* [2003] ECR II-5433, paras. 119–20; Joined Cases T-191, and 212 to 214/98 *Atlantic Container Line AB and Others* v. *Commission* [2003] ECR II-3275; Joined Cases T-5 and 6/00 *Nederlandse Federatieve Vereniging voor de Groothandel op Electrotechnisch Gebied* v. *Commission* [2003] ECR II-5761, para. 296; and Case T-87/05 *Energias de Portugal* v. *Commission* [2005] ECR II-3745, para. 119. Cf. Case C-207/01 *Altair Chimica SpA* v. *ENEL Distribuzione SpA* [2003] ECR I-8875, paras. 30–1; and Case C-198/01 *Consorzio Industrie Fiammiferi* v. *Autorità Garante della Concorrenza e del Mercato (CIF)* [2003] ECR I-8055, paras. 51 and 56–7.

[88] Case C-198/01 *Consorzio Industrie Fiammiferi* v. *Autorità Garante della Concorrenza e del Mercato (CIF)* [2003] ECR I-8055, para. 1, case summary.

of infringing Article 81 EC even where an (illegal) State measure requiring or reinforcing their behaviour exists. In the *Consiglio Nazionale degli Spedizionieri Doganali (CNSD)* Case, the Court of First Instance found that, precisely because national legislation at issue allowed the undertakings involved to determine the scope for effective competition in the sector, they were capable of infringing Article 81.[89] In fact, the finding that the undertakings involved were not constrained by public interest considerations, when setting tariffs led to illegal delegation in *Commission v. Italy*, necessarily implied that the undertakings involved enjoyed a sufficient margin of freedom to infringe the competition rules.

Hence, where national legislation leaves undertakings a sufficient margin of freedom either to compete, or to restrain competition at their own initiative, the competition rules apply in spite of the existence of the regulatory measure in question. The applicability of the competition rules in principle does not depend on whether or not the regulatory measure infringes competition law. Nevertheless, as was seen in relation to *effet utile* (and as will be seen in relation to Article 86 EC below), if State measures restrict competition in pursuit of a legitimate public policy objective, the Court is likely to find the private arrangements involved acceptable as well. Where there is a link between a cartel arrangement and national legislation that restricts competition, both the private arrangement and the national legislation are likely to fall foul of the competition rules and *effet utile* respectively.

4.5. Free movement or competition rules?

The logical consequence of the *Reiff, Meng,* and *OHRA* trilogy would seem to be that State measures not 'linked' to private concerted action would instead fall under Article 28.[90] However, the relationship between the competition rules and the free movement provisions remains complex:

- In the first place, the Court has not always been clear about the question of whether the competition rules and the free movement rules in fact pursue what is fundamentally the same objective.

---

[89] Case T-513/93 *CNSD* [2000] ECR II-1807, paras. 71 ff. See the earlier discussion of Case C-35/96 *Italian Customs Agents* [1998] ECR I-3851.
[90] This is fervently pleaded by Van der Esch, 'Loyauté Fédérale et Subsidiarité', (1994) 30 CDE 523.

– Second, it is not clear on what basis it decides to resolve cases based on one set of rules, rather than another, even where – as a result of its own functionalist case law – both sets of rules are in principle applicable.

In *Van de Haar*, the Court held that:

Article 28 of the Treaty, which seeks to eliminate national measures capable of hindering trade between Member States, pursues an aim different from that of Article 81, which seeks to maintain effective competition between undertakings.[91]

However, in the *Leclerc* Cases, less than a year later, the Court stated that the fundamental aim of the free movement and competition rules was the same:

Articles 2 and 3 of the Treaty set out to establish a market characterised by the free movement of goods where the terms of competition are not distorted. That objective is secured *inter alia* by Article 28 et seq. . . . and by Article 81 et seq.[92]

Here, it went on to find it 'appropriate' to consider the competition rules read in conjunction with Articles 5 and 3(f) (now Articles 10 and 3(g)) first, followed by Article 30 EC (now Article 28). In subsequent case law, the Court generally appears to start with the *effet utile* test and to continue with Article 28 EC only if no infringement of the competition rules is found, as measures that infringe the *effet utile* are in general likely to be contrary to free movement rules in any event.[93] In the context of services, this approach seems confirmed in *Job Centre Coop* and *Raso*, where the Court found 'no need' to answer questions relating to Article 59 (now Article 49) because it had already found the measure in question contrary to Articles 86 and 90(1) (now Articles 82 and 86(2)).[94] In *Bosman*, however, the Court declined to discuss the UEFA's

---

[91] Joined Cases 177 and 178/82 *Van de Haar and Kaveka* [1984] ECR 1797, para. 14.

[92] Case 229/83 *Au Blé Vert* [1985] ECR 1, para. 9; and Case 231/83 *Cullet* v. *Leclerc* [1985] ECR 305, para. 11.

[93] Case 13/77 *GB-INNO-BM* v. *ATAB* [1977] ECR 2115, para. 35: 'In any case, a national measure which has the effect of facilitating the abuse of a dominant position capable of affecting trade between Member States will generally be incompatible with Articles 28 and 29'. It repeated the formula in Case C-179/90 *Merci* [1991] ECR I-5889, para. 21, where it added: 'in so far as such a measure has the effect of making more difficult and hence of impeding imports of goods from other Member States'.

[94] Case C-55/96 *Job Centre Coop* [1997] ECR I-7119, para. 39; and Case C-136/96 *Raso* [1998] ECR I-533, para. 33. In Case C-70/95 *Sodemare* [1997] ECR I-3395, the Court first held

transfer system under the competition rules as it had already found the arrangement to fall foul of Article 48 (now Article 39) EC.[95]

In some cases, both sets of rules were applied in combination. For example, in *Tankstation 't Heuske*, Dutch rules on shop opening hours were held in accordance with the competition rules for lack of a link with private concerted action and outside of the scope of Article 28 under the *Keck* rule.[96] Of course, such a clearance under both sets of rules is logically consistent with the Court limiting itself to testing against one set of rules if these are found to be infringed (obviating the need to test for the other set).

Because the *effet utile* norm would usually constitute the stricter rule, it makes sense that it would be given precedence. Although the Court has explicitly allowed a de minimis rule for Article 81 EC and ruled out such a rule for Article 28,[97] the reach of the free movement regime for anti-competitive State measures has in practice been limited even further. If no link with concerted behaviour exists, the State measures involved may fall outside the scope of Article 28 EC not only based on the *Keck* rule on (formally non-discriminatory) selling arrangements, but also on the *Peralta* formula. According to *Peralta*, a State measure is not caught if it is not discriminatory, 'its purpose is not to regulate trade' and the restrictive effects which it might have are 'too uncertain and indirect' to be regarded as hindering trade.[98] In competition law terms: there is no appreciable effect on trade.[99] The absence of a link with concerted action in combination with the *Peralta* formula has left outside the scope of Community law, for example: Spanish legislation obliging oil traders to supply at least four islands of the Canaries in *Esso*

---

against application of Article 49 EC for want of a transnational element and then against the combined rule of Articles 3(g), 10, 81, 82 and 86 EC for lack of a link with concerted action.

[95] Case C-415/93 *Bosman* [1995] ECR I-4921, para. 138.

[96] Joined Cases C-401 and 402/92 *Tankstation 't Heuske* [1994] ECR I-2199.

[97] Agreements must 'appreciably' affect trade for purposes of Article 81(1) EC. See Case 5/69 *Völk v. Vervaecke* [1969] ECR 295. On the other hand, Article 28 'does not distinguish according to the degree to which trade is affected'. See Joined Cases 177 and 178/82 *Van de Haar* [1984] ECR 1797, para. 13. See e.g. Oliver, 'Some Further Reflections on the Scope of Articles 28–30 (ex 30–36) EC', (1999) 36 CMLR 783, p. 791 (arguing that the refusal to allow de minimis corresponds to the 'fundamental character' of the four freedoms and that 'the State bears a higher duty than private bodies').

[98] Case C-379/92 *Peralta* [1994] ECR I-3453, para. 24.

[99] Joined Cases C-215 and 216/96 *Carlo Bagnasco et al. v. Banca Popolare di Novara soc. coop. arl. and Cassa di Risparmio di Genova e Imperia SpA (Bagnasco)* [1999] ECR I-135.

Española;[100] Italian transport-tariff arrangements in *Spediporto*;[101] Italian legislation establishing a licensing system for new shops in *DIP*;[102] and giving an undertaking the exclusive right to provide mooring services in the ports of Genova and La Spezia in *Corsica Ferries France*.[103]

When Articles 82 and 86(1) EC are applied in conjunction with the Article 28 EC test, the results are similar, but less obviously consistent. As the granting of exclusive rights as such does not infringe Article 82 EC, in *La Crespelle*, where the alleged price abuse was not a direct consequence of the legal measure in question and might therefore have been found to constitute an abuse on account of the undertaking concerned in its own right, the Court decided against applying Articles 82 and 86(1) EC. Instead, it found that the State measure requiring imported bovine semen to be stored at centres with exclusive territorial rights for storage and insemination 'that applies at the stage immediately following importation and imposes an economic burden on importers' to be 'liable to restrict the volume of imports'.[104] It did so without even mentioning *Keck*. A similar conclusion prohibiting certain exclusive territorial rights for meat traders was reached based on Article 28 EC in *Ligur Carni*.[105]

In *Banchero*, however, the Italian tobacco monopoly with its exclusive licensing of tobacco retail outlets survived scrutiny under Articles 82 and 86(1) EC because the arrangement did not induce abuse of a dominant position and fell outside of the scope of Article 28 EC under the *Keck* rule.[106] Likewise, in *Commission* v. *Greece*, where the Article 86 EC issue was not raised, the Court held the monopoly of pharmacies on the sale of infant-formula milk to be outside the scope of Article 28 EC, explicitly citing the *Keck* rule. The main differences with *La Crespelle* and *Ligur Carni* appear to be that in the Greek infant formula milk case (as in *Banchero*) the State measures involved did not mandate the monopoly traders to levy charges for their services and the traders did not enjoy territorial exclusivity.[107]

---

[100] Case C-134/94 *Esso Española* v. *Comunidad Autónoma de Canarias (Esso Española)* [1995] ECR I-4223, para. 24.

[101] Case C-96/94 *Spediporto* [1995] ECR I-2883, para. 41.

[102] Joined Cases C-140 to 142/94 *DIP* [1995] ECR I-3257, para. 29.

[103] Case C-266/96 *Corsica Ferries France* [1998] ECR I-3949, para. 31.

[104] Case C-323/93 *La Crespelle* [1994] ECR I-5080, para. 29.

[105] Joined Cases C-277, 318 and 319/91 *Ligur Carni* [1993] ECR I-6621.

[106] Case C-387/93 *Giorgio Domingo Banchero* [1995] ECR I-4663.

[107] Case C-391/92 *Commission* v. *Greece* [1995] ECR I-1621. Advocate General Lenz relied explicitly on *La Crespelle* and *Ligur Carni* to plead for the applicability of Article 28 EC. *Ibid.*, para. 21 of the Opinion.

4.6. Conclusion

So far, our discussion has focused on cases where the Court attempted to draw a line between such activities related to the public sphere as might be precluded from the application of the competition rules altogether and activities that should be subject to closer scrutiny. The focus of this was the application of free movement to private parties and the application of the competition rules to public bodies.

It has become clear that the Court takes a functional approach to free movement and consequently appears headed for recognising horizontal direct effect, i.e. subjecting private parties to the free movement rules. Concerning the application of the competition laws, however, in a number of cases where restrictions were self-evident and no formal public interest exceptions existed, the Court has compensated this by not applying the competition rules to certain activities with a public interest dimension. *Wouters* and *Albany* are prime examples of this.

As regards the application of the competition rules to public bodies, teleology is central due to the concept of *effet utile* as based on the good faith clause of the Treaty as an agreement between Member States. In practice, however, a link with pre-existing illegal private restrictions of competition is required. If a link between State regulation and concerted action is established, the question arises if the undertakings involved are protected from the application of the competition rules. The answer is in essence straightforward: if national legislation leaves undertakings a sufficient degree of freedom either to compete or to restrain competition at their own initiative, the competition rules apply to them.

On balance, so far, the *effet utile* line of case law, which initially appeared to herald a new age with the end of corporatism and State-organised collusive practices, has proven to be a damp squib. As is demonstrated by *Librandi* and *Arduino*, the procedural guarantees required to avoid illegal forms of delegation of decision-making are by now minimal. *CIF* may give a new lease of life to *effet utile* by enabling its application by national competition authorities at least in theory, but in the absence of more regular support by the Court, few authorities are likely to take up this invitation to test the limits of their credibility.

In Part II, we move to examine the various heads under which closer scrutiny is exercised, and where various economic and non-economic public interest justifications may come into play in conjunction with the application of the rules on commercial monopolies, competition, special and exclusive rights, and state aids.

PART II · THE PUBLIC PRIVATE INTERFACE: ARTICLES 31, 86 AND 87–88 EC

The second part of this text will deal with three sets of rules that were designed to deal with the interface between the public and the private spheres as such. These are Article 31 EC, on commercial State monopolies; Article 86 EC, which deals with special and exclusive rights, as well as with services of general economic interest; and finally Articles 87 and 88 EC, dealing with State aid.

5 Article 31 EC: commercial state monopolies

5.1. Introduction

Article 31 EC deals with the position of commercial State monopolies, in particular in so far as they introduce discrimination regarding the conditions under which goods are procured and marketed (for example, in the case of import and export monopolies). As such, it forms a *lex specialis* in relation to the general rules pertaining to the trade in goods[1] – and following the end of the transitional period it is, like Article 28 EC, directly effective.[2] Also, in dealing with State monopolies, Article 31

---

[1] There is a long-standing debate regarding whether Article 31 EC applies to trade in services. Although the Court has consistently held that Article 31 EC *cannot* relate to a monopoly over the provision of services, it has recognised that services monopolies may indirectly influence trade in goods, in particular in cases where a services monopoly entails discrimination against imported goods. Cf. Case 155/73 *Giuseppe Sacchi (Sacchi)* [1974] ECR 409, para. 10; Case 271/81 *Société Coopérative d'Amélioration de l'Élevage et d'Insémination Artificielle du Béarn* v. *Lucien J. M. Mialocq et al.* [1983] ECR 2057, para. 8; Case 30/87 *Bodson* [1988] ECR 2479, para. 10; Joined Cases C-46/90 and 93/91 *Lagauche and Evrard* [1993] ECR I-5267, para. 33; Case C-17/94 *Criminal Proceedings against Denis Gervais et al.* [1995] ECR I-4353, para. 35; and Case C-6/01 *Associação Nacional de Operadores de Máquinas Recreativas (Anomar) et al.* v. *Portugal* [2003] ECR I-8621, paras. 58 ff. Importantly for the application of Article 31 EC, electricity is considered a good under Community law. Cf. Case 6/64 *Costa* v. *ENEL* [1964] ECR 585; confirmed in Case C-393/92 *Gemeente Almelo et al.* v. *Energiebedrijf IJsselmij NV (Almelo)* [1994] ECR I-1477, para. 28 (with reference to Case 6/64 *Costa* v. *ENEL* [1964] ECR 585). Noted by Hancher (1995) 32 CMLR 305. See generally e.g. Slot, 'Energy and Competition' (1994) 31 CMLR 511; A. Rinne, *Die Energiewirtschaft zwischen Wettbewerb und öffentlicher Aufgabe* (Baden-Baden: Nomos, 1998); D. Geradin (ed.), *The Liberalisation of Electricity and Natural Gas in the European Union* (Deventer: Kluwer, 2001); and M. Klasse, *Gemeinschaftsrechtliche Grenzen für staatlich veranlasste Wettbewerbsbeschränkungen* (Baden Baden: Nomos, 2006).

[2] Case 45/75 *Rewe-Zentrale des Lebensmittel-Grosshandels GmbH* v. *Hauptzollamt Landau/Pfalz (Rewe)* [1976] ECR 196, para. 24; Case 59/75 *Pubblico Ministero* v. *Flavia Manghera et al. (Manghera)* [1976] ECR 91, para. 16; Case 91/78 *Hansen* v. *Hauptzollamt Flensburg (Hansen)* [1979] ECR 935, para. 16; Case C-361/90 *Commission* v. *Portugal* [1993] ECR I-95; and Case

EC bridges the free movement and competition rules. Article 31 EC does not require national monopolies of a commercial character to be abolished, nor, as demonstrated by *Costa*,[3] is it illegal to create new commercial State monopolies.

Instead, Article 31 EC aims to reconcile the existence of such monopolies with the requirements of the establishment and functioning of the internal market – in particular, after the expiration of the transitional period, with the non-discrimination requirement.[4] Thus the Member States are required to 'adjust' the monopolies concerned.

According to the Court, in its 1997 *Franzén* Case:

It is clear not only from the wording of Article 37 [now Article 31] but also from the position which it occupies in the general scheme of the Treaty that the article is designed to ensure compliance with the fundamental principle that goods should be able to move freely throughout the common market, in particular by requiring quantitative restrictions and measures having equivalent effect in trade between Member States to be abolished, and thereby to ensure maintenance of normal conditions of competition between the economies of Member States in the event that a given product is subject, in one or other of those States, to a national monopoly of a commercial character.[5]

Hence, Article 31 EC aims at the elimination of any obstacles to the free movement of goods which may be involved, except, notably, 'such restrictions of trade as are inherent in the existence of the monopolies in question'.[6] In the *Franzén* Case, the Court has further clarified the scope of the Article 31 EC exception to free movement and competition in line with the general rule concerning the exercise of public authority:

C-76/91 *Caves Neto Costa SA* v. *Ministro do Comércio e Turismo and Secretário de Estado do Comércio externo* [1993] ECR I-117, para. 9.

[3] Case 6/64 *Costa* v. *ENEL* [1964] ECR 585, 597–8.

[4] Case 59/75 *Manghera* [1976] ECR 91, para. 9; Case 78/82 *Commission* v. *Italy* [1983] ECR 1955, para. 11; Case C-347/88 *Commission* v. *Greece* [1990] ECR I-4747, para. 42; and Case C-387/93 *Criminal Proceedings against Giorgio Domingo Banchero (Banchero)* [1995] ECR I-4663, para. 27.

[5] Case C-189/95 *Criminal Proccedings against Harry Franzén (Franzén)* [1997] ECR I-5909. Noted by Slot, (1998) 35 CMLR 1183.

[6] Case C-347/88 *Commission* v. *Greece* [1990] ECR I-4747, para. 35. '[T]hus, Article 37 [now Article 31] requires that the organisation and operation of the monopoly be arranged so as to exclude any discrimination between nationals of Member States as regards conditions of supply and outlets, so that trade in goods from other Member States is not put at a disadvantage, in law or in fact, in relation to domestic goods and that competition between the economies of the Member States is not distorted.' Case C-189/95 *Franzén* [1997] ECR I-5909, para. 40.

The purpose of Article 37 [now Article 31] of the Treaty is to reconcile the possibility for Member States to maintain certain monopolies of a commercial character as instruments for the pursuit of public interest aims with the requirements of the establishment and functioning of the common market.[7]

The Court's interpretation of Article 31 EC appears to be in tune with the distinction between the public and private spheres under the competition rules as discussed above with regard to 'economic activities' and 'the exercise of public authority'. Evidently, in the case of commercial State monopolies, there will be no actual competition. Nevertheless, given that *commercial* monopolies are concerned, there can be little argument concerning the fact that, in principle, the activities involved could by definition be carried out by one or several private undertakings with a view to profit. Under such a strict functionalist view, therefore, the very existence of commercial monopolies should be accounted for by legitimate public policy objectives – as they would otherwise be contrary to Community law.

However, it appears that so far the application of Article 31 EC does not require the nature and scope of the legitimate public interest involved, and hence of the necessity and proportionality of any related restrictions on competition, to be determined. It merely involves a strict non-discrimination test.

5.2. Delegation, sub-delegation and private agreements under Article 31 EC

When the issue of whether or not a certain entity is subject to Article 31 EC arises, the Court evaluates if 'the national authorities are in a position to control, direct or appreciably influence trade between the Member States through a body established for that purpose or a delegated monopoly'. This applies to monopolies operated by the State itself, or by means of delegation, either to its territorial sub-units, to undertakings or to groups of undertakings.[8]

Article 31 EC clearly does not cover sub-delegation or arrangements based on private agreements that are one step removed from the exercise of public authority. For example, in *Bodson*, no delegated

---

[7] Case C-189/95 *Franzén* [1997] ECR I-5909, para. 39.
[8] Case 30/87 *Bodson* [1988] ECR 2479, para. 13; Case C-393/92 *Almelo* [1994] ECR I-1477, para. 29; Case C-387/93 *Banchero* [1995] ECR I-4663, para. 26; and Case C-157/94 *Dutch Electricity Monopoly* [1997] ECR I-5699, para. 20.

monopoly in the sense of Article 31 EC was held to exist, as the State had left local authorities the freedom either to deliver funeral services themselves or to contract out for them.[9] Likewise, in the *Almelo* Case, Article 31 EC did not apply, as the State had not granted the electricity distributor concerned an exclusive concession and the supply contracts that contained the contested exclusive purchasing clauses (by virtue of the applicable general conditions for supply) were considered private agreements.[10] The restrictions involved were treated as private restrictions of trade and dealt with under Articles 81, 82 and 86(2) EC. Hence, it appears that the Court applies a formal approach concerning delegation issues. There is a significant analogy here to its requirement, following *Meng*, that a formal link between an illegal private agreement and government policy must exist, for the latter to be subject to the *effet utile* rule.[11]

5.3. Free movement and Article 31 EC

Most important, although Article 31 EC tolerates the existence of commercial monopolies (i.e. sales monopolies), it requires all import and export monopolies to be abolished (this does not affect production monopolies, which are regulated by means of Article 86 EC). Thus, in *Manghera*, the Court held that exclusive import rights inherently involve discrimination prohibited by Article 31 EC, and in the French and Italian *Electricity* cases,[12] that exclusive rights to export products are inherently contrary to Article 31 and must be abolished.[13]

Further, as an elaboration of Article 28 EC, Article 31 EC in most cases follows the case law on measures having equivalent effect to quantitative restrictions on trade, which covers all trading rules that are capable of 'hindering, directly or indirectly, actually or potentially, intra-Community trade'.[14] For example, Article 31 EC follows the general rule that authorities may not fix prices at such a level that the marketing of imported products is impaired.[15] Hence, where, in

---

[9] Case 30/87 *Bodson* [1988] ECR 2479.   [10] Case C-393/92 *Almelo* [1994] ECR I-1477.
[11] See the discussion above in section 4.3.
[12] Case 59/75 *Manghera* [1976] ECR 91, paras. 9–13.
[13] Case C-158/94 *Commission* v. *Italy* [1997] ECR I-5789, paras. 24–5; and Case C-159/94 *Commission* v. *France* [1997] ECR I-5815, paras. 34–5.
[14] Case 8/74 *Dassonville* [1974] ECR 837, para. 5.
[15] Cf. Case 31/74 *Galli* [1975] 47; Case 65/75 *Tasca* [1976] ECR 291; and Case 82/77 *Van Tiggele* [1978] ECR 25.

addition to the existence of a production monopoly, either these monopolies themselves or the State authorities that supervise them fix prices of imported products, both Articles 31 and 28 EC are infringed.[16] Nevertheless, Articles 28 and 31 EC are based on different tests. These rules are complementary rather than alternatives.

As was established in *Cassis de Dijon*, Article 31 EC is 'irrelevant with regard to general provisions which do not concern the exercise by a public monopoly of its specific function – namely, its exclusive right – but apply in a general manner to … production and marketing', regardless of whether such general provisions cover the products that are subject to a commercial monopoly.[17] *Cassis* went on to develop the celebrated proportionality requirement for national measures purportedly serving the general interest in exception to the free movement rules – sacrificing the opportunity to bring the creation and maintenance of commercial monopolies under the same regime. The mandatory fixing of minimum alcohol contents was held to be unacceptable in comparison to less restrictive means designed to service the same public health objective (such as consumer information by means of packaging). Hence, the Court held that:

[R]equirements relating to the minimum alcohol content of alcoholic beverages do not serve a purpose which is in the general interest and such as to take precedence over the requirements of the free movement of goods, which constitutes one of the fundamental rules of the Community.[18]

By relying on this argument, *Cassis* failed to develop the line of reasoning set out as early as *Costa*, that 'any new monopolies or bodies specified in Article 37(1) [now Article 31(1)] are prohibited *in so far as* they tend to introduce new cases of discrimination regarding the conditions under which goods are procured and marketed'.[19] In the subsequent case law the *Cassis* approach has been elaborated to the effect that provisions that are separable from the operation of a commercial monopoly and that do not concern its existence as such or regulate its functioning are subject to the general rule of Article 28 EC and the

---

[16] Case 90/82 *Commission* v. *France* [1983] ECR 2011, paras. 26–8. The fixing of uniform trading margins which do not discriminate against imported products is not caught by Article 37. Cf. Case 78/82 *Commission* v. *Italy* [1983] ECR 1955.

[17] Case 120/78 *Cassis de Dijon* [1979] ECR 649, para. 7.

[18] Case 120/78 *Cassis de Dijon* [1979] ECR 649, paras. 13–14.

[19] Case 6/64 *Costa* v. *ENEL* [1964] ECR 585, 598 (emphasis added).

Article 30 EC exceptions thereto, and are not caught by Article 31 EC. Thus, Articles 31 and 28 EC are complementary.

Moreover, the application of Article 28 is generally considered separately and only after establishing that the measures concerned are not caught by Article 31 EC.[20] This means that measures which merely 'have a bearing upon' the operation of a commercial monopoly will be evaluated under the proportionality requirement of Articles 28 and 30 EC and in line with the recent subsidiarity case law on Article 28 EC. For example, in *Banchero*, the contested measures concerning the Italian marketing system for tobacco products first escaped the scope of Article 31 EC, and next that of Article 28 EC as well, because they were held to concern selling arrangements in the sense of the *Keck* case law.[21] In any event, both under Articles 31 and 28 EC a strict non-discrimination test applies.

5.4. State aids and Article 31 EC

In *Hansen*, the Court found that a *lex specialis* relationship also holds between Article 31 EC and Articles 87 and 88 EC on State aids.[22] Hence:

[T]he operations of a state monopoly are not exempted from the application of Article 37 [now Article 31] by reason of the fact that they may at the same time be classified as an aid within the meaning of the Treaty.

And:

[S]tate measures inherent in the exercise by a state monopoly of a commercial character of its exclusive right must, even where they are linked to the grant of an aid to producers subject to the monopoly, be considered in the light of the requirements of Article 31.[23]

If Article 31 EC applies and prohibits certain measures, Articles 87 and 88 EC need not be considered.

---

[20] Case C-189/95 *Franzén* [1997] ECR I-5909, para. 35; with reference to Case 91/75 *Hauptzollamt Göttingen v. Miritz* [1976] ECR 217, para. 5; Case 120/78 *Cassis de Dijon* [1979] ECR 649, para. 7; and Case 91/78 *Hansen* [1979] ECR 935, paras. 9–10. Cf. Case C-170/04 *Rosengren v. Riksåklagaren* [2007] ECR I-4071, para. 26.

[21] Case C-387/93 *Banchero* [1995] ECR I-4663, para. 34; with reference to Joined Cases C-267 and 268/91 *Keck and Mithouard* [1993] ECR I-6097, para. 16.

[22] Case 91/78 *Hansen v. Hauptzollamt Flensburg (Hansen)* [1979] ECR 935.

[23] Case 91/78 *Hansen v. Hauptzollamt Flensburg (Hansen)* [1979] ECR 935, paras. 9 and 10.

5.5. Public interest exceptions and Article 31 EC

The evaluation of commercial monopolies under Article 31 only regards the rules relating to the existence and operation of the monopoly, and neither requires nor provides for an explicit public interest exception. As regards the existence of import and export monopolies, although it is a *lex specialis* to Article 28 EC, the public interest exceptions provided for in Article 30 EC do not apply under Article 31. In so far as creating and maintaining import and export monopolies is concerned, the prohibition contained in Article 31 EC is clearly intended to be absolute – with two exceptions:

- first, as demonstrated in *Banchero*, the *Keck* rule applies,[24] so exclusively authorised sales outlets for tobacco products could be excused as mere selling arrangements; and
- second, an Article 86(2) EC defence is available, which will be discussed below.

(i) Even for import and export monopolies otherwise strictly prohibited under Article 31 a public interest defence based on Article 86(2) EC is available. In a series of Article 226 EC Treaty infringement actions concerning exclusive rights in national electricity markets, decided in October 1997 – the Dutch, French and Italian *Electricity* cases – the Court made clear that even unmistakable import and export monopolies can still be saved – provided they can be justified under the limited exception for services of general economic interest in Article 86(2) EC:

[T]he objective of Article 37(1) [now Article 31(1)] of the Treaty would not be attained if, in a Member State where a commercial monopoly exists, the free movement of goods from other Member States comparable to those with which the national monopoly is concerned were not ensured.

The existence of exclusive import rights deprives economic operators in other Member States from the opportunity to offer their products to consumers of their choice in the Member State concerned, regardless of the conditions which they encounter in the Member State of origin or in other Member States.

Since the maintenance of the exclusive import and export rights at issue is therefore contrary to Article 37 [now Article 31] of the Treaty, it is unnecessary to consider whether they are contrary to Articles 30 and 34 [now Articles 28 and 29] or, consequently, whether they might possibly be justified under Article 36 [now Article 30] of the Treaty.

[24] Case C-387/93 *Banchero* [1995] ECR I-4663, para. 34.

Nevertheless, it is still necessary to verify whether the exclusive rights at issue might be justified . . . under Article 90(2) [now Article 86(2)] of the Treaty.[25]

Moreover, echoing its earlier 'pre-emption' approach to *effet utile* in *Au Blé Vert*,[26] in the *Electricity* Cases the Court pointedly reminded the Commission that, in the absence of a common energy policy, it was up to the Commission itself to elaborate the Community interest allegedly infringed by the contested measures of the Member States, for example by using its powers to legislate and adopt decisions in individual cases under Article 86(3) EC.[27] The message conveyed was that, unless a Community approach capable of safeguarding the public interest in a more *communautaire* manner was devised, coherent national systems aimed at protecting such public interests would continue to benefit from Article 86(2) EC protection. Hence, Treaty infringement actions based on Article 31 EC do not offer a short cut towards imposing a more liberal Community regime as they must be accompanied by concerted efforts to adequately address the legitimate public interests involved. The Court does not wish to promote liberalisation by means of litigation at the expense of regular harmonisation (based on political decision-making).

(ii) Restrictions that fall short of such import and export monopolies must also pass strict non-discrimination and proportionality tests under Articles 31, respectively 28 and 30. Commercial monopolies involving exclusive rights for imports and exports can thus only be justified under Article 86(2) EC. For restrictions concerning the operation and existence of commercial monopolies that fall short of full import and export monopolies a strict non-discrimination test applies based on Article 31. Restrictions severable from the operation and existence of the monopoly are subject to Articles 28 and 30 EC.

---

[25] Case C-157/94 *Dutch Electricity Monopoly* [1997] ECR I-5699, paras. 24–5; Case C-158/94 *Italian Electricty Monopoly* [1997] ECR I-5789, paras. 33–4; and Case C-159/94 *French ELectricty and Gas Monopoly* [1997] ECR I-5815, paras. 39–42. Cf. Ehricke, 'Zur Konzeption von Art. 37 I und Art. 90 II EGV', (1998) 8 EuZW 1998.

[26] Case 229/83 *Leclerc v. Au Blé Vert* [1985] ECR 1.

[27] Evidently, Article 37 EC cases often have an Article 90 EC dimension, as special and exclusive rights tend to be involved. In *Banchero*, Article 37 EC was not applicable since the State monopoly concerned did not control retailers' purchases or imports, whereas Article 90 EC did not apply as abuse was not inevitable and the Italian tobacco retail system was not manifestly unable to meet demand. Case C-387/93 *Banchero* [1995] ECR I-4663, para. 5; with reference to Case C-41/90 *Höfner and Elsner v. Macroton* [1991] ECR I-1979, para. 31.

This principle was first clearly established in the *Franzén* Case of October 1997 (decided, incidentally, on the same day as the more widely noted *Electricity* Cases) regarding the Swedish licensing system for trade in alcoholic beverages. The Court appears to have used a three-part test:

- the existence of a public interest aim (protecting public health against the dangers of alcohol) – not previously explicitly required – that was not contested, was noted;
- regarding Article 31 EC, a strict non-discrimination test was applied and passed; and
- next, for Articles 28 and 30 EC a strict proportionality test was applied – which the Swedish system failed.

Although the protection of health could in principle have justified a derogation from Article 28 EC, this particular defence failed since the Swedish Government had not established that its licensing system 'was proportionate to the public health aim pursued or that this aim could not have been attained by measures less restrictive of intra-Community trade'.[28] In *Rosengren*, the Court held that the prohibition on private individuals to import alcohol was 'unsuitable' for the achievement of the monopoly's alleged objective, the general limitation of alcohol consumption, 'in light of its rather marginal effects in that regard'.[29]

Similarly, in *Hanner*,[30] the Court found that a retail sales monopoly of medicinal preparations (i.e. a system of pharmacies' monopolies) was not only precluded by Article 31 EC, but could also not benefit from the exception for services of general economic interest in Article 86(2) EC because it lacked a selection system that excluded discrimination against medicinal preparations from other Member States. The strict non-discrimination rule thus applied.

5.6. Proportionality under Article 31 EC

Hence, so far neither the legitimacy nor the proportionality of public interest objectives – relative to the restrictions on free movement involved – are evaluated under Article 31 EC: the key test here remains

---

[28] Case C-189/95 *Franzén* [1997] ECR I-5909, para. 76.
[29] Case C-170/04 *Rosengren* v. *Riksaklågeren* [2007] ECR I-4071, para. 47. Cf. Case C-186/05 *Commission* v. *Sweden* [2007] ECR I-129.
[30] Case C-438/02 *Criminal Proceedings against Krister Hanner* [2005] ECR I-4551, paras. 42–5, 47–9.

non-discrimination. This is unlike the Article 86(2) EC test applicable to import and export monopolies or the Article 28 and 30 EC tests that are applicable to provisions severable from the existence and operation of a commercial monopoly.

Nevertheless, it appears that under Article 31 EC a 'quasi' proportionality test is in fact applied. This is because the Court is willing to accept only such restrictions as are 'inherent in the existence' of the monopoly concerned, and its non-discrimination test is clearly slanted toward checking whether the monopoly displays market oriented behaviour (for example, the application of purely commercial criteria to the selection of products marketed through the monopoly sales system). Given the close link with Articles 28, 30 and 86(2) EC, the Court may well eventually develop a formal proportionality requirement under Article 31 EC.

Consequently, it appears that following the October 1997 judgments the Court applies a three-pronged test:

- a strict non-discrimination test for the existence and operations of commercial monopolies under Article 31 EC itself (mitigated by the *Keck* rule);
- an Article 86(2) EC test for commercial monopolies related to services of general economic interest; and
- an Article 28 and 30 test for non-economic public interest justifications concerning related restrictions.

Jointly, these tests cover all situations caught by Article 31 EC.

5.7. Conclusion

There is but a thin line between the view that commercial monopolies are justified by definition, but any related infringements of Treaty rules must be covered by a public interest exception, and the view that the very existence of commercial monopolies is justifiable only in so far as they rely on public interest exceptions. So far, the Court does not appear to have crossed this line: i.e. commercial monopolies remain justified. We believe that, in accordance with pre-emption, it will strike them down where a Community standard for the public interest concerned is available, as only that would enable it to apply a strict proportionality test to the creation or maintenance of monopoly itself. This squares with the observations concerning the scope of the public sphere under the competition rules made earlier – notably concerning the Court's approach to book price maintenance in *Au Blé Vert*.[31]

The present Article 31 EC loophole, if such it is, is to be found in the loose proportionality test applied under Article 86(2) EC, and the absence of a definition of what constitutes a legitimate 'public interest' that merits exceptions to the competition and free movement rules. In any event, the 1997 *Electricity* Cases indicate a convergence of applicable public interest standards on free movement and competition, which we will examine further under Article 86 EC.

---

[31] Case 229/83 *Leclerc* v. *Au Blé Vert* [1985] ECR 1.

6 Article 86(1): public undertakings, special and exclusive rights

6.1. Introduction

Article 86(1) EC provides a regime for special and exclusive rights in that it highlights the fact that their aexistence is warranted provided the free movement and competition rules are respected. This section will discuss, sequentially:

- the role and structure of Article 86 EC;
- public undertakings, special and exclusive rights;
- the legality of monopoly rights;
- the prohibition on abuse of statutory monopoly rights;
- general public interest defences under Article 86(1) EC;
- convergence between the free movement and competition rules under Article 86 EC;
- delegation of regulatory functions under Article 86 EC; and
- the possibility of pre-emption under Article 86 EC.

The next chapter will then examine the role of Article 86(2) EC, concerning services of general economic interest.

6.2. The role and structure of Article 86 EC

Article 86 EC provides a special regime for public monopolies and for undertakings granted 'special and exclusive rights' by the Member States in respect to both the free movement and the competition rules.

Consequently, Article 86 EC is a key provision as regards the distinction between the public and the private spheres in EU law. It is structured as follows:

- Article 86(1) EC formulates the general rule prohibiting the Member States from taking, concerning public undertakings or undertakings enjoying special and/or exclusive rights, any measures contrary to the rules contained in the Treaty. These Treaty rules are further specified as the anti-discrimination provisions of Articles 28 and 49, the competition rules and the rules on State aids.

- Article 86(2) provides a limited derogation from this general rule for services of a general economic interest and revenue-producing monopolies. This exception is limited to cases where the free movement and competition rules would obstruct such enterprises in the performance of their public interest tasks, and to State measures which do not encroach on the Community interest – repeating the familiar EU law requirements of necessity and proportionality.

- Under Article 86(3) EC the Commission is empowered to enforce the prohibition in Article 86(1) by way of Directives and decisions. As is the case for Article 86 EC itself, such Article 86(3) EC Directives are addressed to the Member States, not to undertakings directly.

Broadly, Article 86 EC fulfils a function similar to that performed by Article 31 EC for commercial monopolies in relation to the free movement of goods and, in the case law of the Court, the two often appear side by side. Like Article 31, Article 86 EC is addressed to the Member States, not to undertakings directly. In summary, it prohibits the Member States from taking, in relation to the specific categories of undertakings mentioned above, any measures contrary to the Treaty, with a limited exception for services of general economic interest. The application of both the general rule and its exception are subject to Commission supervision. As such, Article 86 EC is also an elaboration of the principle of Community 'good faith' set out in Article 10 EC, which formed the basis of the Article 81 EC *effet utile* case law discussed above.

In the words of the Court:

Article 90 [now Article 86] concerns only undertakings for whose actions Member States must take special responsibility by reason of the influence which they may exert over such actions. It emphasises that such rulings, subject to the provisions contained in paragraph 2, are subject to all the rules laid down in the Treaty and, further, requires the Member States to respect those rules in their relations with those undertakings.

That being so, Article 90(1) [now Article 86(1)] must be interpreted as being intended to ensure that the Member States do not take advantage of their relations with those undertakings in order to evade the prohibitions laid down by other Treaty rules addressed directly to them, such as those in Article 30, 34 and 37, [now Articles 28, 29 and 31] by obliging or encouraging those undertakings to engage in conduct which, if engaged in by the Member States, would be contrary to those rules.[1]

Hence, the function of Article 86(1) EC is to bar the Member States from abusing statutory monopolies to circumvent, inter alia, the free movement rules. The Court's reading of Article 86 EC completes the triangle that it has constructed by interpreting the Treaty rules on free movement and competition as being linked across the public/private divide:

- The first leg of this triangle is the Court's reading of the competition rules as intended to bar private restrictive practices replacing quantitative restrictions and measures of equivalent effect, cited in *Consten and Grundig* in 1964.[2]
- The second leg is the *effet utile* approach to the competition rules set out in the 1987 *Van Eycke* case,[3] designed to bar the Member States from depriving these rules of their effect by sanctioning such private restrictions.
- As spelled out in the 1997 *Electricity* Cases, Article 86 EC forms the third link between the private and public regimes concerning the free movement and competition rules, barring restrictions by means of statutory monopolies.

With a series of judgments in the 1990s, the Court has markedly increased the relevance of Article 86 EC. They turned Article 86 EC into a flashpoint for the tensions resulting from the shifting balance between the regime for undertakings subject to the competition rules and the public interest exceptions thereto, concomitant with the liberalisation and privatisation trends, for example in the realm of public utilities.[4] This can be explained largely by the fact that Article 86

---

[1] Case C-157/94 *Dutch Electricity Monopoly* [1997] ECR I-5699, paras. 29–30 with reference to Joined Cases 188, 189 and 190/80 *France, Italy and United Kingdom* v. *Commission (Transparency)* [1982] ECR 2545, para. 12. Noted by Mortelmans, (1998) SEW 30.

[2] Joined Cases 56 and 58/64 *Consten and Grundig* v. *Commission (Consten)* [1966] ECR 299.

[3] Case 267/86 *Pascal Van Eycke* v. *ASPA NV (Van Eycke)* [1988] ECR 4769.

[4] Cf. Bright, 'Article 90, Economic Policy and the Duties of the Member States', (1993) 4 ECLR 263; J. Buendia Sierra, *Exclusive Rights and State Monopolies in EC Law* (Oxford University Press, 1999); Buendia Sierra, 'Article 86 – Exclusive Rights and Other Anti-competitive State Measures' in J. Faull and A. Nikpay (eds.), *The EC Law of Competition* 2nd ed. (Oxford University Press, 2007), p. 593; Devroe, 'Privatisations and Community Law: Neutrality versus Policy' (1997) 34 CMLR 267; Edward and Hoskins, 'Article 90: Deregulation and EC Law: Reflections Arising From the XVI FIDE Conference', (1995) 32 CMLR 157; Ehlermann, 'Neuere Entwicklungen im europäischen Wettbewerbsrecht', (1991) 26 EuR 307; Ehlermann, 'Managing Monopolies: The Role of the State in Controlling Market Dominance in the European Community', (1993) 14 ECLR 61; Gardner, 'The Velvet Revolution: Article 90 and the Triumph of the Free Market in Europe's Regulated Sectors' (1995) 16 ECLR 78; Gyselen, 'State Action and the

EC – unlike Article 31 EC or indeed the competition rules themselves – provides an explicit public interest exception under Article 86(2) EC.

As a result of this case law, Article 86(1) has developed into an independent legal norm, subject to general public interest exceptions, with Article 86(2) EC as a more specific separate norm applicable to services of general economic interest. So far this mainly concerns network industries such as transport (notably including port facilities), energy and telecommunications. Most recently, the effective scope of the Article 86(1) EC prohibition appears to have been determined by reference to two related variables. These are:

- first, the margins left to national public interest considerations such as allowed under Articles 28, 46 and 86(2) EC; and
- second, the degree to which the Community itself has adopted a coherent approach to balancing these public interest requirements with the market freedoms for the sector concerned (or pre-emption).

Such Community 'pre-emption' may occur both under Article 86(3) EC (the Commission acting on its own) or 95 EC (harmonisation by European Parliament and Council) secondary rules and by means of consistent enforcement action. Here, Articles 86(1) and 86(2) EC will first be discussed separately.

6.3. Public undertakings, special and exclusive rights

Article 86 EC covers two types of undertakings: public undertakings and privileged undertakings, which can in turn be subdivided between undertakings granted 'exclusive' and those granted 'special' rights.

The concept of 'public undertaking' was first defined by the Commission in its 1980 Transparency Directive (the first Directive it ever adopted based on Article 86(3) EC) as 'any undertaking over which the public authorities may exercise directly or indirectly a dominant

Effectiveness of the EC Treaty's Competition Provisions', (1989) 26 CMLR 33; Hancher, 'Artikel 90 EEG – Minder troebel, maar nog niet helder', (1993) 41 SEW 328; Lowe, 'Telecommunications Services and Competition Law in Europe', (1994) 5 EBLR 139; Naftel, 'The Natural Death of a Natural Monopoly: Competition in EC Telecommunications after the Telecommunications Terminals Judgment', (1993) 14 ECLR 105; Pappalardo, 'State Measures and Public Undertakings: Article 90 of the Treaty Revisited', (1991) 12 ECLR 29; W. Schroeder and K. Weber (eds.), *Daseinsvorsorge durch öffentliche Unternehmen und das europäische Gemeinschaftsrecht* (Vienna: Manz, 2003); Van Miert, 'Les Missions d'Intérêt Général et l'Article 89§2 du Traité CE dans la Politique de la Commission', (1997) 2 *Il diritto dell'economia* 277.

influence by virtue of their ownership of it, their financial participation therein, or the rules which govern it'.[5] Similarly to the concept of 'control' in the context of merger assessments, dominant influence is assumed to exist where a public administration directly or indirectly controls either a majority of:

- the capital; or
- the related voting rights; or
- the positions of the governing (administrative, managerial or supervisory) bodies of the undertaking.

These definitions have proven lasting.

The Commission first used the concept of 'special and exclusive rights' in its 1988 Terminal Directive that was likewise based on Article 86(3) EC and abolished such rights for telecommunications terminal equipment, albeit without defining them.[6] The Court subsequently struck down the relevant provisions of the Directive in relation to 'special rights' for lack of a definition.[7] In its Services Directive of 1990, also based on Article 86(3) EC,[8] the Commission brought special and exclusive rights under a single definition as 'the rights granted by a Member State or a public authority to one or more public or private bodies through any legal, regulatory or administrative instrument reserving them the right to provide a service or undertake an activity'. Again, the Court struck down the relevant provision as insufficiently precise in relation to special rights,[9] leading to an amendment of the Services Directive with the following definition of the latter:

[R]ights that are granted by a Member State to a limited number of undertakings, through any legislative, regulatory or administrative instrument, which, within a given geographical area,

---

[5] Article 2, Transparency Directive 80/723/EEC, OJ 1980 L195/35. Replaced by Commission Directive 2000/52/EC of 26 July 2000 amending Directive 80/723/EEC on the transparency of financial relations between Member States and public undertakings OJ 2000 L193/75. Cf. Joined Cases 188 to 190/80 *France, Italy and United Kingdom* v. *Commission (Transparency Directive)* [1982] ECR 2545; and Case 118/85 *Commission* v. *Italy* [1987] ECR 2599.

[6] Articles 1 and 2 of Commission Directive 88/301/EEC of 16 May 1988 on competition in the markets in telecommunications terminal equipment (Terminal Directive) OJ 1988 L131/73.

[7] Case C-202/88 *France* v. *Commission (Terminal Directive)* [1991] ECR I-1223.

[8] Commission Directive 90/388/EEC of 28 June 1990 on competition in the markets for telecommunications services (Services Directive) OJ 1990 L192/10.

[9] Joined cases C-271, 281 and 289/90 *Spain, Belgium and Italy* v. *Commission (Services Directive)* [1992] ECR I-5833.

- limits to two or more the number of such undertakings, otherwise than according to objective, proportional and non-discriminatory criteria, or
- designates, otherwise than according to such criteria, several competing undertakings, or
- confers on any undertaking or undertakings, otherwise than according to such criteria, any legal or regulatory advantages which substantially affect the ability of any other undertaking to import, market, connect, bring into service and/or maintain telecommunication terminal equipment in the same geographical area under substantially equivalent conditions.[10]

In 2000, these definitions of exclusive and special rights were incorporated, in generalised terms, by amendment into the Transparency Directive, alongside the definitions of public undertaking and dominant influence.[11]

To be relevant for the purposes of Article 86, the special and exclusive rights concerned have to be created by a State measure, i.e. a public administration acting in its role as public authority. When such an entity is acting as an economic operator, for example, exclusive purchasing contracts may be subject to Articles 81 and/or 82 EC.[12]

6.4. The legality of monopoly rights

There has been much discussion of the per se legality or illegality of State monopolies: the question of whether the creation of a monopoly as such infringes Article 86 EC. In fact, the Court has been remarkably consistent on this count. In its 1974 *Sacchi* ruling,[13] concerning the Italian State monopoly on television broadcasting, the Court confirmed the Member States' rights to confer monopoly:

---

[10] Article 1, Commission Directive 94/46/EC of 13 October 1994 amending Directive 88/301/EEC and Directive 90/388/EEC in particular with regard to satellite communications (Satellite Directive) OJ 1994 L268/15.

[11] Article 2, Commission Directive 2000/52/EC of 26 July 2000 amending Directive 80/723/EEC on the transparency of financial relations between Member States and public undertakings OJ 2000 L193/75. For electronic communications, the concepts of exclusive and special rights are now defined (consistent with the amended Transparency Directive) in Article 1 of Commission Directive 2002/77/EC of 16 September 2002 on competition in the markets for electronic communications networks and services OJ 2002 L249/21.

[12] E.g. Case C-393/92 *Almelo* [1994] ECR I-1477, paras. 30–1. Cf. Buendia Sierra, 'Article 86 – Exclusive Rights and Other Anti-competitive State Measures' in J. Faull and A. Nikpay (eds.), *The EC Law of Competition*, 2nd edn (Oxford University Press, 2007), para. 6.10.

[13] Case 155/73 *Sacchi* [1974] ECR 409.

Nothing in the Treaty prevents Member States *for considerations of public interest, of a non-economic nature,* from removing radio and television transmissions, including cable transmissions, from the field of competition by conferring on one or more establishments an exclusive right to conduct them.[14]

The Court went on to elaborate that whereas neither the creation nor the extension of a monopoly by means of exclusive rights were incompatible with Article 86 EC, the behaviour of the undertakings concerned remained subject to the prohibitions against discrimination and to the competition rules. Hence, it tempered a presumption of per se legality of statutory monopoly by emphasising the applicable behavioural constraints. This is in line with the general logic of Article 82 EC, which does not prohibit the existence or creation of dominant market power as such, but merely forbids abuse thereof.

Moreover, the Court in *Sacchi* clarified the scope of the Article 86(2) EC exception. It held that the application of the competition rules to undertakings charged with the operation of *services of general economic interest* could be limited by the exception of Article 86(2) EC only if it was demonstrated that the prohibitions of the competition rules were 'incompatible with the performance of their tasks'.[15] This established two separate, but similar, regimes for economic and non-economic public interest exceptions.

Finally, the Court underscored that none of the peculiarities of an Article 86 EC regime in a particular case would detract from the fact that the competition rules remained directly enforceable by individuals.[16] Despite various twists and turns, the Court in its subsequent case law has essentially continued down the path marked out in *Sacchi*.

6.5. The prohibition on abuse of statutory monopoly rights

In subsequent cases, the Court initially appeared to retreat from the per se legality position taken in *Sacchi*. It did so by indicating that, in certain cases, awarding special and exclusive rights could be tantamount to inducing or introducing prohibited Article 82 EC dominance abuse. For

---

[14] Case 155/73 *Sacchi* [1974] ECR 409, para. 14 (emphasis added).

[15] Case 155/73 *Sacchi* [1974] ECR 409, para. 15.

[16] 'Even within the framework of Article 90 . . . the prohibitions of Article 86 have direct effect and confer on interested parties rights which the national courts must safeguard.' Case 155/73 *Sacchi* [1974] ECR 409, para. 18. Cf. Case C-179/90 *Merci* [1991] ECR I-5889, para. 23.

example, in *Télé-Marketing*, the Court first confirmed that Article 82 EC continued to apply to statutory monopolies:

> Article 86 [now Article 82] of the Treaty must be interpreted as applying to an undertaking holding a dominant position on a particular market, even where that position is not due to the activities of the undertaking itself but to the fact that by reason of the provisions laid down by law there can be no competition or only limited competition on that market.[17]

It then continued by stating that extending the monopoly in question might constitute an Article 82 EEC abuse:

> An abuse within the meaning of Article 86 is committed where, without any objective necessity, an undertaking holding a dominant position on a particular market reserves to itself or to an undertaking belonging to the same group an ancillary activity which might be carried out by another undertaking as part of its activities on a neighbouring but separate market with the possibility of eliminating all competition from such undertaking.[18]

Likewise, in *RTT*, concerning the Belgian telecommunications monopoly, the Court held that the granting of exclusive rights which extend an existing dominant position could constitute an Article 86 EC infringement.[19] By similar reasoning, conferring rule making powers on a (former) State monopoly was considered prohibited in *British Telecom*[20] and in *ERT*, regarding the statutory cumulation of exclusive rights on television broadcasting and retransmission in Greece.[21]

In subsequent cases, the Court ruled that Articles 86 and 82 EC applied to situations 'where the undertaking in question, merely by exercising the exclusive rights granted to it, *cannot avoid abusing* its dominant position',[22] or where the Member State '*induces*' or '*enables*'

---

[17] Case 311/84 *CBEM* v. *CLT and IBP (Télé-Marketing)* [1985] ECR 3261, para. 18.
[18] Case 311/84 *CBEM* v. *CLT and IBP (Télé-Marketing)* [1985] ECR 3261, para. 16.
[19] Case C-18/88 *RTT* v. *GB-INNO-BM* [1991] ECR I-5941.
[20] Case C-41/83 *Italy* v. *Commission (British Telecom)* [1985] ECR 873.
[21] C-260/89 *ERT* [1991] ECR I-2925.
[22] Case C-41/90 *Höfner* [1991] ECR I-1979, paras. 28–9. Here, the beneficiary of the exclusive rights could not avoid infringing Article 86 EC (although it tolerated competition – in breach of its statutory monopoly), due to its manifest (inbuilt) failure to meet demand for job placement services. Cf. Case C-323/93 *La Crespelle* [1994] ECR I-5080, para. 18; Case C-387/93 *Banchero* [1995] ECR I-4663, para. 51; Case C-242/95 *GT-Link* [1997] ECR I-4449, para. 33; Case C-55/96 *Job Centre Coop* [1997] ECR I-7119, para. 31; Case C-340/99 *TNT Traco SpA* v. *Poste Italiane SpA et al.* [2001] ECR I-4109, para. 44; and Case C-462/99 *Connect Austria* [2003] ECR I-5197, para. 80.

the undertaking concerned to abuse its dominant position.[23] The Court even appeared to suggest the possibility of per se illegality of exclusive rights by ruling that Article 86(1) EC prohibited the granting of exclusive rights 'where such rights are liable to create a situation where the undertaking is *led to infringe* Article 86 EC [now Article 82 EC]'.[24] In this context, it also pointed out that the Member States are required 'not to adopt or maintain in force any measures which may deprive Article 86 [now Article 82] of its effectiveness' (or *effet utile*).[25] Evidently, this stricture could apply even in the absence of evidence of any abusive practices.[26]

More recently, the line adopted has generally been that first set out in *Merci*, i.e. to underline that granting exclusive rights is not as such illegal, but to find an infringement:

if the undertaking in question, merely by exercising the exclusive rights granted to it, is led to abuse its dominant position or if such rights are liable to create a situation in which that undertaking is led to commit such abuses.[27]

In fact, if Article 86 is to remain consistent with the general approach towards dominance under Article 82, the per se illegality of exclusive rights under Article 86(1) EC is inconceivable for at least two good reasons:

-   dominance is established based on the definition of a relevant product and geographic market, an analysis not made here; and
-   dominance is not illegal per se, only dominance abuse is.

(i) Definition of a relevant market: The first issue is that of market definition. In a number of cases the Court ruled that an enterprise granted

---

[23] Cf. Case C-18/93 *Corsica Ferries Italia* [1994] ECR I-1783, para. 43 (induces); Case C-203/96 *Dusseldorp* [1998] ECR I-4075, para. 61 (enables); and Case C-242/95 *GT-Link* [1997] ECR I-4449, para. 34 (induces).

[24] Case C-260/89 *ERT* [1991] ECR I-2925, para. 38.

[25] Case C-260/89 *ERT* [1991] ECR I-2925, para. 35. Cf. Case 13/77 *GB-INNO-BM* v. *ATAB* [1977] ECR 2115, paras. 30–5; and Case C-320/91 *Corbeau* [1993] ECR I-2533, para. 11.

[26] Inversely, in Case C-179/90 *Merci* [1991] ECR I-5889, where an array of abuses was involved in the monopoly provision of docking services, the Court held that the exclusive right concerned induced the beneficiary to commit abuse.

[27] Case C-179/90 *Merci* [1991] ECR I-5889, para. 17; Case C-136/96 *Raso* [1998] ECR I-533, para. 27; Case C-266/96 *Corsica Ferries France* [1998] ECR I-3949, para. 40; Joined Cases C-115, 116, 117 and 119/97 *Brentjens* [1999] ECR I-6025, para. 93; and Case C-219/97 *Drijvende Bokken* [1999] ECR I-6121, para. 83; Case 209/98 *Entreprnørforeningens Affalds/ Miljøsektion* v. *Københavns Kommune (Sydhavnens)* [2000] ECR I-3743, para. 66.

a legal monopoly by definition has a dominant position.[28] However, as confirmed in *Bodson*, a determination of the relevant market is required in order to establish the existence of a dominant position – albeit that doing so may be facilitated by the existence of a legal monopoly.[29] At least in theory, however, a monopoly right may be more limited in scope than the relevant market to an extent that the dominance threshold is not reached.

(ii) Dominance is not illegal per se: Second, and likewise consistent with its general Article 86 EC case law, the Court holds that maintaining or creating a dominant position – and by extension a legal monopoly – itself is not as such illegal.[30] This is also consistent with the Court's approach to Article 31 EC, which appreciates separately the restrictions inherent in the existence of commercial monopolies and any other restrictions.

The question, therefore, is not whether exclusive rights are allowed; rather, it is:

- in which cases they are allowed only in so far as the free movement and competition rules are not infringed by the exercise of these exclusive rights; and
- when public interest exceptions may in addition justify certain infringements of the free movement and competition rules.

The next section will examine these two issues.

---

[28] Cf. Case C-260/89 *ERT* [1991] ECR I-2925, para. 31; Case C-179/90 *Merci* [1991] ECR I-5889, para. 14; Case C-18/93 *Corsica Ferries Italia* [1994] ECR I-1783, para. 40; Case C-320/91 *Procureur du Roi* v. *Paul Corbeau* [1993] ECR I-2533; and Case C-242/95 *GT-Link* [1997] ECR I-4449, para. 35. In Case C-41/90 *Höfner* [1991] ECR I-1979, the Court stated that 'an undertaking with a legal monopoly may be regarded as occupying a dominant position within the meaning of Article 86 of the Treaty'. *Ibid.*, para. 28.

[29] Case 30/87 *Bodson* [1988] ECR 2479, paras. 26–9. This more standard approach to dominance under Article 82 EC based on market definition has also been adopted in more recent Article 86 EC cases such as: Case C-475/99 *Glöckner* [2001] ECR I-8089; and Case C-82/01 P *Aéroports de Paris* [2002] ECR I-9297.

[30] Case C-41/90 *Höfner* [1991] ECR I-1979, para. 29. Cf. Case 311/84 *Télé-Marketing* [1985] ECR 3261, para. 17; Case C-260/89 *ERT* [1991] ECR I-2925; Case C-179/90 *Merci* [1991] ECR I-5889, para. 16; Case C-18/93 *Corsica Ferries Italia* [1994] ECR I-1783, para. 42; Case C-320/91 *Corbeau* [1993] ECR I-2533, para. 11; Case C-323/93 *La Crespelle* [1994] ECR I-5080, para. 18; Case C-387/93 *Banchero* [1995] ECR I-4663, para. 51; Case C-266/96 *Corsica Ferries France* [1998] ECR I-3949, para. 41; Case C-67/96 *Albany* [1999] ECR I-5751, para. 93; Joined Cases C-115, 116, 117 and 119/97 *Brentjens* [1999] ECR I-6025, para. 93; Case C-219/97 *Drijvende Bokken* [1999] ECR I-6121, para. 83; and Case 209/98 *Sydhavnens* [2000] ECR I-3743; paras. 66 ff.

6.6. General public interest defences under Article 86(1) EC

As the Court stated in *Sacchi*, exclusive rights are in any event permitted under Article 86(1) EC for reason of non-economic public interest considerations. This suggests that, depending on whether Article 86(1) is applied in conjunction with Articles 28, 49 and/or 82 EC, various public interest defences can be invoked – for example, based on Article 30 or 46 EC.[31] This means that, in the context of statutory monopolies, public interest defences could in theory justify certain infringements of Articles 28 and 49 EC.

In practice, however, there appear to be few instances where infringements of Articles 28 and 49 EC have actually been exempted from the Article 86(1) EC prohibition based on public interest exceptions under the free movement rules. (An exception is the *Crespelle* Case, discussed below.[32]) The Court has recognised that, for example, cultural objectives[33] and protection of the fundamental right of freedom of expression[34] in principle constitute legitimate public interest objectives that a national broadcasting policy may pursue consistent with Article 56 EC. However, attempts to salvage national broadcasting monopolies restrictive of Article 56 EC based on such public interest arguments have typically failed on non-discrimination and proportionality (including necessity) grounds.[35] Notably, the 'least restrictive means' proportionality test when applied under both Article 30 and 46 EC is, in most cases, prohibitive.[36]

---

[31] Cf. Case 33/74 *Van Binsbergen* [1974] ECR 1299; Case 279/80 *Webb* [1981] ECR 3305; Case 62/79 *SA Coditel et al.* v. *SA Ciné Vog Films et al.* [1980] ECR 881; Case 52/79 *Procureur du Roi* v. *Debauve* [1980] ECR 833; and Case 352/85 *Bond van Adverteerders* v. *Netherlands* [1988] ECR 2085.

[32] Case C-323/93 *La Crespelle* [1994] ECR I-5080.

[33] Case C-288/89 *Goudse Kabel* [1991] ECR I-4007; Case C-353/89 *Mediawet* [1991] ECR I-4069; Case C-148/91 *Veronica Omroep Organisatie* v. *Commissariaat voor de Media* [1993] ECR I-487; and Case C-23/93 *TV10 SA* v. *Commissariaat voor de Media* [1994] ECR I-4795.

[34] Cf. Case C-260/89 *ERT* [1991] ECR I-2925; and Case C-353/89 *Mediawet* [1991] ECR I-4069; Case C-23/93 *TV10 SA* v. *Commissariaat voor de Media* [1994] ECR I-4795.

[35] Case C-288/89 *Goudse Kabel* [1991] ECR I-4007; Case C-353/89 *Mediawet* [1991] ECR I-4069; and cf. Case C-260/89 *ERT* [1991] ECR I-2925.

[36] Case C-288/89 *Goudse Kabel* [1991] ECR I-4007; Case C-353/89 *Mediawet* [1991] ECR I-4069; Case C-412/93 *Leclerc-Siplec* [1995] ECR I-179; Case C-384/93 *Alpine Investments BV* v. *Minister van Financiën* [1995] ECR I-1141; Joined Cases C-34, 35 and 36/95 *Konsumentombudsmannen* v. *De Agostini*, [1997] ECR I-3843, 2. This case law converges with that on free movement. Cf. Joined Cases C-267 and 268/91 *Keck* [1993] ECR I-6097; Case C-292/92 *Hünermund* [1993] ECR I-6787. Cf. Fernández Martín and O'Leary,

For Article 82 EC, for which the Treaty does not provide a general non-economic public interest exemption (as Article 86(2) EC is limited to the general *economic* interest), the picture is more varied.

On the one hand, certain types of abuses, such as price discrimination and abusive pricing, if induced by the government measures concerned, have in some instances been dealt with forcefully.[37] Exclusive rights linked with inability to meet demand, and tying practices, fared likewise.[38] On the other hand, in the absence of a clear link between an (alleged) abuse and the State measure granting the exclusive right, national monopolies and collectively dominant positions have been left untouched under Article 86(1) EC – without reference to any public interest justifications that would be key in assessing the legality of measures infringing the free movement rules.

A clear illustration of this is found in the *Crespelle* Case, where the exclusive rights that left undertakings free to determine price levels based on a nationwide system of regional monopolies themselves were not held to induce price abuse, in spite of the fact that the dominance which made price abuse possible had been created by means of contiguous exclusive rights.[39] Article 82 was therefore not held applicable. Although the exclusive rights concerned were found to constitute barriers to trade under Article 28 EC, the Court held they were covered by Article 30 on health grounds given that health conditions in intra-Community trade in bovine semen were not yet fully harmonised – i.e. the absence of pre-emption – provided the restrictions involved were

---

'Judicially-Created Exceptions to the Free Provision of Services' in M. Andenas and W.-H. Roth (eds.), *Services and Free Movement in EU Law* (Oxford University Press, 2002), p. 163.

[37] 'The Member State infringes the prohibitions . . . if, by approving the tariffs adopted by the undertaking, it induces it to abuse its dominant position inter alia by applying dissimilar conditions to equivalent transactions with its trading partners within the meaning of Article 86(c) of the Treaty.' Case C-18/93 *Corsica Ferries Italia* [1994] ECR I-1783, para. 45; Case C-242/95 *GT-Link* [1997] ECR I-4449, paras. 38 ff; and Case C-136/96 *Raso* [1998] ECR I-533, paras. 30–1. Likewise in Case 30/87 *Bodson* [1988] ECR 2479, where it was charged that unfair prices formed part of the concession contract, the Court held that Article 86(1) precluded public authorities from imposing price conditions that were contrary to Article 82 EC.

[38] Case C-41/90 *Höfner* [1991] ECR I-1979; Case C-55/96 *Job Centre Coop* [1997] ECR I-7119, paras. 32 ff; and Case C-179/90 *Merci* [1991] ECR I-5889.

[39] Case C-323/93 *La Crespelle* [1994] ECR I-5080, paras. 20–1. This ruling – including its pre-emption aspect – presages the approach later taken in the 1997 *Electricity* Cases that will be discussed in detail in the next chapter. Case C-157/94 *Dutch Electricity Monopoly* [1997] ECR I-5699; Case C-159/94 *French Electricity and Gas Monopoly* [1997] ECR I-5815; and Case C-158/94 *Italian Electricty Monopoly* [1997] ECR I-5789.

proportionate (a matter left to the national court to decide, presumably on the basis of the 'manifestly disproportionate' standard).

The next section will concern the link between Article 82 EC abuse and infringements of the free movement rules.

6.7. Convergence between free movement and competition rules under Article 86 EC

Abuse of Article 82 EC and infringements of the free movement rules can evidently coincide. For example, the Court has tended to find that statutory monopolies which induce Article 82 EC abuse almost by definition involve infringements of Articles 28 and 46 EC. Already in its 1977 Case *GB-INNO-BM* v. *ATAB*, the Court stated that:

In any case, a national measure which has the effect of facilitating the abuse of a dominant position capable of affecting trade between Member States will generally be incompatible with Articles 30 and 34 [now Articles 28 and 29], which prohibit quantitative restrictions on imports and exports and all measures having equivalent effect.[40]

In its 1991 *Porto di Genova* Case, it confirmed this view:

As regards the interpretation of Article 30 [now Article 28] of the Treaty . . . it is sufficient to recall that a national measure which has the effect of facilitating the abuse of a dominant position capable of affecting trade between Member States will generally be incompatible with that article.[41]

Based on analogous reasoning, the Court has on occasion neglected even to examine Article 49 EC on the grounds that a potential infringement of Article 82 EC would suffice.[42] Finally, recalling that Articles 28 and 49 EC must in any event be 'interpreted in the light of' the principle of free competition in open markets, it has repeatedly confirmed that the Commission can use its Article 86(3) EC powers to elaborate the Member States obligations that ensue from the directly effective free movement provisions.[43]

---

[40] Case 13/77 *GB-INNO-BM* v. *ATAB* [1977] ECR 2115, para. 35.

[41] Case C-179/90 *Merci* [1991] ECR I-5889, para. 21.

[42] Case C-55/96 *Job Centre Coop* [1997] ECR I-7119, para. 39; and Case C-136/96 *Raso et al.* [1998] ECR I-533, para. 33.

[43] C-202/88 *Terminal Directive* [1991] ECR I-1223, paras. 41, 43 (with reference to Case 229/83 *Au Blé Vert* [1985] ECR 1, para. 9); and Joined Cases C-271, 281 and 289/90 *Services Directive* [1992] ECR I-5833.

The distinction between Member States' actions and those of entities awarded special and exclusive rights – and in particular delegation – forms the subject of the next section.

6.8. Delegation of regulatory functions under Article 86 EC

Delegation is relevant under Article 86 EC where the entities involved combine the exercise of certain regulatory powers with the offering of related goods and services in the market.

(i) In the first place, as regards the Member States, it is illegal to award special and exclusive rights that include regulatory duties placing an undertaking 'at an obvious advantage over its competitors'.[44] Hence, in RTT v. GB-INNO-BM, the Court held that:

Articles 3(f), 90 and 86 of the EEC Treaty [now Articles 3(g), 86 and 82 EC] preclude a Member State from granting to the undertaking which operates the public telecommunications network the power to lay down standards for telephone equipment and to check that economic operators meet those standards when it is itself competing with those operators on the market for that equipment.[45]

In Decoster, the Court ruled that 'it makes no difference whether those combined functions are carried out by a body which is legally separate from the State or a Ministry'.[46] In either case, Articles 3(g), 82 and 86 of the Treaty precluded national rules that prohibited economic operators from marketing of terminal equipment without type-approval certificates, where there was no guarantee that the body responsible for type-approval was independent from operators offering goods and/or services in the sector.[47] As appears self-evident, and was also highlighted in Decoster and in a number of related cases, the limits imposed by EU law are stricter where secondary legislation exists that specifically requires such regulatory independence, such as Article 6 of Terminal Directive 88/301, which required that responsibility for drawing up specifications, monitoring their application and granting type approval

---

[44] Cf. Case C-18/88 RTT v. GB-INNO-BM [1991] ECR I-5941, paras. 25–6; and Case C-202/88 Terminal Directive [1991] ECR I-1223, paras. 51–2.
[45] Case C-18/88 RTT v. GB-INNO-BM [1991] ECR I-5941, para. 28.
[46] Case C-69/91 Ministère Public v. Decoster [1993] ECR I-5335, para. 21.
[47] Case C-69/91 Ministère Public v. Decoster [1993] ECR I-5335, para. 22.

would be entrusted to a body independent of public or private undertakings offering goods in the sector.[48]

(ii) Second, as regards the undertaking concerned, the exercise of such regulatory powers can lead to a finding that it infringed the competition rules. In *Commission v. Italy*, the Court agreed that the Commission was entitled to apply Article 86 EC to the regulatory functions assigned to British Telecom as follows:

The power conferred on BT to introduce schemes has been strictly limited to laying down provisions relating to the scale of charges and other terms and conditions under which it provides services for users. In the light of the wording of those provisions it must further be acknowledged that the United Kingdom legislature in no way predetermined the content of the schemes, which is freely determined by BT.

In those circumstances, the schemes referred to by the contested decision must be regarded as an integral part of BT's business activity.[49]

It followed from this finding that the rule-making powers involved constituted part of BT's business activity and that they could be subjected to scrutiny under Article 86 EC.

Hence, as was found for *effet utile* above, the delegation of rule-making powers based on exclusive and special rights can be illegal, as can the exercise of such delegated rule-making powers.

(iii) Third, however, as was likewise found in relation to effet utile, *the delegation of rule-making functions is saved when the exercise of regulatory powers by the undertaking involved is justified by public interest, and adequate procedural guarantees ensure these powers cannot be abused.* Thus, in the absence of pre-emption by more specific secondary rules of Community law, in *Lagauche*, the Court found the examination of type approval applications by the State monopoly RTT acceptable, as the applicable criteria were defined by State measures:

in contrast to the situation in the GB-INNO-BM case, it is the minister who determines the technical requirements necessary for type-approval of such equipment and the detailed rules concerning that approval, and he does so within the framework of his powers to regulate radiocommunications in

---

[48] Cf. Case C-92/91 *Ministère Public* v. *Taillandier* [1993] ECR I-5383; Case C-69/91 *Ministère Public* v. *Decoster* [1993] ECR I-5335; and Joined Cases C-46/90 and 93/91 *Lagauche and Others* [1993] ECR I-5267. On other aspects of the interpretation of Article 28 EC and Directive 88/301, see Case C-314/93 *Ministère Public* v. *François Rouffeteau and Robert Badia* [1994] ECR I-3257. Cf. Case C-80/92 *Commission* v. *Belgium* [1994] ECR I-1019.

[49] Case C-41/83 *Italy* v. *Commission (British Telecom)* [1985] ECR 873, paras. 19–20.

Belgian territory. While it is true that the RTT is authorised . . . to undertake and operate any radiocommunication service, it is clear . . . that its sole task as regards the type-approval of transmitting or receiving equipment is to check that such equipment complies with the requirements determined by the minister.[50]

In this case setting, the tasks involved were apparently so mechanical as to leave such minimal freedom of appreciation that no illegal delegation was found – even although, as was seen above, making interested parties responsible for type approval has in fact been contested regularly.

   (iv) *The technical complexity of the regulatory task may require it to be performed by an undertaking, provided there is adequate judicial scrutiny.* More remarkably, both as regards the application of Articles 82 and 86 EC, and as regards Article 28 EC, the very complexity of the task involved may justify leaving regulatory responsibility with an undertaking, including a significant degree of discretion, provided that its decisions are subject to judicial scrutiny (similar to its decision on the setting of legal fees in Arduino[51]). In *RTT* v. *GB-INNO-BM*, the Court found that this test had not been met:

If there were no possibility of any challenge before the courts, the authority granting type-approval could adopt an attitude which was arbitrary or systematically unfavourable to imported equipment. Moreover, the likelihood of the authority granting type-approval adopting such an attitude is increased by the fact that the procedures for obtaining type-approval and for laying down the technical specifications do not involve the hearing of any interested parties. . . . therefore . . . Article 30 of the Treaty precludes a public undertaking from being given the power to approve telephone equipment which is intended to be connected to the public network and which it has not supplied if the decisions of that undertaking cannot be challenged before the courts.[52]

In *Albany*, *Brentjens*, and *Drijvende Bokken*, however, this test was met where a sectoral pension fund enjoyed both an exclusive right and the power to grant exemption from mandatory affiliation to this fund. First, in line with *Lagauche*, the Court found that if the State measure

---

[50] Joined Cases C-46/90 and 93/91 *Lagauche and Others* [1993] ECR I-5267, para. 49. As, in addition, telecommunication and radiocommunication systems of the Member States had not been harmonised, requiring such type approval to guard against electromagnetic interference even from equipment already certified in other Member States was allowed.

[51] Case C-35/99 *Criminal Proceedings against Manuele Arduino* [2002] ECR I-1529.

[52] Cf. Case C-18/88 *RTT* v. *GB-INNO-BM* [1991] ECR I-5941, paras. 35–6.

concerned set out the conditions under which the sectoral pension fund could grant exemptions in a binding manner, they were not likely to lead to the abuse of this power.[53] Next, it considered that the power to allow withdrawal from the pension fund 'involves an evaluation of complex data relating to the pension schemes involved and the financial equilibrium of the fund, which necessarily implies a wide margin of appreciation'. In fact, only the fund itself apparently disposed of the information necessary to make the decisions involved. Hence:

In view of the complexity of such an evaluation and of the risks which exemptions involve for the financial equilibrium of a sectoral pension fund and, therefore, for performance of the social task entrusted to it, a Member State may consider that the power of exemption should not be attributed to a separate entity.

The fact that the criteria to be applied by the undertaking involved had been defined in a State measure was a first guarantee of objectivity. The only additional guarantee that the Court required to ensure that the application of these criteria was not abusive was judicial review – in effect holding the private undertaking involved in the exercise of public authority to an administrative review standard:

It should be noted, however, that national courts adjudicating, as in this case, on an objection to a requirement to pay contributions must subject to review the decision of the fund refusing an exemption from affiliation, which enables them at least to verify that the fund has not used its power to grant an exemption in an arbitrary manner and that the principle of non-discrimination and the other conditions for the legality of that decision have been complied with.[54]

Consequently, the exclusive right awarded to the pension fund involved did not infringe Articles 82 and 86 EC, and extensive regulatory powers may be delegated to undertakings in conjunction with such rights.[55]

---

[53] Case C-67/96 *Albany* [1999] ECR I-5751, paras. 118–121; Joined Cases C-115, 116, 117 and 119/97 *Brentjens* [1999] ECR I-6025, paras. 118–21; and Case C-219/97 *Drijvende Bokken* [1999] ECR I-6121, paras. 108–11.
[54] Case C-67/96 *Albany* [1999] ECR I-5751, paras. 120–1; Joined Cases C-115, 116, 117 and 119/97 *Brentjens* [1999] ECR I-6025, paras. 120–1; and Case C-219/97 *Drijvende Bokken* [1999] ECR I-6121, paras. 110–11.
[55] Where public involvement is more intensive, the point is reached where the entity involved may no longer be an undertaking. Thus in Case C-218/00 *Cisal* [2002] ECR I-691, where the amount of benefits and the amount of contributions to an insurance scheme were subject to State supervison, and where this scheme was based on solidarity, management of such a scheme was not found to be an economic activity, and the body concerned therefore did not constitute an undertaking. Cf. Joined Cases C-264, 306, 354 and 355/01 *AOK* [2004] ECR I-2493.

Where the Commission disagrees, it must either legislate itself under Article 86(3) EC or propose legislation for adoption by the European Parliament and the Council, for example based on Article 95 EC. This brings us to the topic of pre-emption.

6.9. Pre-emption under Article 86 EC?

The Commission is, in principle, competent to elaborate the scope of Article 86 EC – in particular, both the scope of the Article 86(1) EC prohibition and that of the Article 86(2) EC exemption. It may do so by means of Article 86(3) EC Commission Directives (adopted without formal recourse to the Council and European Parliament)[56] and Decisions. It has wide discretion in deciding whether or not to act under Article 86(3) EC.[57] The choice between using a Directive and a Decision depends on whether the Commission's objective is to specify in general terms the obligations arising under the Treaty (Directive) or to assess a specific situation in one or more Member States and to assess its consequences in Community law (Decision).[58]

Notably, in its 1991 *Terminal Directive* Case, the Court stated that special and exclusive rights were not by definition compatible with the Treaty, and that this compatibility was to be established by reference to the free movement and competition rules.[59] It upheld the Commission's competence to interpret and elaborate the resulting obligations under Article 86(1) EC, to the point of permitting the Commission to – eventually – abolish all relevant exclusive rights in the telecommunications sector by means of (sector-specific) Article 86 (3) EC Directives.

---

[56] This concerned, in particular, the Terminal Directive 88/301/EEC, OJ 1988 L131/72, and the Services Directive 90/388/EEC, OJ 1990 L192/10. The single precedent for these liberalisation Directives was the Transparency Directive 80/723/EEC, OJ 1980 L195/35. Subsequent Article 86(3) EC liberalisation Directives in the telecommunications sector and concerning financial transparency were not only submitted to the European Parliament and Council for voluntary consultation, but were also structured as 'amendments' to the three original Article 86(3) EC Directives.

[57] Joined Cases C-48 and 66/90 *Netherlands et al.* v. *Commission (Courier Services)* [1992] ECR I-565; Case C-107/95 P *Bundesverband der Bilanzbuchhalter et al.* v. *Commission* [1997] ECR I-947, para. 27.

[58] Case C-163/99 *Portugal* v. *Commission (Airport Landing Charges)* [2001] ECR I-2613, para. 28.

[59] C-202/88 *Terminal Directive* [1991] ECR I-1223. Confirmed in Joined Cases C-271, 281 and 289/90 *Services Directive* [1992] ECR I-5833. Cf. Case C-353/89 *Mediawet* [1991] ECR I-4069, paras. 34–5.

In *Terminal Directive*, the Court made clear that the scope of the Commission's powers under Article 86(3) EC depended on the specific Treaty provisions that were applied in conjunction with Article 86(1) EC. In this sense, Article 86(1) EC could be seen as a reference clause.[60] For example, concerning Article 28 EC, the Court noted that the Commission had correctly taken into account the essential requirements to which the Council itself had agreed in the context of Article 95 EC harmonisation legislation for the sector. Hence, the Commission had not exceeded its powers in withdrawing the relevant exclusive import and marketing rights.[61] Moreover, the applicant Member States had, remarkably enough, neglected to challenge the Commission view on Article 86(2) EC – allowing the Court to focus exclusively on Articles 86(1) and 86(3) EC without entering the discussion on public justifications concerning services of general economic interest.[62]

This also explains why the *Terminal Directive* and *Services Directive* Cases came to form the high water marks of success in the Commission's drive toward convincing the Court to accept per se illegality of exclusive rights. The Council had agreed on the relevant harmonised standards which allowed the Commission to elaborate the Member States' Article 86(1) EC obligations. The Member States failed to contest the Commission's assertion that Article 86(2) EC did not apply, thereby possibly conceding the only point that might have won their case for them.

Subsequently, by applying classic 'salami' tactics, the Commission gradually removed special and exclusive rights from all telecommunications markets slice by slice by means of successive amendments to the Article 86(3) EC liberalisation Directives. However, given democratic objections against liberalisation by Commission fiat, and because the favourable political and economic conditions in the telecommunications sector (technological change, global pressure and a growing internal coalition in favour of reform) were not reproduced elsewhere, Article 86(3) EC Directives were not used in comparable network sectors (for example, energy and transport).

---

[60] *In casu*, this concerned Articles 30, 37, 59 and 86 EC.
[61] Case C-202/88 *Terminal Directive* [1991] ECR I-1223, paras. 33–40.
[62] In preamble 11 to the contested Commission Directive 88/301/EEC on competition in the markets in telecommunications terminal equipment, OJ 1988 L131/72, the Commission had stated that Article 90(2) did not apply. Case C-202/88 *Terminal Directive* [1991] ECR I-1223, para. 13. The Court nevertheless used the occasion for an *obiter dictum* on Article 86(2) in paras. 11–12.

Admittedly, the 1993 *Corbeau* Case concerning the legality of the Belgian postal monopoly appeared to point in the same direction. The Court seemed to suggest – albeit ambiguously – that statutory monopolies which lack (or extend beyond) a public interest justification under Article 86(2) EC are contrary to Community law.[63] However, there is no evidence that the Court intended this dictum to extend beyond services of general economic interest to cover exclusive rights at large.[64] Moreover, it indicated a significant degree of freedom concerning the practices acceptable under the Article 86(2) EC public interest defence for services of general economic interest, including, inter alia, the right to engage in discrimination and cross-subsidisation.[65] Inversely, a statutory monopoly conferred on an undertaking entrusted with the operation of services of general economic interest that goes beyond what can be justified under Article 86(2) EC infringes Article 86(1) EC, as it impairs the *effet utile* of Article 82 EC.[66]

Hence, as was first indicated in *Sacchi*, in many cases the scope of Article 86(2) EC ultimately determines whether the creation of a statutory monopoly or the behaviour of such a monopoly are prohibited or exempted on public interest grounds. As will be seen in the next chapter, the scope of this exemption is in turn largely determined by the question of whether a Community regime is in place.

---

[63] C-260/89 *ERT* [1991] ECR I-2925, paras. 33–4; Case C-320/91 *Corbeau* [1993] ECR I-2533, noted by Gilliams (1994) 42 SEW 515; Hancher (1994) 31 CMLR 105. Cf. Wachsmann and Berrod, 'Les Critères de Justification des Monopoles: un Premier Bilan après l''Affaire *Corbeau*', (1994) 30 RTDE 39.

[64] The Court in reference to Article 86(1) EC, stated: 'That provision necessarily implies that the Member States may grant exclusive rights to certain undertakings and thereby grant them a monopoly.' Case C-157/94 *Dutch Electricity Monopoly* [1997] ECR I-5699, para. 27. Although this may also at a later stage be construed as an implict reference to undertakings exemptable under Article 86(2) EC, it is held here that, to date, there is no evidence that Case C-202/88 *Terminal Directive* [1991] ECR I-1223 and Case C-320/91 *Corbeau* [1993] ECR I-2533 signify a departure from the earlier case law.

[65] Case C-320/91 *Corbeau* [1993] ECR I-2533, paras. 12–20; and Case C-393/92 *Almelo* [1994] ECR I-1477.

[66] Case C-320/91 *Procureur du Roi* v. *Paul Corbeau* [1993] ECR I-2533, para. 11. Cf. Case C-260/89 *Elliniki Radiophonia Tileorassi* v. *Dimotiki Etairia Pliroforissis and Sotirios Kouvelas (ERT)* [1991] ECR I-2925, para. 35; Case 66/86 *Ahmed Saeed Flugreisen and Silver Line Reisebüro GmbH* v. *Zentrale zur Bekämpfung unlauteren Wettbewerbs e.V.* [1989] ECR 803, paras. 48 and 56; Joined Cases 209 to 213/84 *Asjes* [1986] ECR 1425, paras. 70 ff.

6.10. Conclusion

Article 86 EC on exclusive and special rights is an elaboration of the principle of Community 'good faith' set out in Article 10 EC that formed the basis of the Article 81 EC *effet utile* case law. The function of Article 86(1) EC is to bar the Member States from abusing statutory monopolies to circumvent the free movement and the competition rules. Provisions at odds with Article 82 are likely to also infringe the free movement rules.

Neither the creation nor the extension of a monopoly by means of exclusive rights is incompatible with Article 86 EC. However, exclusive and special rights involving distortions of competition are illegal, barring the exceptions provided in Article 86(2) EC and elsewhere in the Treaty. If exclusive and special rights are contested as constituting (part of) an Article 82 EC abuse under Article 86(1), no public interest derogations exist. However, the abuse test requires the existence of a formal link between the award of the special or exclusive right and the alleged abuse. Where Article 86(1) is applied in combination with Articles 28 and 49 EC (free movement), non-economic justifications in the general interest may be considered.

The Court's reading of Article 86 EC completes the triangle that links the Treaty rules on free movement and competition across the public/private divide:

- the Court's reading of the competition rules as intended to bar private restrictive practices replacing quantitative restrictions and measures of equivalent effect;
- the *effet utile* approach to the competition rules to bar the Member States from depriving these rules of their effect by sanctioning such private restrictions; and
- Article 86 EC forms the third link between the private and public regimes concerning the free movement and competition rules, barring restrictions by means of statutory monopolies.

The effective scope of the Article 86(1) EC prohibition is determined by, on the one hand, the margins left to national public interest considerations such as allowed under Articles 28, 46 and 86(2) EC and, on the other hand, pre-emption. It is illegal to award special and exclusive rights that include regulatory duties placing an undertaking 'at an obvious advantage over its competitors' and the exercise of regulatory powers can lead to a finding of an infringement of the competition rules. However, the delegation of rule-making functions is saved when the exercise of regulatory powers by the undertaking involved is justified by the public interest. Adequate procedural guarantees ensure that these powers cannot be abused. For instance, the technical complexity of regulatory task may require it to be performed by an undertaking, provided there is adequate judicial scrutiny.

With these observations we now come to Article 86(2) EC on services of general economic interest.

7 Article 86(2) EC: derogation for services of general economic interest (SGEI)

7.1. Introduction

Article 86(2) EC has been at the heart of much recent debate on the relative merits of liberalisation of public services.[1] In the process, a new Article 16 EC was added by the Amsterdam Treaty that is a monument of vagueness:

Without prejudice to Articles 73, 86 and 87, and given the place occupied by services of general economic interest in the shared values of the Union as well as their role in promoting social and territorial cohesion, the Community and the Member States, each within their respective powers and within the scope of application of this Treaty, shall take care that such services operate on the basis of principles and conditions which enable them to fulfil their missions.

Perhaps most noteworthy is the fact that this leaves the existing rules on services of economic interest of Article 86 and on State aids of Article 87 untouched.[2] A crucial amendment is found in the following addition

---

[1] Cf. the successive communications from the Commission: *Services of general interest in Europe*, OJ 1996 C281/3; *Services of general interest in Europe*, OJ 2001 C17/4; *Report to the Laeken European Council – Services of general interest*, COM(2001) 598 final; *Green paper on services of general interest*, COM(2003) 270 final; *White paper on services of general interest*, COM(2004) 374 final; *Implementing the Community Lisbon programme: social services of general interest in the European Union*, COM(2006) 177 final.

[2] See the Opinion of AG Poaires Maduro in Case C-205/03 P *FENIN* v. *Commission* [2006] ECR I-6295, n. 35 (Article 16 EC 'does not constitute a restriction on the scope of Article 86(2) EC, but instead provides a point of reference for the interpretation of that provision'). Article 73 EC refers to aids in the transport sector that are held compatible with the Treaty if they meet the needs of the coordination of transport or represent reimbursement for public service obligations. Cf. Rodrigues, 'Les Services Publics et le Traité d'Amsterdam-Genèse et Portée Juridique du Projet de Nouvel Article 16 du Traité CEE', [1998] *Revue du Marché Unique Européen* 37; and Ross, 'Article 16 and Services of General Interest: from Derogation to Obligation?', (2000) 25 *European Law Review* 22.

introduced by the Lisbon Treaty to what now is set to be Article 14 of the Treaty on the Functioning of the European Union:

The European Parliament and the Council, acting by means of regulations in accordance with the ordinary legislative procedure, shall establish these principles and set these conditions without prejudice to the competence of the Member States, in compliance with the Treaties, to provide, to commission and to fund such services.[3]

The choice of *regulations* is significant in that it makes it likely that the Member States' freedom to define services of general economic interest will be reduced.

In addition, the Lisbon Treaty also adds an interpretative protocol:

Article 1

The shared values of the Union in respect of services of general economic interest within the meaning of Article 14 of the Treaty on the Functioning of the European Union include in particular:

- the essential role and the wide discretion of national, regional, and local authorities in providing, commissioning and organising services of general economic interest as closely as possible to the needs of users;
- the diversity between various services of general economic interest and the differences in the needs and preferences of users that may result from different geographical, social or cultural situations;
- a high level of quality, safety and affordability, equal treatment and the promotion of universal access and of user rights.

Article 2

The provisions of the Treaties do not affect in any way the competence of Member States to provide, commission and organise non-economic services of general interest.

The protocol appears to add little of substance as regards services of general economic interest themselves, other than highlighting once again the topicality of this issue and the deep concerns held by Member States that something essential may slip from their control. The provision on 'non-economic services of general interest', absurd as it may be,[4] need not detain us here.

---

[3] *Mutatis mutandis*, the paragraph is identical to Article III-122, Treaty establishing a constitution for Europe, OJ 2004 C310.
[4] Is Article 141 EC no longer to apply to public librarians?

A less substantive additional tribute paid to the special role of services of general economic interest is found in Article 36 of the Charter on fundamental rights:

The Union recognises and respects access to services of general economic interest as provided for in national laws and practices, in accordance with the Treaty establishing the European Community, in order to promote the social and territorial cohesion of the Union.

Champions of the *service public* have won very little if anything at all by these changes and – given the proposed rule-making clause – may have lost ground. Meanwhile, the case law of the Court has progressed further to limit the scope for special and exclusive rights, as well as the exemption for services of general economic interest. Of particular practical importance have been the Court's recent judgments in the *Altmark Trans* and *Enirisorse* cases, which set out the conditions under which compensation for services of general economic interest does not constitute State aid.[5] These judgments were subsequently fleshed out by a Commission notice and decision based on Article 86(3) EC, which, given the emphasis on the Court's case law, will not be described in detail here.[6]

This chapter will deal successively with the following eight topics:

- the role and structure of Article 86(2) EC;
- Article 86(2) EC derogation and direct effect;
- the scope of the Article 86(2) EC derogation;
- the 'economic' nature of SGEI;
- proportionality and Article 86(2) EC;
- 'pre-emption' and Article 86(2) EC;
- private restraints on competition and Article 86(2) EC; and
- Article 86(2) EC and State aid.

Following a short summary of conclusions on these topics related to services of general economic interest, the last chapter of this book will deal with State aid.

---

[5] Case C-280/00 *Altmark Trans* [2003] ECR I-7747; Joined Cases C-34 to 38/01 *Enirisorse SnA v. Ministero delle Finanze (Enirisorse)* [2003] ECR I-14243.
[6] *Community framework for State aid in the form of public service compensation*, OJ 2005 C297/04; and *Commission Decision of 28 November 2005 on the application of Article 86(2) of the EC Treaty to State aid in the form of public service compensation granted to certain undertakings entrusted with the operation of services of general economic interest*, OJ 2005 C312/67.

7.2. The role and structure of Article 86(2) EC

Article 86(2) EC provides a limited exception to the Treaty rules for undertakings charged with services of general economic interest. As such, it forms an independent norm for such services.[7] Other exclusive and special rights must be tackled under Article 86(1) EC in combination with Article 82 EC or Articles 28 and/or 49 EC. Moreover, as a derogation from the rules of the Treaty, Article 86(2) EC must be interpreted restrictively.[8]

The essence of the wording and purpose of Article 86(2) EC can be found in the Court's ruling in *Terminal Directive*:

Article 86(2) provides that undertakings entrusted with the operation of services of general economic interest are to be subject . . . in particular to the rules on competition, in so far as the application of such rules does not obstruct the performance, in law or in fact, of the particular tasks assigned to them, on condition, however, that the development of trade is not affected to such an extent as would be contrary to the interests of the Community.

In allowing derogations to be made from the general rules of the Treaty on certain conditions, that provision seeks to reconcile the Member States' interest in using certain undertakings, in particular in the public sector, as an instrument of economic and fiscal policy with the Community's interest in ensuring compliance with the rules on competition and the preservation of the unity of the common market.[9]

---

[7] See generally e.g. Kovar, 'Droit Communautaire et Service Public: Esprit d'Orthodoxie ou Pensée Laïcisée', (1996) 32 RTDE 215, 493; Scott, 'Services of General Interest in EC Law: Matching Values to Regulatory Technique in the Public and Privatised Sectors,' (2000) 6 ELJ 310; Szyszczak, 'Public Services in Competitive Markets', (2001) 21 YEL 35; Napolitano, 'Towards a European Legal Order for Services of General Economic Interest', (2005) 11 EPL 565; T. Prosser, *The Limits of Competition Law – Markets and Public Services* (Oxford University Press, 2005); Prosser, 'Competition Law and Public Services. From Single Market to Citizenship Rights', (2005) 11 EPL 543; Moral Soriano, 'Public Services: The Role of the European Court of Justice in Correcting the Market' in D. Coen and A. Héritier (eds.), *Refining Regulatory Regimes: Utilities in Europe* (Cheltenham: Elgar, 2005), p. 183; J.-V. Louis and S. Rodrigues (eds.), *Les Services d'Intérêt Économique Général et l'Union Européenne* (Brussels: Bruylant, 2006); and E. Szyszczak, *The Regulation of the State in Competitive Markets in the EU* (Oxford: Hart, 2007), p. 211 et seq.

[8] Case 127/73 *BRT* v. *SABAM and NV Fonior* [1974] ECR 313, para. 19; and Case T-260/94, *Air Inter SA* v. *Commission* [1997] ECR II-997, para. 135. Note, however, AG Alber's reading of Article 16 EC and Article 36 of the Charter as underlining 'the importance of this exception as an expression of a fundamental value judgment of Community law'. Case C-340/99 *TNT Traco SpA* v. *Poste Italiane SpA et al.* [2001] ECR I-4109, para. 94 of the Opinion.

[9] This is the *obiter dictum* on Article 86(2) in Case C-202/88 *Terminal Directive* [1991] ECR I-1223, paras. 11–12. The submissions concentrated on Articles 86(1) and 86(3) EC. See section 7.9. below.

Hence, the objective of Article 86(2) EC is to balance the competition rules with the use of public undertakings and statutory monopolies for purposes of legitimate public policy. Specifically – and unlike the Article 86(1) EC defence available under the free movement rules – this concerns a public interest defence based on economic arguments against full competition.

In order to apply the Article 86(2) EC justification to an exclusive right, a court must determine the necessary scope of the exemption required to enable the undertaking or undertakings involved to meet the relevant public interest objectives. Since the 1993 *Corbeau* Case, this evaluation involves:

> – first, a justification of the restrictions on competition and free movement imposed, or of granting of the exclusive right concerned, based on legitimate public interest grounds, as concerning 'services of general economic interest'; and
> – second, a proportionality test.

In addition, it is necessary to determine that the obligation to provide services in the public interest is ultimately based on a public act, and also, to determine whether there is an effect on trade between the Member States.

Much as they appear to follow literally from the wording of Article 86 (2) EC, applying these tests is not straightforward.

(i) Definition: As regards the definition of a service of general economic interest: a fixed EU law definition does not exist, neither in the Treaty, nor in secondary legislation, nor in the case law. Nor, in spite of the publication of no fewer than five Commission Communications on the topic, has the Commission proposed a definition (arguably it has carefully avoided doing so instead).[10] At the present stage, this should therefore be a relatively straightforward test to see if the Member States have bothered to specify their public interest objectives and to impose the related tasks on a particular entity or group by means of a legal act.

(ii) Proportionality: As regards proportionality, things are considerably more complicated: EU law recognises two fundamentally different types of proportionality tests: namely, whether the 'least restrictive

---

[10] Cf. *Services of general interest in Europe*, OJ 2001 C17/4; *Report to the Laeken European Council – Services of general interest*, COM(2001) 598; *Green paper on services of general interest*, COM(2003) 270; *White paper on services of general interest*, COM(2004) 374 and COM(2004) 374 final; and *Implementing the Community Lisbon programme: social services of general interest in the European Union*, COM(2006) 177 final.

means' were used, or whether the means used were 'not manifestly disproportionate'. Clearly, the type of test applied will largely determine the scope that remains for national measures in practice.

(iii) Which forum: Also, the issue of which forum determines whether the Article 86(2) EC derogation applies is evidently of the greatest importance. If the Member States themselves could do so autonomously, Article 86(2) EC would in effect constitute a blank cheque for intervention by means of national statutory monopolies. If instead only the Community institutions were competent, this would allow for a restrictive view on the scope of the exemption, with significant potential deregulatory effects that might be difficult to defend politically.

In practice, a balancing mechanism has been established on all of these issues. We will examine how this balance is struck in relation to the issues of direct effect, the scope of the derogation and pre-emption. We start with the preliminaries: direct effect.

7.3. Article 86(2) EC derogation and direct effect

In at least some of its early case law, the Court rejected the direct effect of Article 86(2) EC, stating that the appraisal of this provision depended upon 'the objectives of general economic policy pursued by the States under supervision of the Commission' and that hence 'Article 90(2) [now Article 86(2)] cannot *at the present stage* create individual rights which the national Court must protect'.[11] Already in 1973, however, in *BRT* v. *SABAM*, it held, apparently in contradiction to this view, that:

It is . . . the duty of the national court to investigate whether an undertaking which invokes the provisions of Article 90(2) [now Article 86(2)] for the purposes of claiming a derogation from the rules of the Treaty has in fact been entrusted by a Member State with the operation of services of general economic interest.[12]

This might still be taken to refer only to a duty to verify that some general interest obligations had in fact been conferred as a matter of

---

[11] Case 10/71 *Ministère Public of Luxembourg* v. *Madeleine Hein* [1971] ECR 723, paras. 14–15. Cf. Case 172/82 *Fabricants Raffineurs d'Huile de Graissage* v. *Inter-Huiles* [1983] ECR 555, para. 15.
[12] Case 127/73 *BRT* v. *SABAM and NV Fonior* [1974] ECR 313, para. 22.

applicable national law. However, in its ruling on *Sacchi* of the same year, the Court stated that:

[E]ven within the framework of Article 86 . . . the prohibitions of Article 82 have a direct effect and confer on the interested parties rights which the national courts must safeguard.[13]

There can thus be no doubt that Article 86(2) EC has direct effect.

(i) After some further twists and turns of the case law, at least since the early 1990s there can no longer be any doubt that national courts are instrumental in determining, directly, the scope of the Article 86(2) EC derogation. In *British Telecom*, the Court observed that the application of Article 86(2) EC was not left to the discretion of the Member State which had charged the undertaking involved with a task of general economic interest, but was subject to monitoring by the Commission.[14] In a number of subsequent cases such as *ERT* and *Corbeau*, the Court held that national courts should determine whether in specific cases the Article 86(2) EC exemption could be successfully invoked.[15] The direct effect issue was definitively resolved in a series of preliminary rulings concerning the directly effective provisions of (the Article 86(3) EC-based) Terminal Directive 301/88 before national courts: i.e. *Lagauche, Decoster and Taillandier.*[16]

Because Article 86(2) EC is directly effective, it may be invoked – and its scope determined – in national courts. In order to apply the Article 86(2) EC justification to an exclusive right, a court must determine the necessary scope of the exemption required to enable the undertaking or undertakings involved to meet the relevant public interest objectives.

(ii) The evaluation of the necessary scope of the Article 86(2) exemption involves both a justification of the exclusive right as requisite for the performance of a service of general economic interest and a proportionality test.[17] The obligation to perform services in the public interest must be based on a public act.[18] Finally, the effect on trade between the Member States may not

---

[13] Case 155/73 *Sacchi* [1974] ECR 409, para. 18.

[14] Case C-41/83 *British Telecom* [1985] ECR 873, para. 30.

[15] Case C-260/89 *ERT* [1991] ECR I-2925, para. 34; Case C-320/91 *Corbeau* [1993] ECR I-2533, para. 20; and Case C-393/92 *Almelo* [1994] ECR I-1477, para. 43.

[16] Joined Cases C-46/90 and 93/91 *Lagauche* [1993] ECR I-5267; Case C-69/91 *Decoster* [1993] ECR I-5335; and Case C-92/91 *Taillandier* [1993] ECR I-5383, noted by Hancher (1994) 31 CMLR 857.

[17] Case C-320/91 *Procureur du Roi* v. *Paul Corbeau* [1993] ECR I-2533, para. 14.

[18] Case 127/73 *BRT* v. *SABAM and NV Fonior* [1974] ECR 313, para. 20.

harm the Community interest. It is very important to note, therefore, that the restrictions concerned must be proportional both in relation to the general economic interest at national level and to the Community interest concerned.

Finally, the Court of Justice has developed a restrained approach to Article 86(2) EC on grounds that strongly resemble the pre-emption doctrine.[19] It tends to respect the jurisdiction of the national courts and the wisdom of national governments, unless very clear-cut cases of infringement are involved, or a sufficient degree of harmonisation of the relevant general economic interest standards has occurred for the Community to have occupied the field.

7.4. The scope of the Article 86(2) EC derogation

In most early Article 86 EC cases, there was no substantive discussion on the scope of Article 86(2) EC. This changed with the 1993 Belgian postal monopoly case *Corbeau* and *Almelo*, decided in 1994, concerning the Dutch electricity market. In both cases, the Court suggested that, where legitimate services of general economic interest are involved, not merely some restrictions of competition may be allowed, but even elimination of all competition in the market concerned can be justified.

Specifically, the Court stated in *Corbeau* concerning Article 86(2):

That latter provision . . . permits the Member States to confer on undertakings to which they entrust the operation of services in the general economic interest, exclusive rights which may hinder the application of the rules of the Treaty on competition in so far as restrictions on competition, or even the exclusion of all competition, by other economic operators are necessary to ensure the performance of the particular tasks assigned to the undertakings possessed of the exclusive rights.[20]

In *Almelo*, the Court repeated that:

Article 90(2) [now 86(2)] of the Treaty provides that undertakings entrusted with the operation of services of general economic interest may be exempted from the application of the competition rules of the Treaty in so far as it is

---

[19] Cf., generally, Cross, 'Pre-emption of Member State Law in the European Economic Community: A Framework for Analysis', (1992) 29 CMLR 447; and Weatherill, 'Preemption, Harmonisation and the Distribution of Competence to Regulate the Internal Market' in C. Barnard and J. Scott (eds.), *The Law of the Single Market – Unpacking the Premises* (Oxford: Hart, 2002), p. 41.

[20] Case C-320/91 *Corbeau* [1993] ECR I-2533.

necessary to impose restrictions on competition, or even to exclude all competition, from other operators in order to ensure the performance of the particular tasks assigned to them.[21]

These positions are relatively clear. Jointly, they settle the per se legality/illegality debate: even special and exclusive rights can be compatible with the Treaty – and can continue to be created – (as by extending this logic, so can lesser restrictions) in so far as this is necessary to deliver services of general economic interest.[22] The following remain to be determined:

> – the way in which the existence of a service of general economic interest may be determined; and
> – what the legitimate scope of the related restrictions on competition actually is.

Equally important is that *Almelo* and *Corbeau* also indicated that the legitimate scope of the restrictions involved is established by reference to a proportionality test ('restrictions ... *necessary* to ensure performance'), applied in relation to the relevant public interest objective. Yet this still leaves a significant margin of appreciation. Moreover, what constitutes a service of general economic interest in the first place is even less self-evident and will therefore be discussed first.

7.5. Services of general 'economic' interest

A logical prerequisite to establishing whether or not services are of general economic interest would seem to be the ability to draw a distinction between 'economic' and 'non-economic' services. Unlike services of a non-economic nature, services of an economic nature are subject to the freedom to provide services, the freedom of establishment, the competition and State aid rules. Services of economic nature are subject to both non-economic and economic (Article 86(2) EC) public interest derogations. As discussed earlier, the starting point here is that 'any activity consisting in offering goods and services on a given market is an economic activity'.[23]

---

[21] Case C-393/92 *Almelo* [1994] ECR I-1477, para. 46.

[22] Consequently, these cases were initially celebrated as a starting point for a Community concept of 'service public'. Cf. Belloubet-Frier, 'Service Public et Droit Communautaure', (1994) 20 *Actualité Juridique- Édition Droit Administratif* 270, p. 283 ff.

[23] Case C-35/96 *Italian Customs Agents* [1998] ECR I-3851, para. 36, paraphrasing Case 118/85 *Transparency Directive* [1987] ECR 2599, para. 7. Cf. Joined Cases C-180 to 184/98

However, it is evident that opinions on whether particular activities can and should be provided based on market principles can vary considerably across time and space. As the Commission warned the Laeken Council in 2001, incorporating a fixed classification of services as economic or non-economic in any kind of official text could artificially arrest and perpetuate an existing situation that was in fact an amalgam of different factual settings in various stages of development to the detriment of future social and economic progress.[24] Hence there is no definition or even a standard list of services of general economic interest in Community law. Nor can there be a definitive list. If a list were to exist it would have to be open-ended and subject to regular updates.

In its first Communication on the subject in 1996, which attempts to systemise the Community approach to services of general interest, of general economic interest, public service and universal service, the Commission offers only the following descriptive and non-exhaustive clarification:

This is the term used in Article 90 [now Article 86] of the Treaty and refers to market services which the Member States subject to specific public service obligations by virtue of a general interest criterion. This would tend to cover such things as transport networks, energy and communications.[25]

After seven years of consultation and discussion, in its Green Paper of 2003, the Commission deals with the matter as follows:

The term 'services of general economic interest' is used in Articles 16 and 86(2) of the Treaty. It is not defined in the Treaty or in secondary legislation. However in Community practice there is broad agreement that the term refers to services of a economic nature which the Member states or the Community subject to specific public services obligations by virtue of a general interest criterion. The concept of services of general economic interest thus covers in particular certain services provided by the big network industries such as transport, postal services, energy and communications. However, the term also extends to any other economic activity subject to public service obligations.[26]

Pavlov [2000] ECR I-6451, para. 75; Case C-475/99 *Glöckner* [2001] ECR I-8089, para. 19; Case 218/00 *Cisal* [2002] ECR I-691, para. 23; and Case C-82/01 P *Aéroports de Paris* v. *Commission* (*Aéroports de Paris*) [2002] ECR I-9297, para. 75.

[24] COM(2001) 598, *Report to the Laeken European Council – Services of general interest*, para. 30.

[25] COM(96) 443, *Services of General Interest in Europe*, p. 2.

[26] COM(2003) 270, *Green Paper on Services of General Interest*, p. 7.

Since then, the social service of general interest has been identified as a subset, although 'under Community law, social services do not constitute a legally distinct category of service within services of general interest'.[27] The specific characteristics of such social services of general economic interest are listed as including one or more of the following:

- they operate on the basis of solidarity, in particular by the non-selection of risks or the absence, of equivalence between individual contributions and benefits;
- they are comprehensive and integrate the response to differing needs;
- they are not for profit;
- they include the participation of voluntary workers;
- they are strongly rooted in (local) cultural traditions; and
- an asymmetric relationship between providers and beneficiaries that requires third-party financing.[28]

Clearly, there is a large number of services that might qualify based on meeting at least one of these criteria (albeit qualify for what? – a question wisely left open).

The same reasons – any fixed definition would not only be highly contentious, but might foreclose desirable future developments – presumably explain why the Court itself has not established a definition of services of general economic interest. Instead, in each relevant case before it, the Court decides on the merits of the case at hand – and only if Article 86(2) EC is invoked by the parties involved – whether it appears that a particular service could be regarded as being one that is of general economic interest. At present, therefore, services of general economic interest very much remain a 'public interest defence'.[29]

In *Almelo*, for example, the Court pointed to the objective of ensuring the supply of energy in part of the Netherlands' territory. The undertaking concerned was obligated to provide all consumers 'uninterrupted supplies of electricity in sufficient quantities to meet demand at

---

[27] COM(2006) 177, *Implementing the Community Lisbon programme: social services of general interest in the European Union*, p. 4.
[28] *Ibid.*, pp. 4–5. It should be noted that health services are not covered by this communication, given that they are subject to a separate communication the Commission is presently preparing.
[29] It goes beyond the remit of this book to examine whether (and/or under which circumstances) it could make sense to use the legal category of services of general economic interest pro-actively, as a safe haven e.g. for those hospital services or pension rights that do not lend themselves to market-based provision.

any given time, at uniform rates, and on terms which may not vary save in accordance with objective criteria applicable to all customers'.[30] These criteria were found in the applicable national law. The approach in *Corbeau* was not only similarly descriptive, but also highlighted similar elements of universality, uniformity, continuity, and tariff control:

> it cannot be disputed that the Régie des Postes is entrusted with a service of general economic interest consisting in the obligation to collect, carry and distribute mail on behalf of all users throughout the territory of the Member States concerned, at uniform tariffs and on similar quality conditions, irrespective of the specific situations or the degree of economic profitability of each individual operation.[31]

These rulings appear to locate the competence to designate services as being of general economic interest at Member State level. This approach is consistent with that which the Commission subsequently set out in its 1996 Communication. The Commission stated that the Community approach to the broader category of general interest services rests on two pillars:

> *Neutrality* as regards the public or private status of companies and their employees, as guaranteed by Article 295 of the Treaty. The Community has nothing to say on whether companies responsible for providing general interest services should be public or private and is not, therefore, requiring privatisation. Moreover, the Community will continue to clamp down on unfair practices, regardless of whether the operators concerned are private or public.
>
> The Member States' *freedom* to determine what are general interest services, to grant the special or exclusive rights that are necessary to the companies responsible for providing them, regulate their management and, where appropriate, fund them, in conformity with Article 86 of the Treaty.[32]

---

[30] Case C-393/92 *Almelo* [1994] ECR I-1477, para. 48.

[31] Case C-320/91 *Procureur du Roi* v. *Paul Corbeau* [1993] ECR I-2533, para. 15.

[32] Cf. COM(96) 443, *Services of General Interest in Europe*, at p. 5 (emphasis in the original). At the time it issued this communication, the Commission was labouring to fend off an attack on its Article 86 EC powers. In the run-up to the 1996/1997 Intergovernmental Conference that led to the Amsterdam Treaty, proposals to curtail Article 86, and/or add an Article 86a EC for services of general economic interest abounded. Cf. L. Grand, J. Vandamme and F. Van der Mensbrugghe (eds.), *Vers un Service Public Européen* (Paris: ASP Europe, 1996). The Commission tried to anticipate this by proposing a relatively harmless statement as Article 3(u) EC instead. The outcomes were Article 16 and the Protocol on Public Broadcasting. Given this context, these documents represent efforts at political damage control rather than a conclusive

The Court of First Instance has brought the point home forcefully. In *Olsen*, it made clear that Member States have a wide discretion to define what they regard as services of general economic interest, subject to review by the Commission only to a standard of 'manifest error'.[33] In *BUPA*, it responded to allegations that the Commission had 'delegated' the definition of an SGEI to Ireland and elaborated as follows:

> The prerogative of the Member State concerning the definition of SGEIs is confirmed by the absence of any competence specially attributed to the Commission and by the absence of a precise and complete definition of the concept of SGEI in Community law. The determination of the nature and scope of an SGEI mission in specific spheres of action which either do not fall within the powers of the Community, within the meaning of the first paragraph of Article 5 EC, or are based on only limited or shared Community competence, within the meaning of the second paragraph of that Article, remains, in principle, within the competence of the Member States. . . . That division of powers is also reflected, generally, in Article 16 EC.[34]

Member States are, however, required to ensure that 'certain minimum criteria common to every SGEI mission within the meaning of the EC Treaty' are satisfied, notably, the presence of an act of the public authority and 'the universal and compulsory nature of that mission'.[35]

  (i) Services of general economic interest are defined in line with subsidiarity and pre-emption: The approach to services of general economic interest in the course of several revisions of the Treaty is intended to be in line with subsidiarity. On the one hand, it leaves the Member States complete liberty to identify services of general interest, subject to the free movement rules and the Treaty's non-economic public interest exceptions. On the other hand, the Community itself claims at least a

---

Commission legal position. Competition DG Commissioner Van Miert has clearly indicated its political nature, as opposed to the more subtle view as expressed in the Court's Article 86(2) EC case law. Cf. Van Miert, 'Les Missions d'Intérêt Général et l'Article 90§2 du Traité CE dans la Politique de la Commission', (1997) 2 *Il diritto dell'economia* 277, at p. 278.

[33] Case T-17/02 *Fred Olsen* v. *Commission* [2005] ECR II-2031, para. 216, with a rather misleading reference to Case T-106/95 *FFSA and Others* v. *Commission* [1997] ECR II-229, para. 99. There, the Court merely noted that Article 86(2) EC required 'the Commission to take account, in exercising that discretion, of the demands inherent in the particular tasks of the undertakings concerned', and noted that Member States 'may in some instances have a sufficient degree of latitude in regulating certain matters, such as, in the present case, the organisation of public services in the postal sector'.

[34] Case T-289/03 *BUPA* v. *Commission*, judgment of 12 February 2008, nyr, para. 167.

[35] Case T-289/03 *BUPA* v. *Commission*, judgment of 12 February 2008, nyr, para. 172.

concurrent competence for services of general *economic* interest – which, under the Treaty, it lacks for services concerning non-economic activities such as education and social security, and matters of vital national interest (for example, security and justice). This explains why, under current Treaty rules, services of general economic interest can – by means of pre-emption – in principle be brought under a general Community regime, whereas other general public services cannot. In the Commission's view, services of general economic interest (whether defined or not) are an EU law category.[36]

(ii) Liberalisation creates the need for defining services of general economic interest: Services of general *economic* interest are in principle subject to the single market rules. As individual sectors are more or less gradually exposed to market forces, this can lead to the need for developing a general economic interest criterion at EU level, as was the case for universal services in the telecommunications sector.[37] There, vaguely defined public service obligations appeared doomed to condone 'natural monopoly' for perpetuity. Thus, concerning the monopoly for the establishment and operation of the public telecommunications network, the Court could still hold in the 1991 *RTT* Case that:

> At the present stage of development of the Community, that monopoly, which is intended to make a public telephone network available to users, constitutes a service of general economic interest within the meaning of Article 90(2) [now Article 86(2)] of the Treaty.[38]

Prospective market entrants looked forward to a time when the conditions under which the services of general economic interest would be provided would have been redefined in competitive terms – as they were eventually when the relevant general economic interest standard for universal service (concerning access to telecommunications services

---

[36] Van Miert, 'Les Missions d'Intérêt Général et l'Article 89§2 du Traité CE dans la Politique de la Commission', (1997) 2 *Il diritto dell'economia* 277, at pp. 279–80.

[37] Not suprisingly, this is also the example elaborated by Van Miert, *ibid*. Note that the universal service criterion is not only evolutionary (it may expand in scope over time), but also leaves room for additional obligations to be defined at national level, provided these are consistent with EU law. It should also be noted that the initial abolition of exclusive rights on importation and the marketing of terminal equipment was based on the respect of 'essential requirements' that had been defined in Council Directive 86/361/EEC of 24 July 1986 on the initial stage of the mutual recognition of type approval for telecommunications terminal equipment (Type Approval Directive) OJ 1986 L217/21. Cf. Case C-202/88 *Terminal Directive* [1991] ECR I-1223, paras. 37 ff.

[38] Case C-18/88 *RTT* [1991] ECR I-5941, para. 16 (emphasis added).

and facilities) was established at EU level.[39] This enabled competitive provision of this particular public good to be guaranteed, i.e. in a form no longer requiring reliance on monopoly rights, which in turn allowed full liberalisation to proceed.

Generally, the Commission communications on general interest services have advocated a sector-specific approach based on consensus- (or at least coalition-) building by means of consultation.[40] It is worth underlining that, as the examples of telecommunications and energy show, consultation aimed at defining the objectives of general economic interest can enable the Community to tackle the liberalisation of hitherto intractable services. In order to launch sectoral liberalisation successfully, it appears plausible that initially amorphous public interest issues must first be identified, agreed, defined and, thus circumscribed, ring-fenced as narrowly as possible to create maximum scope for the market process.[41] The service of general economic interest is thus reduced to a 'hard core' (or *noyau dur*) with as little disturbing effect on the competitive provision of the services concerned – based on the criterion of 'necessity'.

The distinction between services of general interest and services of general economic interest reflects the general understanding of subsidiarity as restricted to areas of concurrent competence. In practice, both strands converge progressively, primarily by means of harmonisation. This is further promoted by the amendment of the provisions of the current Article 16 EC Treaty in the Lisbon Treaty. It adds to a text that is essentially identical to Article 16 EC a mandate to Parliament and Council to define these principles and conditions by

---

[39] Directive 98/10/EC of the European Parliament and of the Council of 26 February 1998 on the application of open network provision (ONP) to voice telephony and on universal service for telecommunications in a competitive environment, OJ 1998 L101/24; Directive 2002/22/EC of the European Parliament and of the Parliament of 7 March 2002 on universal service and users' rights relating to electronic communications networks and services, OJ 2002 L108/51.

[40] The subsequent discussion is reflected in the Commission's *Services of general interest in Europe*, OJ 2001 C17/4; *Report to the Laeken European Council – Services of general interest*, COM(2001) 598; *Green paper on services of general interest*, COM(2003) 270; *White paper on services of general interest*, COM(2004) 374 and COM(2004) 374 final; and *Implementing the Community Lisbon programme: social services of general interest in the European Union*, COM (2006) 177 final.

[41] It may then turn out that competitive market outcomes eliminate the scarcity of certain services that originally held back liberalisation. Who today still looses much sleep over universal service provision in telecommunications? Yet ten years ago political feelings ran strong on this issue.

legislative means. This is in line with the Commission's view of services of general economic interest as a category of EU law and may well provide additional scope for it to elaborate its 86(3) EU practice.

Beyond defining public service missions in the context of harmonisation, this means clarifying and simplifying the legal framework for the compensation of public service obligations and providing a clear and transparent framework for the selection of undertakings entrusted with a service of general interest.[42] An important example of what this might mean is provided by the framework for State aid in relation to services of general economic interest set out by the Court, which will be discussed in the final section of this chapter.

7.6. Proportionality and Article 86(2) EC

As was discussed above, services of general economic interest are defined nationally, at least initially, within the general framework of the internal market obligations of the Member States. The main legal criteria that are then applied to determine the scope of the restrictions on competition mandated by the provision of service of general economic interest are the principles of proportionality and necessity. In *Almelo*, the Court stated that this means that '[r]estrictions on competition from other economic operators must be allowed in so far as they are *necessary* in order to enable the undertaking entrusted with such task of general interest to perform it'.[43] In *Corbeau*, the Court stated that Article 86(2):

permits the Member States to confer on undertakings to which they entrust the operation of services of general economic interest, exclusive rights which may hinder the application of the rules of the Treaty on competition in so far as restrictions on competition, or even the exclusion of all competition, by other economic operators are necessary to ensure the performance of the particular tasks assigned to the undertakings possessed of the exclusive rights.

Likewise in *Corbeau*, inversely, it also elaborated the limits on these restrictions, i.e. they may not go beyond what is necessary and

---

[42] *White paper on services of general interest*, COM(2004) 374.
[43] Case C-393/92 *Almelo* [1994] ECR I-1477, para. 46.

specifically may not cover markets that can be dissociated from the service of general economic interest at hand:

the exclusion of competition is not justified as regards specific services dissociable from the service of general interest . . . in so far as such specific services, by their nature and the conditions in which they are offered, such as the geographical area in which they are provided, do not compromise the economic equilibrium of the service of general economic interest performed by the holder of the exclusive right.[44]

However, the restrictions at hand may cover related markets that may be necessary to cross-subsidise general economic interest activities, as in the case of universal service.[45] Hence, in particular in *Corbeau* and in *Almelo*, it had appeared that the acceptable restrictions were closely related to the economic equilibrium of the statutory monopoly, in so far as this equilibrium might be jeopardised by the obligation to provide services of general economic interest of a universal service nature.[46] However, in the *Electricity* cases, the Court refused to endorse the view that the financial equilibrium of the undertaking involved itself need be at stake in order to make a successful appeal to protection under Article 86(2) EC:

it is not necessary, in order for the conditions for the application of Article 86(2) of the Treaty to be fulfilled, that the financial balance or economic viability of the undertaking entrusted with the operation of a service of general economic interest be threatened. It is sufficient that, in the absence of the rights at issue, it would not be possible for the undertaking to perform the particular tasks entrusted to it, defined by the obligations and constraints to which it is subject.

Moreover, it follows from the Corbeau judgment . . . that the conditions for the application of Article 90(2) [now Article 86(2)] are fulfilled in particular if maintenance of those rights is necessary to enable the holder of them to perform the tasks of general economic interest assigned to it under economically acceptable conditions.[47]

---

[44] Case C-320/91 *Corbeau* [1993] ECR I-2533, para. 19.

[45] Cf. Hancher and Buendia Sierra, 'Cross-subsidisation and EC Law' (1998) 35 CMLR 901.

[46] Cf. Case C-320/91 *Corbeau* [1993] ECR I-2533, para. 19; and Case C-393/92 *Almelo* [1994] ECR I-1477, para. 49. An example where the Court found a need for such cross-subsidisation to exist (between emergency and non-emergency medical transport services) is Case C-475/99 *Glöckner* [2001] ECR I-8089.

[47] Case C-157/94 *Dutch Electricity Monopoly* [1997] ECR I-5699, paras. 52–3; Case C-159/94 *French Electricity and Gas Monopoly* [1997] ECR I-5815, paras. 95–6, with reference to Case C-320/91 *Corbeau* [1993] ECR I-2533, paras. 14–16. Noted by Slot, (1998) 35 CMLR 1183.

Hence, the survival of the undertaking enjoying a statutory monopoly need not hang in the balance: at issue is merely its ability to perform the general economic interest services under economically acceptable conditions (i.e. based on costs, plus a reasonable rate of return).[48] Moreover, as will be seen below, Article 86(2) EC applies to a statutory monopoly's prerogative of performing general economic interest services single-handedly, if the Member State so chooses. This is the case even where competitive provision might in theory be possible, until Community pre-emption has occurred. Until such time, the conditions under which general economic interest services are provided is a matter of national law. When balancing the general economic interest against the Community interest, the Court does not require the Member State to depart radically from established national policy objectives:

Article 86(2) seeks to reconcile the Member States' interest in using certain undertakings, in particular in the public sector, as an instrument of fiscal policy, with the Community's interest in ensuring compliance with the rules on competition and the preservation of the unity of the common market.

The Member States' interest being so defined, they cannot be precluded, when defining the services of general economic interest which they entrust to certain undertakings, from taking account of objectives pertaining to their national policy or from endeavouring to attain them by means of obligations and constraints which they impose on such undertakings.[49]

The Commission has always maintained that, as an exception to the Treaty rules, the Article 86(2) EC exemption should be interpreted strictly. That is, any Member State wishing to benefit from this derogation is shouldered with the burden of proof, in particular under

---

[48] Case C-280/00 *Altmark Trans* [2003] ECR I-7747, paras. 89–93. Cf. Joined Cases C-34 to 38/01 *Enirisorse SnA* v. *Ministero delle Finanze (Enirisorse)* [2003] ECR I-14243, paras. 31 ff. Elaborated in *Community framework for State aid in the form of public service compensation*, OJ 2005 C297/04; and *Commission Decision of 28 November 2005 on the application of Article 86(2) of the EC Treaty to State aid in the form of public service compensation granted to certain undertakings entrusted with the operation of services of general economic interest*, OJ 2005 C312/67.

[49] Case C-157/94 *Dutch Electricity Monopoly* [1997] ECR I-5699, paras. 39–40; Case C-159/94 *French Electricity and Gas Monopoly* [1997] ECR I-5815, paras. 55–6. The same formula is used in Case C-67/96 *Albany* [1999] ECR I-5751, paras. 103–4; Joined Cases C-115, 116, 117 and 119/97 *Brentjens* [1999] ECR I-6025, paras. 103–4; and Case C-219/97 *Drijvende Bokken* [1999] ECR I-6121, paras. 93–4. Cf. Case C-393/92 *Almelo* [1994] ECR I-1477, para. 46: 'In that regard, it is necessary to take into consideration the economic conditions in which the undertaking operates, in particular the costs which it has to bear and the legislation . . . to which it is subject'.

a strict proportionality test.[50] This would require the Member State concerned to demonstrate that it has used the least restrictive means to achieve a service of general economic interest, where possible by reference to a Community standard. However, it is clear from the case law already cited that, in practice, the Court does not impose the full burden of proof on the Member States and is prepared to give precedence to national measures. Pre-emption and the burden of proof regarding proportionality are therefore closely linked. As will be seen, this can be understood on the basis of the pre-emption type approach that it developed most extensively in the 1997 *Electricity Cases*.

7.7. 'Pre-emption' and Article 86(2) EC

Leaving aside the issue of developing a Community standard for particular general interest services, as well as the political difficulties involved in deciding the core values concerned, defining the general public interest under Article 86(2) EC is at least in theory relatively unproblematic because it is in the first instance left to the Member States to do so. As former competition Commissioner Van Miert confirms, it is the Article 86(2) EC proportionality test that appears the most daunting because this is the part that the European institutions – the Court and the Commission – will scrutinise:

Le problème de l'article 90(2) [now Article 86(2)] du traité, s'il existe, est celui du *contrôle de la proportionalité des moyens* utilisés par les États membres ou par les entreprises pour assurer leur missions du intérêt général. La définition de ces missions n'a presque jamais fait l'objet de controverses.[51]

The proportionality test poses national courts the unenviable task of balancing national public interests against the Community interest. Evidently, in most cases alternative means of providing services of general economic interest would be imaginable that are at least in

---

[50] Case C-331/88 *Queen* v. *Minister of Agriculture, Fisheries and Food and Secretary of State for Health, ex parte: Fedesa et al. (Fedesa)* [1990] ECR I-4023, paras. 13 and 14.

[51] 'If there is a problem with Article 90(2) [now 86(2)], it is that of verifying the proportionality of the means used by the Member States or of the undertakings concerned to achieve their public interest objectives. The definition of the latter has hardly ever given rise to controversy.' Van Miert, 'Les Missions d'Intérêt Général et l'Article 90§2 du Traité CE dans la Politique de la Commission', (1997) 2 *Il diritto dell'economia* 277, at pp. 280–1 (emphasis in the original).

theory less onerous than statutory monopoly and more readily compatible with the internal market.[52] Yet, however attractive such alternatives may be in theory, unless they are firmly embedded in the political and economic systems of the Member States, simply imposing them by judicial means is clearly another matter. Furthermore, national courts are not obligated to hazard this slippery slope. Sectors where there are Community rules governing the matter excepted, Member States have a wide margin of discretion in the definition of services that could be classified as being services of general economic interest.[53] In the absence of harmonisation – or pre-emption – national courts can avoid getting caught up in comparative regulatory politics by the simple device of merely controlling for 'manifest errors'.[54] Key to this issue is the 1990 agriculture case *Fedesa*. Here, the Court distinguished between the 'manifestly disproportionate' and 'least restrictive means' regimes as follows in a case regarding the legality of a number of Council Directives in the agricultural field:

The Court has consistently held that the principle of proportionality is one of the general principles of Community law. By virtue of that principle, the lawfulness of the prohibition of an economic activity is subject to the condition that the prohibitory measures are appropriate and necessary in order to achieve the objectives legitimately pursued by the legislation in question; when there is a choice between several appropriate measures recourse must be had to the least onerous, and the disadvantages caused must not be disproportionate to the aims pursued.

However, with regard to judicial review of compliance with those conditions it must be stated that in matters concerning the common agricultural policy the Community legislature has a discretionary power which corresponds to the political responsibilities given to it by Articles 40 and 43 of the Treaty. Consequently, the legality of a measure adopted in that sphere can be affected only

---

[52] In Case C-202/88 *Terminal Directive* [1991] ECR I-1223, para. 41, the Court famously clarified the internal market concept as follows: '. . . Articles 2 and 3 of the Treaty set out to establish a market characterised by the free movement of goods where the terms of competition are not distorted' (with reference to Case 229/83 *Leclerc* v. *Au Blé Vert* [1985] ECR 1, para. 9).

[53] Cf. Commission Decision on the application of Article 86(2) of the EC Treaty to State aid in the form of public service compensation granted to certain undertakings entrusted with the operation of services of general economic interest, OJ 2005 C312/67 preamble, consideration 7; and para. 9 of the Communication of the Community framework for State aid in the form of public service compensation, OJ 2005 C297/4.

[54] This is the solution proposed by then Justice Edwards and his law clerk Hoskins, 'Article 90: Deregulation and EC Law: Reflections Arising from the XVI FIDE Conference' (1995) 32 CMLR 157.

if the measure is manifestly inappropriate having regard to the objective which the competent institution is seeking to pursue.[55]

It is submitted here that regarding the Member States the same logic applies, but with a reverse outcome: where there is no Community norm that has occupied the field (pre-emption), the lighter 'manifestly disproportionate' administrative law test prevails; where pre-emption has occurred, Member States may only intervene based on 'the least restrictive means'.

This takes the sting out of the Article 86(2) EC proportionality test in those cases where the Community interest has not yet been defined by means of pre-emption: any reasonably effective system designed to provide a service of general economic interest will then be acceptable as a matter of EU law.

In its preliminary rulings under Article 234 EC the Court has left the national courts free to take this view. It might still have been thought that, given the opportunity to adopt a strict interpretation of the scope of Article 86(2) EC itself, the Court of Justice would have acted accordingly – even if only to safeguard the unity of Community law. However, when faced with the Article 226 EC Treaty infringement cases concerning national electricity monopolies in the Netherlands, France and Italy, the Court has clearly opted for judicial restraint:

Whilst it is true that it is incumbent upon a Member State which invokes Article 86(2) to demonstrate that the conditions laid down by that provision are met, that *burden of proof cannot be so extensive as to require the Member States*, when setting out in detail the reasons for which, in the event of elimination of the contested measures, the performance, under economically acceptable conditions, of the tasks of general economic interest which it has entrusted to an undertaking would, in its view, be jeopardised, *to go even further and prove, positively, that no other conceivable measure, which by definition would be hypothetical, could enable those tasks to be performed* under the same conditions.[56]

Concerning the proportionality issue, the Court further pointed out that the Commission had restricted itself to making legal arguments and had not demonstrated that alternative means of achieving the general economic interest at hand were a tenable proposition. Hence, it

---

[55] Case C-331/88 *Fedesa* [1990] ECR I-4023, paras. 13–14, with reference to Case 265/87 *Schraeder* [1989] ECR 2237, paras. 21–2.

[56] Case C-157/94 *Dutch Electricity Monopoly* [1997] ECR I-5699, para. 58; Case C-159/94 *French Electricity and Gas Monopoly* [1997] ECR I-5815, para. 101; and Case C-158/94 *Italian Electricity Monopoly* [1997] ECR I-5789, para. 54 (emphasis added).

held that it could not, 'undertake an assessment, necessarily extending to economic, financial and social matters, of the means which a Member State might adopt' to assure this general economic interest.[57] This could still be read to mean that the least restrictive means test must be done in its actual setting, not that a least restrictive means test was rejected in favour of the 'manifestly disporportionate' standard.

However, the Court went on to show that the Commission had neglected to elaborate on the nature of the Community interest involved – even in terms of the effect on Community trade.[58] It clearly held that the Commission should have acted under Article 86(3) EC to back up its allegations:

it was incumbent on the Commission, in order to prove the alleged failure to fulfil obligations, to define, subject to review by the Court, the Community interest in relation to which the development of trade must be assessed. In that regard, it must be borne in mind that Article 86(3) of the Treaty expressly requires the Commission to ensure the application of that article and, where necessary, to address appropriate Directives or Decisions to Member States.[59]

Specifically, the Court held that the Commission should have demonstrated how '*in the absence of a common policy* in the area concerned, development of direct trade between producers and consumers, in parallel with the development of trade between major networks, would have been possible'.[60] Likewise, therefore, the Court dismissed the Commission's argument on this count.[61]

---

[57] Case C-157/94 *Dutch Electricity Monopoly* [1997] ECR I-5699, para. 63; and Case C-159/94 *French Electricity and Gas Monopoly* [1997] ECR I-5815, para. 106.

[58] Case C-157/94 *Dutch Electricty Monopoly* [1997] ECR I-5699, paras. 66–73; and Case C-159/94 *French Electricity and Gas Monopoly* [1997] ECR I-5815, paras. 109–16. The French Government had even gone to the length of making arguments on the development of Community trade in electricity that the Commission had neglected.

[59] Case C-157/94 *Dutch Electricity Monopoly* [1997] ECR I-5699, para. 69; and Case C-159/94 *French Electricity and Gas Monopoly* [1997] ECR I-5815, para. 113.

[60] Case C-157/94 *Dutch Electricity Monopoly* [1997] ECR I-5699, para. 58; and Case C-159/94 *French Electricity and Gas Monopoly* [1997] ECR I-5815, para. 71 (emphasis added). Cf. Joined Cases C-147 and 148/97 *Deutsche Post* [2000] ECR I-3061. Here, in the absence of agreements on terminal dues between postal operators that would allow Deutsche Post to execute its public service task in a financially balanced manner, legislation allowing Deutsche Post to charge international mail at (higher) national rates did not cause it to infringe Article 86 EC.

[61] The Commission cannot be forced to act under Article 86(3) EC. Case T-32/93 *Ladbroke Racing* [1994] ECR II-1015; and Case T-84/95 *Bundesverband der Bilanzbuchhalter* [1995] ECR II-103.

Hence, in the absence of solid Commission evidence, the Court will not consider itself bound to judge on the feasibility of alternative regulatory solutions, even if these may theoretically be more consistent with EU law. This means that it will in such cases not apply the 'least restrictive means' test, but the 'manifestly inappropriate' test. In *Albany*, *Brentjens* and *Drijvende Bokken*, the Court repeated this point forcefully in relation to social security schemes:

it must be emphasised that, in view of the social function of supplementary pension schemes and the margin of appreciation enjoyed, according to settled case law, by the Member States in organising their social security systems, it is incumbent on each Member State to consider whether, in view of the particular features of its national pension system, laying down minimum requirements would still enable it to ensure the level of pension which it seeks to guarantee in a sector by compulsory affiliation to a pension fund.[62]

The Court's stance on this issue makes it likely that national courts will be even more reticent to substitute their own judgment of the appropriate means to reach generally accepted public interest objectives for that of their national administrations. The result is that a least restrictive means test applies only where Community standards for services of general economic interest have been set (examples could be found, for example, in the telecommunications, postal, energy and transport sectors[63]). Where they have not, the burden of proof is reversed and placed on the Commission if the Member State concerned is capable of mounting a prima facie case that it has developed a reasonable approach to address what is apparently a service of general economic interest, a service defined at national level.

---

[62] Case C-67/96 *Albany* [1999] ECR I-5751, para. 122; Joined Cases C-115, 116, 117 and 119/97 *Brentjens* [1999] ECR I-6021, para. 122; and Case C-219/97 *Drijvende Bokken* [1999] ECR I-6121, para. 112. With reference to Case 238/82 *Duphar et al.* [1984] ECR 523, para. 16; Joined Cases C-159 and 160/91 *Poucet and Pistre* [1993] ECR I-637, para. 6; and Case C-70/95 *Sodemare* [1997] ECR I-3395, para. 27. NB: by contrast in Case C-18/88 *RTT* v. *GB-INNO-BM* [1991] ECR I-5941, para. 22, the Court held that essential requirements could be achieved by less restrictive means (as set out in Terminal Directive 88/301/EEC). The essential requirements themselves had been set out in the Council's Type Approval Directive 86/361/EEC (OJ 1986 L217/21).

[63] Examples for these sectors can be found via the relevant section of the website of DG Competition at: http://ec.europa.eu/comm/competition/liberalisation/legislation/legislation.html (accessed 10 June 2008).

7.8. Private restraints on competition and Article 86(2) EC

There can of course be no doubt that Article 86(2) EC applies not only to public undertakings, but also to private undertakings performing services of general economic interest.[64] However, for Article 86(2) EC to apply, it is necessary that such private undertakings have in fact been entrusted with the operation of services of general economic interest by means of a State measure – although no particular legal form is required, it is necessary that a legal act is involved. This was first established clearly in relation to private companies responsible for collective exploitation of copyright, which sought to rely on general statutory provisions intended to protect such rights.[65] The Court subsequently repeated this in its 1997 ruling on the *French Electricity and Gas Monopoly* case:

It is true that, for an undertaking to be regarded as entrusted with the operation of a service of general economic interest within the meaning of Article 90 (2) [now Article 86(2)] of the Treaty, it must have been so entrusted by an act of public authority . . .[66]

However, that does not mean that a legislative measure or regulation is required. The Court has already recognised that an undertaking may be entrusted with the operation of services of general economic interest through the grant of a concession governed by public law . . . That is so a fortiori where such concessions have been granted in order to give effect to obligations imposed on undertakings which, by statute, have been entrusted with the operation of services of general economic interest.[67]

Any attempt to invoke the Article 86(2) EC exemption thus requires proof of a legal act that spells out the public interest service involved. Article 86(2) EC cannot be invoked for private restraints of competition, nor can its criteria be applied independently by the Commission in the context of Article 81(3) EC, as was demonstrated by the 1996 *Métropole*

---

[64] Case 127/73 *BRT v. SABAM and NV Fonior* [1974] ECR 313, paras. 19–20.

[65] Case 127/73 *BRT v. SABAM and NV Fonior* [1974] ECR 313, para. 22–3; and Case 7/82 *GVL v. Commission* [1983] ECR 483, paras. 29 ff.

[66] Case C-159/94 *Commission v. France* [1997] ECR I-5815, para. 55, with reference to Case 127/73 *BRT v. SABAM and NV Fonior* [1974] ECR 313, para. 20; and Case 66/86 *Ahmed Saeed Flugreisen and Silver Line Reisebüro GmbH v. Zentrale zur Bekämpfung unlauteren Wettbewerbs e.V.* [1989] ECR 803, para. 55.

[67] Case C-159/94 *French Electricity and Gas Monopoly* [1997] ECR I-5815, para. 66 (with reference to Case C-393/92 *Almelo* [1994] ECR I-1477, para. 47).

judgment of the Court of First Instance. For the first time ever, it struck down a Commission clearance under Article 81(3) EC, on the grounds that the Commission had inappropriately based its Decision on an alleged 'public interest mission' of the constituent members of the EBU, the European public broadcasters' union. The Court of First Instance ruled that:

the Decision never started out from the principle that all members of the EBU are broadcasters entrusted with a mission of general economic interest involving their being subject to obligations under their statutes by virtue of an official act.[68]

At issue were not exclusive rights that EBU members had been awarded by their national governments, if any, but the exclusive rights to their pooled resources, denied to non-members. Even if all EBU members were charged with a public interest mission, the Commission could not assume the conditions for the application of Article 81(3) EC were met merely because of this. If the conditions of Article 86(2) EC could be applied by analogy under Article 81(3) EC 'in the context of an overall assessment', this required an assessment of the indispensable nature of exclusive rights to transmit certain sports events: i.e. a proportionality test. Moreover, as part of the same 'overall assessment', the State aid rules would have to be considered, because any public service obligations to which the EBU members were subject were likely to be off-set by preferential financial arrangements:

In any event, the Commission would not be justified in taking into account, for the purposes of exemption pursuant to Article 85(3) [now Article 81[(3)], the burdens and obligations arising for the members of the EBU as a result of a public mission, unless it also examined . . . the other relevant aspects of the case, such as the possible existence of a system of financial compensation for those burdens and obligations, without prejudice to Articles 92 and 93 [now Articles 87 and 88] of the Treaty.[69]

Hence, an appropriate test would have been whether, in view of the balance between public service obligations and the financial benefits intended to compensate for these obligations, a demonstrable need for

---

[68] Joined Cases T-528, 542, 543 and 546/93 *Métropole Télévision et al.* v. *Commission* (*Métropole*) [1996] ECR II-649, para. 113. Cf. the continuation of this saga in Case T-206/99 *Métropole Télévision* v. *Commission* [2001] ECR II-1057; and Case T-354/00 *M6* v. *Commission* [2001] ECR II-31.

[69] Joined Cases T-528, 542, 543 and 546/93 *Métropole* [1996] ECR II-649, para. 121.

additional private restraints on competition could have been shown. This would have had to amount to demonstrating an objective necessity of the restraints on competition involved. In the absence of a direct link with a State measure setting out the scope of the obligations involved, it is difficult to see how such a test could be met. Recently, the Court has greatly clarified the relation between public service obligations and compensation in the context of State aids.

7.9. Article 86(2) EC and State aid

The Member States' freedom concerning services of general economic interest extends to the financing of these services. Financing mechanisms applied range from direct financing from the general State budget to cross-subsidies in the context of special and exclusive rights, contributions by participants, tariff averaging and financing based on solidarity. In the absence of harmonisation (pre-emption), this freedom is limited only by the condition that such financing must not distort competition in the sense of the rules on State aid set out in Articles 87 and 88 of the Treaty.[70]

A key question in this context is whether aid is involved: essentially this appears to revolve around a proportionality test. Early case law of the Court in *Used Oils* held that an indemnity granted in relation to the imposition of certain obligations concerning waste oil collection and disposal did not involve aid provided it did not exceed the actual costs (and a reasonable profit) of these services.[71] Likewise, in *Ferring*, the Court held that a tax on direct sales by pharmaceutical laboratories amounted to State aid to wholesale distributors 'only to the extent that the advantage in not being assessed to the tax on direct sales of medicines exceeds the additional costs that they bear in discharging the public service obligations imposed on them by national law'.[72] The effect of the tax in this case would be to put the laboratories and the wholesale distributors 'on an equal footing' whereas otherwise the latter would be at a disadvantage given obligations to keep a minimum range of medicines stocked, and to ascertain various types of deliveries within set time limits. Conversely:

---

[70] COM(2003) 270, *Green Paper on Services of General Interest*, pp. 13–14.
[71] Case 240/83 *Procureur de la République* v. *Association de défense des brûleurs d'huiles usagée (Used Oils)* [1985] ECR 531, paras. 3 and 18.
[72] Case C-53/00 *Ferring SA* v. *Agence Centrale des Organisms de Sécurité Sociale (Ferring)* [2001] ECR I-9067, para. 29.

That Article 90(2) [now Article 86(2)] of the Treaty is to be interpreted as meaning that it does not cover tax advantages enjoyed by undertakings entrusted with the operation of a public service . . . in so far as that advantage exceeds the additional costs of performing the public service.[73]

Building on *Used Oils* and *Ferring*, in *Altmark Trans* the Court stated:

It follows from those judgments that, where a State measure must be regarded as compensation for the services provided by the recipient undertakings in order to discharge public service obligations, so that those undertakings do not enjoy a real financial advantage and the measure does not have the effect of putting them in a more favourable competitive position than the undertakings competing with them, such a measure is not caught by Article 87(1) of the Treaty.[74]

The Court then set out a four-part test to determine whether or not, in the context of Article 86(2) EC, a State aid might be involved:

First, the recipient undertaking must actually have public service obligations to discharge, and the obligations must be clearly defined. . . .

Second, the parameters on the basis of which the compensation is calculated must be established in advance in an objective and transparent manner, to avoid it conferring an economic advantage which may favour the recipient undertaking over competing undertakings. . . .

Third, the compensation cannot exceed what is necessary to cover all or part of the costs incurred in the discharge of public service obligations, taking into account the relevant receipts and a reasonable profit for discharging those obligations. . . .

Fourth, where the undertaking which is to discharge public service obligations, in a specific case, is not chosen pursuant to a public procurement procedure which would allow for the selection of the tenderer capable of providing those services at the least cost to the community, the level of compensation needed must be determined on the basis of an analysis of the costs

---

[73] Case C-53/00 *Ferring* [2001] ECR I-9067, para. 33.
[74] Case C-280/00 *Altmark Trans* [2003] ECR I-7747, para. 87. See e.g. Nicolaides, 'Compensation for Public Service Obligations: The Floodgates of State Aid', (2003) 24 ECLR 561; Merola and Medina, 'De l'Arrêt Ferring à l'Arrêt Altmark: Continuité ou Revirement dans l'Approche des Services Publics?', (2003) *Cahiers de Droit Européen* 639; Biondi, 'Justifying State Aid: The Financing of Services of General Economic Interest' in T. Tridimas and P. Nebbia (eds.), *European Union Law for the Twenty-First Century* (Oxford: Hart, 2004), Vol. 2, p. 259; Szyszczak, 'Financing Services of General Economic Interest', (2004) 67 *Modern Law Review* 982; Bovis, 'Financing Services of General Interest, Public Procurement and State Aids: The Delineation Between Market Forces and Protection in the European Common Market', [2005] *Journal of Business Law* 1; and Gromnicka, 'Services of General Economic Interest in the State Aids Regime: Proceduralisation or Political Choices?', (2005) 11 *European Public Law* 429.

which a typical undertaking, well run and adequately provided . . . so as to be able to meet the necessary public service requirements, would have incurred in discharging those obligations . . .[75]

Compensation for public service missions that meets these criteria will not constitute State aid. If such compensation does not meet these criteria, it will be subject to the State aid rules.[76] Beyond establishing the distinction between what is aid and what is not, these criteria establish, in passing, a minimum set of rules with which public service missions must comply to enjoy the benefit of the Article 86(2) EC exemption. The Commission has since seized on this judgment to issue a Notice and an Article 86(3) EC Decision to elaborate a general framework for State aid in the form of public service compensation based on the *Altmark Trans* ruling.[77] It is logical that the Commission should do so, because elaborating its powers concerning State aids when covered by a clear Court ruling raises no issues of concurrent powers and pre-emption: it is simply clarifying the law as it stands, not making new law.

7.10. Conclusion

The Article 86 EC standard is that exceptions to the free movement and competition rules may extend to the granting of (public or private) monopolies, so long as their mere creation does not make abuse unavoidable, or they are otherwise clearly linked to abuse.[78] At least since the early 1990s there can no longer be any doubt that national courts are instrumental in determining, directly, the scope of the Article 86(2)

---

[75] Case C-280/00 *Altmark Trans* [2003] ECR I-7747, paras. 89–93. Cf. Joined Cases C-34 to 38/01 *Enirisorse SnA v. Ministero delle Finanze (Enirisorse)* [2003] ECR I-14243, paras. 31 ff. The *Enirisorse* case finally clarified that collecting and allocating (part of) charges levied on other undertakings to the benefit of an undertaking charged with services of general economic interest may constitute State aid.

[76] Note, however, that CFI did not strictly impose the third and fourth Altmark criteria in its case on the Irish risk equalisation scheme for private health insurance in Case T-289/03 *BUPA v. Commission*, judgment of 12 February 2008, nyr, paras. 241 ff. This is due to the fact that ex ante compensation in the context of risk equalisation for health insurers is designed to promote competition on the merits, including on costs, and therefore precludes full (ex post) compensation of costs related to the provision of a service of general economic interest.

[77] *Community framework for State aid in the form of public service compensation*, OJ 2005 C297/04; and *Commission Decision of 28 November 2005 on the application of Article 86(2) of the EC Treaty to State aid in the form of public service compensation granted to certain undertakings entrusted with the operation of services of general economic interest*, OJ 2005 C312/67.

[78] Case C-323/93 *La Crespelle* [1994] ECR I-5080; and Case C-179/90 *Merci* [1991] ECR I-5889.

EC derogation. This involves both a justification of the exclusive right in public interest terms and a proportionality test. Any restrictions concerned must be proportional both in relation to the general economic interest at national level, and to the Community interest concerned.

Services of general economic interest are defined in line with subsidiarity and pre-emption: where there is no Community norm that has occupied the field (pre-emption), the lighter 'manifestly disproportionate' administrative law test prevails; where pre-emption has occurred, Member States may only intervene based on 'the least restrictive means'. At the same time, liberalisation creates the need for defining services of general economic interest.

Over time, Article 86(2) EC has variously been interpreted as a dead letter, an apparent exception to a liberalisation rule and an apparent general waiver which only fails to apply if the full application of the competition rules would not impede fulfilling nationally defined general economic interest objectives. This latter reading seriously undermines the proportionality test which is key to a strict interpretation of Article 86 EC (a strict interpretation which, as it concerns an exception to some of the most fundamental rules of the internal market, would be appropriate).

One way out of this stalemate occurs where the Community can preempt autonomous Member State action. This would be the case where either the Commission has sufficient confidence to provide a coherent Article 86(3) EC framework, as in the case of State aids, or the Council achieves political agreement on harmonised standards.

Moreover, finding a majority in favour of harmonisation or relying on the independent powers of the Commission may not always be necessary. As social services become increasingly difficult to fund without a significant degree of recourse to the market mechanism, in the context of liberalisation, Member States may be hampered by the competition and free movement rules in protecting core public services. This means they may eventually favour a formal legal act to bring that core within the haven of services of general economic interest. It should be noted that in such a setting there is almost by definition a more market-based alternative available as the basis for a more stringent proportionality test.

Consequently, it is submitted here that services of general economic interest may instead of being used as an ad hoc legal defence come to be applied as a full-fledged legal instrument, if not the main source of exceptions to market freedoms in the social sphere.

8   Articles 87–88 EC: State aid

8.1. Introduction

The State aid rules aim to provide a level playing field in the internal market, combating foreclosure of market entry as well as distortions of competition by governmental favouritism at the expense of the public purse and/or contributions by market participants. Although today almost all governments subscribe to the view that economic performance based on subsidies and handouts is unsustainable, this remains a sensitive area, in particular where distressed sectors are involved. Now most Member States have surrendered their monetary management to the European Central Bank and the European System of Central Banks subsidies is one of the few ways of influencing the economy that is left.

The Treaty's provisions on State aid have arguably gained in significance over the decades, for two main reasons. First, widespread privatisation across the Member States has resulted in public authorities looking for alternative methods of public intervention and market manipulation, many of which are subject to scrutiny under the State aid rules rather than, say, Article 86. Second, the Court's interpretation of the main provisions to apply far beyond mere subsidies and other blunt financial handouts has led them to acquire 'constitutional' significance for being used to separate legitimate mechanisms and methods of State intervention from illegal protectionism.[1]

---

[1] See e.g. Ross, 'State Aids – Maturing into a Constitutional Problem', (1995) 15 YEL 79; Bacon, 'State Aids and General Measures', (1997) 17 YEL 269; and Biondi and Rubini, 'Aims, Effects, and Justifications: EC State Aid Law and Its Impact on National Social Policies' in M. Dougan and E. Spaventa (eds.), *Social Welfare and EU Law* (Oxford: Hart, 2005), p. 79.

The State aid regime is a notoriously complex area of EC law,[2] notably because of the procedural intricacies involved in the notification and recovery schemes.[3] This chapter, as throughout this book, will focus on selected issues related to the demarcation of the public and private spheres. First, the chapter discusses the definition of the State itself for purposes of the personal scope of Article 87 EC. The analysis then moves on to the material scope of the provison. The third section discusses the criterion of a financial burden on the State to distinguish public from 'private' aid. The fourth section looks at the ways in which the Court attempts to separate State aid from general measures of economic policy. The fifth section then discusses the 'private investor principle' before, finally, placing the State aid rules in the context of other internal market rules, most importantly Article 86(2) EC.

8.2. Public or private bodies

Article 87(1) EC prohibits aid granted 'by a Member State' or 'through State resources'. From early case law, the Court has taken this to express that:

there is no necessity to draw any distinction according to whether the aid is granted by the State or by public or private bodies established or appointed by it to administer the aid. In applying Article 92 [now Article 87] regard must primarily be had to the effects of the aid on the undertakings or producers favoured and not on the status of the institutions entrusted with the distribution and administration of the aid.[4]

---

[2] See e.g. A. Biondi, P. Eeckhout and J. Flynn (eds.), *The Law of State Aid in the European Union* (Oxford University Press, 2004); L. Hancher, P. J. Slot and T. R. Ottervanger (eds.), 2nd rev. edn, *EC State Aids*, (London: Sweet & Maxwell, 2006); C. Quigley, *European State Aid Law* 2nd rev. edn (Oxford: Hart, 2007); Knaul and Pérez Flores, 'State Aid' in J. Faull and A. Nikpay (eds.), *The EC Law of Competition*, 2nd edn (Oxford University Press, 2007), p. 1703.

[3] Aid needs to be notified under Article 88(3) EC. Infringement of that obligation automatically renders the aid unlawful, putting national courts and authorities under the obligation to recover the aid. This all becomes rather complicated if the Commission subsequently – in the context of a complaint procedure – finds the aid to be compatible under Article 87 EC. See e.g. Case C-368/04 *Transalpine Ölleitung* [2006] ECR I-9957. Things get really out of hand if the Court of First Instance then annuls the favourable Commission Decision. See Case C-199/06 *CELF*, judgment of 12 February 2008, nyr. There remains, of course, the possibility that the Court of Justice then annuls the CFI decision.

[4] Case 78/76 *Steinike and Weinlig* v. *Commission* [1977] ECR 595, para. 21. In later case law, the Court used more forceful language, holding that such a distinction was

The aid must still be 'imputable' to the State. For a while, this seemed to imply not much more than the search for indicators of institutional public 'control' familiar from the case law on Article 28 and the Transparency Directive discussed earlier.[5] Thus, in *Van der Kooy*, the Court attributed to the Netherlands favourable tariffs set by the *Gasunie* by virtue of a classic catalogue of criteria: 50 per cent of shares were held by the State, half of the members of the supervisory board were appointed by the State, and the Minister had discretion to approve the tariffs set.[6] In its 2002 Decision in *Stardust Marine*,[7] however, the Court struck down a Commission Decision for attributing financial support measures to the State on the sole basis of the fact that they were taken by public undertakings:

[T]he mere fact that a public undertaking is under State control is not sufficient for measures taken by that undertaking to be imputed to the State. It is also necessary to examine whether the public authorities must be regarded as having been involved, in one way or another, in the adoption of those measures.[8]

However:

On that point, it cannot be demanded that it be demonstrated, on the basis of a precise inquiry, that in the particular case the public authorities specifically incited the public undertaking to take the aid measures in question. . . . It must be accepted that the imputability to the State of an aid measure taken by a public undertaking may be inferred from a set of indicators arising from the circumstances of the case and the context in which that measure was taken.[9]

The *Van der Kooy* criteria then are reclassified as forming part of this 'set of indicators', together with others such as: the undertaking's integration into the structures of the public administration; the nature of its activities and the exercise of the latter on the market in normal conditions of competition with private operators; the intensity of the

---

'inappropriate' or 'should not be drawn'. See e.g. Case C-305/88 *Italy* v. *Commission* [1991] ECR I-1603, para. 13; and Case C-126/01 *GEMO* [2003] ECR I-13769, para. 23.
[5] Transparency Directive 80/723/EEC (OJ 1980 L195/35).
[6] Joined Cases 67, 68 and 70/85 *Van der Kooy* [1988] ECR 219, paras. 35–8. See also Case 303/88 *Italy* v. *Commission* [1991] ECR I-1433, para. 12; and Case C-305/88 *Italy* v. *Commission* [1991] ECR I-1603, para. 14.
[7] Case C-482/99 *France* v. *Commission* [2002] ECR I-4397. Noted by Hancher (2003) 40 CMLR 739.
[8] Case C-482/99 *France* v. *Commission* [2002] ECR I-4397, para. 52.
[9] Case C-482/99 *France* v. *Commission* [2002] ECR I-4397, paras. 53 and 55.

supervision of the public authorities over the management of the undertaking; 'or any other indicator showing, in a particular case, an involvement by the public authorities in the adoption of a measure or the unlikelihood of their not being involved'.[10]

8.3. Public or private funds

It has long been unclear whether the distinction between aid granted 'by a Member State' or 'through State resources' sees *only* to the personal scope of Article 87 EC, or to the material scope as well. The argument could well be made, of course, that *any* advantage granted by the State, whether financed 'through State resources' or not, is capable of distorting competition in the internal market.[11] The Court, however, insists on a financial burden on the State ever since *Van Tiggele*. There, it held of Article 92 that:

[w]hatever definition must be placed upon the concept of 'aid' within the meaning of that article, it is clear from the wording thereof that a measure characterised by the fixing of minimum retail prices with the objective of favouring distributors at the exclusive expense of consumers cannot constitute an aid within the meaning of Article 87. The advantages which such an intervention in the formation of prices entails for the distributors of the

---

[10] Case C-482/99 *France v. Commission* [2002] ECR I-4397, para. 56. Cf. Case C-345/02 *Pearle* [2004] ECR I-7139, para. 37.
[11] This line of thought is strengthened by the Court's long-standing willingness to expand the substantive definition of aid beyond mere subsidies to 'interventions which, in various forms, mitigate the charges which are normally included in the budget of an undertaking and which, without therefore being subsidies in the strict meaning of the word, are similar in character and have the same effect'. The formula goes back to the decision in the ECSC Case 30/59 *Gezamenlijke Steenkoolmijnen in Limburg* [1961] ECR 1, 19 and has been repeated ever since. See e.g. Case C-143/99 *Adria Wien* [2001] ECR I-8365, para. 38. To decide what is 'normally' included in undertakings' budgets is not, of course, a value-free exercise. In *GEMO*, the Court implicitly relied on the 'polluter pays' principle to hold that the costs associated with the disposal of carcasses and slaughterhouse waste are 'inherent' in the activities of farmers and slaughterhouses. The State's organisation of such disposal, free of charge, was hence held to constitute State aid. Case C-126/01 *GEMO* [2003] ECR I-13769, paras. 31–3. In *France v. Commission*, the French Government tried to argue that a relief on social security contributions was targeted specifically at offsetting the additional costs associated with the implementation of a sectoral collective bargaining agreement and should hence be condoned. The Court held that, since undertakings are bound to observe collective bargaining agreements either by contract or regulation, the associated costs are included 'by their nature' in the budgets of undertakings. Case C-251/97 *France v. Commission* [1999] ECR I-6639, para. 40.

product are not granted, directly or indirectly, through state resources within the meaning of Article 87.[12]

The Commission has twice tried to convince the Court to widen the notion of State aid as a matter of principle to measures which grant advantages to certain undertakings without being financed through State resources. The first of these 'private aid' theories was raised in a 1985 case concerning a 'solidarity grant' to poor French farmers paid from the operating surplus of a private agricultural credit fund.[13] With Article 88(2) EC proceedings well under way, the Commission accepted the French argument that no 'State aid' was involved for lack of public funds being transferred. Taking the view, however, that the decision to finance the solidarity grant 'must have been the result of encouragement and pressure from the public authorities', the Commission started infringement proceedings under Article 226 EC, arguing that the grant constituted 'a measure having an equivalent effect to State aid' and holding France accountable under Article 10 EC, because a 'Member State cannot avoid its obligations by entrusting to an economic agent the implementation of a measure which, if it were taken by the State directly, would be incompatible with the Treaty'.[14]

This attempt to hold Member States responsible for 'private aid' bears a striking resemblance to the solution accepted fifteen years later by the Court in the context of Article 28 EC.[15] However, in *Commission v. France*, the Court would have none of it, largely on the basis of the difference in procedural guarantees afforded by Articles 88 and 226 EC respectively.[16] Holding the Article 226 application to be inadmissible, the Court seemed to imply that the case could have been dealt with effectively under the 'normal' State aid rules. After pointing out that the allocation of the fund's profits did not become definitive until approved by the public authorities, the Court said in *dictum*:

As is clear from the actual wording of Article 87(1), aid need not necessarily be financed from State resources to be classified as State aid.[17]

---

[12] Case 82/77 *Van Tiggele* [1978] ECR 25, paras. 24 and 25.
[13] Case 290/83 *Commission v. France* [1985] ECR 439.
[14] Case 290/83 *Commission v. France* [1985] ECR 439, para. 9.
[15] See above, section 4.2.
[16] Case 290/83, *Commission v. France* [1985] ECR 439, paras. 17 and 18.
[17] Case 290/83 *Commission v. France* [1985] ECR 439, para. 14.

That particular statement, however, has tacitly but probably definitively been overruled by the Court's relying on *Van Tiggele* in *Sloman Neptun*, where it held unambiguously that advantages granted from other resources than those of the State fall outside the scope of Article 87.[18] It is now clear, then, that the distinction between aid granted 'by a Member State' and 'through State resources' sees *only* to the provision's personal scope and has no bearing on the nature of the aid.

The Commission, undeterred, tried out another theory of private aid in *Preussen Elektra*, where the measure at issue obliged electricity supply companies to purchase from producers of renewable energy against fixed prices. This time, the Commission relied on the analogy with the court's combined reading of Articles 81 and 82 with Article 10 in the *effet utile* case law on anti-competitive State measures to convince the Court to catch measures decided on by the State, but financed by private undertakings. The Court gave the theory short shrift:

[I]t is sufficient to point out that, unlike Article 81 of the Treaty, which concerns only the conduct of undertakings, Article 87 of the Treaty refers directly to measures emanating from the Member States. In those circumstances, Article 87 of the Treaty is in itself sufficient to prohibit the conduct by States referred to therein and Article 10 of the Treaty cannot be used to extend the scope of Article 87 to conduct by States that does not fall within it.[19]

What we have, then, are two separate and cumulative conditions:[20] the measure must be imputable to the State and it must entail a transfer of State resources. If one but not the other is found, the measure will not be considered State aid. Thus, for example, in *GEMO*, the Court found

---

[18] Joined Cases C-72 and 73/91 *Sloman Neptun* v. *Bodo Ziesemer* [1993] ECR I-887, para. 19. See further e.g. Case C-379/98 *Preussen Elektra* [2001] ECR I-2099, para. 58; and Case C-345/02 *Pearle* [2004] ECR I-7139, para. 36. Confusion was reintroduced by the Court of First Instance in Case T-67/94 *Ladbroke* v. *Commission* [1998] ECR II-1, paras. 108 et seq., where it suggested that a measure designating sums that would otherwise accrue to the Treasury constituted an advantage 'granted through State resources'. On appeal, the Court of Justice agreed, adding the unhelpful consideration that the sums constantly remained 'under public control'. Case C-83/98 P *France* v. *Commission* [2000] ECR I-3471, para. 50. Noted by Hancher (2002) 39 CMLR 865. Cf. Biondi, 'Some Reflections on the Notion of "State Resources" in European Community State Aid Law', (2007) 30 *Fordham International Law Journal* 1426.

[19] Case C-379/98 *Preussen Elektra* [2001] ECR I-2099, paras. 64 and 65.

[20] Case T-351/02 *Deutsche Bahn* [2006] ECR II-1047, para. 103. See further e.g. Case C-482/99 *France* v. *Commission* [2002] ECR I-4397, para. 24; and Case C-126/01 *GEMO* [2003] ECR I-13769, para. 24.

that the removal and disposal of slaughterhouse waste was both 'organised' *and* financed by the State, even if the actual service was carried out by private undertakings.[21] In *Pearle*, however, the Court of Justice satisfied itself that the measure at issue, an advertising campaign financed from compulsory levies on members of a trade association, was both financed entirely from those levies *and* was not the result of 'the initiative' of a public body.[22] In *Deutsche Bahn*, finally, the Court of First Instance refused to classify a tax exemption on aviation fuel as State aid since the measure was taken as a consequence of Germany's obligations under Community law and could hence not be 'imputed' on the State.[23]

8.4. General measures and State aid

The condition of a financial burden was resurrected in the 1993 case of *Sloman Neptun* not to save 'private aid', but to save State measures which, by granting certain undertakings or sectors derogations from onerous legislative constraints, give advantages that on all other requirements of Article 87 would surely constitute aid. Thus the Court refused to extend the definition of 'State aid' to exemptions from certain labour contract standards for shipping undertakings since these did not seek 'to create an advantage which would constitute an additional burden for the State', but merely 'to alter in favour of shipping undertakings the framework within which contractual relations are formed between those undertakings and their employees'.[24] The ensuing financial consequences for the State, in terms of differences in the calculations of social security contributions and loss of tax revenue, were dismissed by the Court as 'inherent in the system'.[25] Although

---

[21] Case C-126/01 *GEMO* [2003] ECR I-13769, paras. 26 and 27.

[22] Case C-345/02 *Pearle* [2004] ECR I-7139, paras. 36 and 37.

[23] Case T-351/02 *Deutsche Bahn* [2006] ECR II-1047, para. 102. The obligation arises from Article 8(1)(b) of Directive 92/81 on the harmonisation of the structures of excise duties on mineral oils OJ 1992 L316/12.

[24] Joined Cases C-72 and 73/91 *Sloman Neptun* [1993] ECR I-887, para. 21. Noted by Slot (1995) 31 CMLR 137. The case dealt with the possibility for German shipping undertakings to employ foreign seamen at conditions worse than those granted to German seamen under German law. See also Case C-189/91 *Petra Kirsammer* [1993] ECR I-6185. Noted by Horspool (1994) 31 CMLR 1115. The case dealt with exemption from the regime of protection for unfair dismissal for SMEs.

[25] Joined Cases C-72 and 73/91 *Sloman Neptun* [1993] ECR I-887, para. 21.

these cases remain controversial,[26] they are coherent with the Court's 'subsidiarity case law' in other fields decided around the same time.[27]

The Court went even further in the 1998 *Viscido* Case, where it denied that relaxing labour market standards for a single undertaking, the *Ente Poste Italiane*, constituted aid. In a particularly concise judgment, it simply held that 'non-application of generally applicable legislation concerning fixed-term employment contracts to a single undertaking does not involve any direct or indirect transfer of State resources to that undertaking'.[28] According to Advocate General Jacobs, the purpose of the measure was 'to remove legal constraints which might hinder the smooth transformation of the Italian Postal Administration into a public undertaking'.[29] Seen in this light, *Viscido* seems in line with the Commission practice of linking authorisations of aid to privatisation measures.[30] The importance of that policy context was confirmed in *Danske Busvognmaend*.[31] There, the Court of First Instance was asked to rule on the validity of the Danish Government's decision to pay out bonuses to public officials to convince them to turn their public employment contracts into 'normal' private law contracts with a newly privatised transport company. The Court held:

[T]he measure in question has been introduced to replace the privileged and costly status of the officials employed by Combus with the status of employees

---

[26] Advocate General Darmon in both cases argued forcefully for a broader definition of 'aid', specifically through the concept of 'derogation', which to his mind, is far more suitable than the identification of certain beneficiaries to distinguish between general economic policy and 'aid'. See especially point 55 of his opinion in Joined Cases C-72 and 73/91 *Sloman Neptun* [1993] ECR I-887. Arguing along similar lines, Slotboom, 'State Aid in Community Law – A Broad or Narrow Definition', (1995) 20 ELR 289. See also Winter, 'Re (de)fining the Notion of State Aid in Article 87 (1) of the EC Treaty', (2004) 41 CMLR 475.

[27] Explicitly relating these cases to the 'subsidiarity' case law on Article 86, Ross, 'State Aids – Maturing into a Constitutional Problem', (1995) 15 YEL 79. Explicitly relating this case law to the Court's 'subsidiarity' case law on Article 28, Davies, 'Market Integration and Social Policy in the Court of Justice', (1995) 24 *Industrial Law Journal* 49.

[28] Joined Cases C-52 to 54/97 *Epifanio Viscido and Others* v. *Ente Poste Italiane* [1998] ECR I-2629, para. 14.

[29] Opinion in Joined Cases C-52/97 to 54/97 *Epifanio Viscido and Others* v. *Ente Poste Italiane* [1998] ECR I-2629, para. 14.

[30] See e.g. Commission Decision 94/1073/EC, OJ 1994 L386/1 *(Bull)* and Commission Decision 95/547/EC, OJ 1995 L308/92 *(Crédit Lyonnais)*. Contrast Evans, 'Privatisation and State Aid Control in EC Law', (1997) 18 ECLR 259; and Devroe, 'Privatizations and Community Law: Neutrality Versus Policy', (1997) 34 CMLR 267. Cf. Verhoeven, 'Privatisation and EC Law: Is the European Commission "Neutral" with respect to Public versus Private Ownership of Companies?', (1996) 45 ICLQ 861.

[31] Case T-157/01 *Danske Busvognmaend* [2004] ECR II-917.

of other bus transport undertakings competing with Combus. The intention was thus to free Combus from a structural disadvantage it had in relation to its private-sector competitors. ... Moreover, instead of paying the DKK 100 million directly to the officials employed by Combus, the Danish Government could have obtained the same result be reassigning those officials within the public administration, without paying any particular bonus, which would have enabled Combus to employ immediately employees on a contract basis falling under private law.[32]

Focusing on the 'financial burden' test will exclude many, but not all, measures that could plausibly be considered to be measures of general economic policy. The other test available to the Court is the one of 'selectivity', a condition stemming from the prohibition in Article 87 EC to favour *certain* undertakings or the production of *certain* goods. From the *Kimberley Clark* Case onwards, it is clear that any scheme that grants a measure of discretion to public authorities in the choice of beneficiaries, the amounts of aid granted and the conditions under which assistance is provided will fall foul of the test. In that case, the Court struck down the financial participation by the French *Fonds National d'Emploi* (FNE) in the social plan of an undertaking in the process of restructuring, objecting to the latitude enjoyed by the FNE.[33] The position was later confirmed in Italian cases concerning the discretion conferred on the Minister for Industry to authorise large insolvent undertakings to continue trading under special administration.[34] Objectivity alone, however, will not save measures from being selective.[35] Nor is it a matter of a limited number of clearly identifiable beneficiaries, as the Court has been making increasingly clear. It is now standing case law that:

neither the high number of benefiting undertakings nor the diversity and importance of the industrial sectors to which to those undertakings belong

---

[32] Case T-157/01 *Danske Busvognmaend* [2004] ECR II-917, para. 57.

[33] Case C-241/94 *France* v. *Commission* [1996] ECR I-4551, paras. 21–4. Lyon-Caen, 'Le Financement Public d'un Plan Social est-il Condamné par le Droit Communautaire?', [1997] *Droit Social* 185, p. 188, speaks of 'l'impérialisme toujours plus affirmé d'une analyse des dispositifs juridiques réduite à leur effets réels ou potentiels sur le marché' ('an ever more imperialist interpretation of legal provisions reducing their meaning to their real or potential effects on the market').

[34] Case C-200/97 *Ecotrade* [1998] ECR I-7907, para. 40; and Case C-295/97 *Piaggio* [1999] ECR I-3735, para. 39. See further e.g. Case C-256/97 *DMT* [1999] ECR I-3913, para. 27; and Joined Cases T-92 and 103/00 *Álava* v. *Commission* [2002] ECR II-1385, para. 31.

[35] See Case C-75/97 *Belgium* v. *Commission (Maribel)* [1999] ECR I-3671, para. 27; Case T-55/99 *CETM* [2000] ECR II-3207, para. 40; and Case C-501/00 *Spain* v. *Commission* [2004] ECR I-6717, para. 121. See Kurcz and Vallindas, 'Can General Measures Be . . . Selective? Some Thoughts on the Interpretation of a State Aid Definition', (2008) 45 CMLR 159.

provide any grounds for concluding that a State initiative constitutes a general measure of economic policy.[36]

Indeed, more recently still the Court has taken to stating bluntly that meaures that do not apply to *all* economic operators cannot be considered part of a general policy.[37]

Instead, the Court has taken to requiring that measures are 'justified by the nature and the general scheme of the system of which they are part'.[38] Recently, the Court has formalised the test thus:

[T]he concept of State aid does not refer to State measures which differentiate between undertakings and which are, therefore, prima facie, selective where that differentiation arises from the nature or the overall structure of the system of charges of which they are part.[39]

In *CETM*, the Court of First Instance made it abundantly clear that more is involved than the mere listing of laudable objectives that the measure in question may be thought to further. In that case, Spain argued that a subsidy on the purchase of commercial vehicles was 'in the interest of environmental protection and improving road safety'. If that argument were followed, the Court held:

it would be sufficient for the public authorities to invoke the legitimacy of the objectives which the adoption of an aid measure sought to attain for that

---

[36] Case C-143/99 *Adria Wien* [2001] ECR I-8365, para. 48. Noted by Golfinopoulos, (2003) 24 ELR 543. The formula finds its origins in Case C-75/97 *Belgium* v. *Commission (Maribel)* [1999] ECR I-3671, para. 32.

[37] See Case C-66/02 *Italy* v. *Commission* [2005] ECR I-10901, para. 99; Case C-148/04 *Unicredito* [2005] ECR I-11137, para. 49; Case C-222/04 *Cassa di Risparmio di Firenze* [2006] ECR I-289, para. 135; and Joined Cases C-393/04 and 41/05 *Air Liquide* [2006] ECR I-5293, para. 32.

[38] Case C-143/99 *Adria Wien* [2001] ECR I-8365, para. 42. The Court traces the test back to Case 173/73 *Italy* v. *Commission* [1974] ECR 709, para. 15, where it observed that reductions of social charges pertaining to family allowances for the textile sector could not find any justification 'on the basis of the nature or general scheme' of the Italian social security system. The formula then remained dormant for twenty-five years, until it was resurrected in Case C-75/97 *Belgium* v. *Commission (Maribel)* [1999] ECR I-3671, para. 33. See further e.g. Case C-351/98 *Spain* v. *Commission* [2002] ECR I-8031, para. 41; Case C-159/01 *Netherlands* v. *Commission* [2004] ECR I-4461, para. 42; Case C-308/01 *GIL Insurance* [2004] ECR I-1477, para. 73; and Case C-148/04 *Unicredito* [2005] ECR I-11137, para. 51. See also Case C-351/98 *Spain* v. *Commission* [2002] ECR I-8031, para. 42.

[39] Case C-88/03 *Portugal* v. *Commission* [2006] ECR I-7115, para. 52. Noted by Winter, (2008) 45 CMLR 183.

measure to be regarded as a general measure outside the scope of Article 87(1) of the Treaty.[40]

To avoid this, the question appears to be whether the measure results directly from 'the basic or guiding guidelines' of the system. The Court distinguishes here between objectives 'extrinsic' to the system and the mechanisms 'inherent' in the system which are necessary for the achievement of those objectives.[41] Although it is not entirely clear what this amounts to, it seems as if the Court is setting up obstacles to the use of social security and tax systems for 'extrinsic' social, or even economic, objectives. In *Portugal* v. *Commission*, the Court objected to an overall reduction in corporation and income tax for undertakings in the Azores designed to compensate for the competitive disadvantage of being located on a far-away island. Here, the Court paradoxically objected to the general nature of the measure, applying as it did to all economic operators 'without any distinction as to their financial circumstances', since this could not ensure that 'for purposes of redistribution the criterion of the ability to pay is observed'. In summary, then, 'the fact of acting on the basis of a regional development or social cohesion policy is not sufficient in itself to justify a measure adopted within the framework of that policy'.[42] In *Spain* v. *Commission*, the Court objected to regional tax deductions related to export activities:

[I]n order to justify the contested measures with respect to the nature or the structure of the tax system of which those measures form part, it is not sufficient to state that they are intended to promote international trade. It is true that such a purpose is an economic objective, but it has not been shown that that purpose corresponds to the overall logic of the tax system in force in Spain, which is applicable to all undertakings.[43]

In *GIL Insurance*, on the other hand, the British Government decided to close the gap between Insurance Premium Tax and VAT after finding that the difference was widely used to manipulate the relative price of sale and rental of appliances and that of the associated insurance. The Court found this measure to be justified by the general nature of the tax

---

[40] Case T-55/99 *CETM* [2000] ECR II-3207, para. 53.
[41] Case C-88/03 *Portugal* v. *Commission* [2006] ECR I-7115, para. 81.
[42] Case C-88/03 *Portugal* v. *Commission* [2006] ECR I-7115, para. 82. It should be noted that the Court's objection should be read in the context of its having decided that the relevant legal framework for the determination of selectivity was the whole of Portugal, not just the Azores.
[43] Case C-501/00 *Spain* v. *Commission* [2004] ECR I-6717, para. 124.

system since it was designed to offset losses of revenue and to rebalance terms of condition.[44]

8.5. Public and private investors

Given the fact that the Treaty explicitly enshrines its accommodation of the mixed economy in Article 295 EC,[45] European law cannot be used to prevent or discourage State participation in the economy. The Court tries to solve the obvious tension between this cardinal principle and the State aid regime by subjecting public intervention in the market to the 'normal' rules of the market. As the Court formulates:

> Pursuant to the principle that the public and private sectors are to be treated equally, capital placed directly or indirectly at the disposal of an undertaking by the State in circumstances which correspond to normal market conditions cannot be regarded as State aid.[46]

In practice, this translates into the controversial 'private investor test', by which the State is held to the standard of behaviour of a putative private market actor.[47] The decisive question in measuring public shareholding in private undertakings is then:

> whether in similar circumstances a private shareholder, having regard to the foreseeability of obtaining a return and leaving aside all social, regional-policy and sectoral considerations, would have subscribed the capital in question.[48]

This private investor test is not an inflexible short-term profit maximisation standard. The Court has refined the private investor test to allow for long-term perspectives, and classifies as aid only those public

---

[44] Case C-308/01 GIL Insurance [2004] ECR I-1477, paras. 73 et seq.

[45] 'This Treaty shall in no way prejudice the rules in Member States governing the system of property ownership.'

[46] Case C-303/88 Italy v. Commission (ENI-Lanerossi) [1991] ECR I-1433, para. 20; Case C-39/94 SFEI v. La Poste [1996] ECR I-3547, para. 60; and Case C-482/99 France v. Commission [2002] ECR I-4397, para. 69.

[47] See e.g. Karydis, 'Le Principe de "l'Opérateur Économique Privé", Critère de Qualification des Measures Étatiques, en tant qu'Aides d'Etat, au Sens de l'Article 87 (1) du Traité CE', (2003) 39 RTDE 389; and Parish, 'On the Private Investor Principle', (2003) 28 ELR 70–89.

[48] Case 234/84 Belgium v. Commission [1986] ECR 2281, para. 14. Cf. Case C-142/87 Belgium v. Commission (Tubemeuse) [1990] ECR I-959. It is probably enough for a State to show that private investors did in fact participate on the same conditions as the public authorities to satisfy the test. See Case T-296/97 Alitalia v. Commission [2000] ECR II-3871, paras. 85 et seq.

investments that 'disregard any prospect of profitability, even in the longer term'.[49] In *Alfa Romeo*, the Court allowed for the theory that bigger companies can afford lavish long-term investments and held it 'necessary to consider whether in similar circumstances a private investor of a size comparable to that of the bodies administering the public sector might have provided capital of such an amount'.[50] When the Commission attempted to use a stricter approach, in a 1996 case, its reasoning was dismissed as follows:

the Commission merely stated, without adequate explanation, that the stock market price is the sole determining factor in valuing shares. That view is too formal, rigid and restrictive. To apply that criterion absolutely and unconditionally, to the exclusion of all other elements, constitutes a purely mechanical exercise which can scarcely be reconciled with the system of the market economy and the economic choices made in present case by undertakings of substantial size guided by prospects of profitability in the longer term.[51]

In the same vain, the Court of First Instance refused in *BAI* and in *P&O* to allow the province of Vizcaya to keep a ferry line running in low season by purchasing vast amounts of travel vouchers without showing 'actual and genuine' need, even if the vouchers were bought at regular prices.[52] On appeal in *P&O*, the issue of principle was raised as to whether the criterion of 'need' is compatible with the Court's exhortations that the private investor test should be based on 'objective and verifiable' elements.[53] That appeal, however, was dimissed on procedural grounds since the issue was considered *res judicata* on the basis of the (unappealed) judgment in *BAI*.[54]

---

[49] Case C-303/88 *Italy* v. *Commission (ENI-Laneroussi)* [1991] ECR I-1433, para. 22. It should be noted that the Court of First Instance is even more lenient in the parallel 'private creditor' test, where it will allow generous terms of debt restructuring. See Case T-152/99 *Hijos de Andrés Molina* [2002] ECR II-3049, paras. 165 et seq.

[50] Case C-305/89 *Italy* v. *Commission (Alfa Romeo)* [1991] ECR I-1603, para. 19. Cf. Case C-482/99 *France* v. *Commission* [2002] ECR I-4397, para. 70; and Case C-334/99 *Germany* v. *Commission* [2003] ECR I-1139, para. 133.

[51] Joined Cases C-329/93, 62 and 63/95 *Germany and Others* v. *Commission* [1996] ECR I-5151, para. 36.

[52] Case T-14/96 *Bretagne Angleterre Irlande (BAI)* v. *Commission* [1999] ECR II-139, paras. 75 et seq.; and Joined Cases T-116 and 118/01 *P&O European Ferries (Vizcaya)* v. *Commission* [2003] ECR II-2957, paras. 115 et seq.

[53] Joined Cases C-83, 93 and 94/01 P *Chronopost* v. *Commission* [2003] ECR I-6993, para. 39.

[54] Joined Cases C-442 and 471/03 P *P&O European Ferries (Vizcaya)* v. *Commission* [2006] ECR I-4845, paras. 38 et seq.

One of the problems with the test is the gap between what a private investor would do and what a rational public authority should do. Two examples may suffice. In a case against Spain, the Commission had allowed financial subsidies to textile and footwear producers when these were still State-owned under the derogation for depressed economic sectors.[55] It objected, however, when Spain privatised the companies and took share capital at unrealistic prices. When the Commission found that Spain failed the 'private investor test', Spain attempted to argue that the solution chosen was preferable to liquidating the companies, with the subsequent costs that would entail. The Court held:

A distinction must be drawn between the obligations which the State must assume as owner of the share capital of a company and its obligations as a public authority. Since the three companies in question were constituted as limited companies, the Patrimonio del Estado, as owner of the share capital, would have been liable for their debts up to the liquidation value of their assets. That means in the present case that the obligations arising from the cost of redundancies, payment of unemployment benefits and aid for the restructuring of the industrial infrastructure must not be taken into consideration for the purpose of applying the private investor test.[56]

Similarly, in a more recent case against Germany, the Court was prepared to calculate the difference between the measure at stake – 'privatising' the failing steel firm *Gröditzer Stahlwerke* for a negative sale price of 340 million DM – and the cost of winding up the company, but only to the extent that the costs of the latter operation resulted from operations that, by themselves, a private investor would have been prepared to undertake. The Court thus subtracted from the winding-up costs all losses resulting from guaranteed loans that in themselves were to be considered State aid and, more poignantly, the 22 million for the cost of a social plan and 87 million for clearing the site, to end up with 292 million DM, markedly less than Germany's calculation of 450 million DM and considerably less than the cost of privatising.[57] The counterpart of this reasoning is that costs incurred to fulfil 'typical'

---

[55] Under Article 93(3)(c) EC, 'aid to facilitate the development of certain economic activities or of certain economic areas' may be held compatible with the common market.

[56] Joined Cases C-278 to 280/92 *Spain v. Commission* [1994] ECR I-4103, para. 22.

[57] Case C-344/99 *Germany v. Commission* [2003] ECR I-1139, paras. 133 et seq.

obligations of a public authority, such as investments in infrastructure and training, are not considered aid.[58]

8.6. State aid and other internal market rules

As early as 1977, the Court had ambiguously summarised the relationship between the Treaty provisions concerning State aid on the one hand and services of general economic interest on the other. It stated that 'it follows from Article 86 of the Treaty that, save for the reservation in Article 86(2), Article 87 covers all private and public undertakings and all their production'.[59] What that 'reservation' exactly amounts to is open for interpretation. The Court of Justice in *Banco Exterior de España*[60] gave this a procedural reading. It held that aid granted to an undertaking covered by Article 86(2) EC fell into the category of aid that 'may be considered incompatible with the common market', and thus extended the Commission's power to review aid under Article 88 to aid granted to undertakings covered by Article 86(2).[61]

The Court of First Instance, in its 1997 judgment in *FFSA v. Commission*, on the other hand, gave the reservation substantive meaning by explicitly extending the *Corbeau* case law to State aid. It held that aid granted to an undertaking falling under Article 86(2) EC specifically for the purpose of offsetting the additional costs of carrying out services in the general economic interest, and not exceeding those costs, falls outside the scope of Article 87 EC altogether.[62] Moreover, it confirmed the pre-emption approach:

in the absence of Community rules governing the matter, the Commission has no power to take a position on the organisation and scale of the public service task assigned to a public undertaking or on the expediency of the political choices made in this regard by the competent national authorities, provided

---

[58] Case C-255/91 *Matra v. Commission* [1993] ECR I-3202, para. 29.
[59] Case 78/76 *Steinike* [1977] ECR 595, para. 18 of the judgment. See generally, Deckert and Schroeder, 'Öffentliche Unternehmen und EG-Beihilferecht', (1998) 33 EuR 291.
[60] Case C-387/92 *Banco Exterior de España* [1994] ECR I-877.
[61] Case C-387/92 *Banco Exterior de España* [1994] ECR I-877, paras. 17–18. The characterisation of a State measure as 'aid' is a responsibility of both national courts and the Commission, given the direct effect granted to Article 87. Nevertheless, the Court allows the Commission broad discretion in cases where 'complex economic appraisals' are necessary. Cf. Case C-56/93 *Belgium v. Commission* [1996] ECR I-723, paras. 10–11. Cf. Case C-39/94 *SFEI v. La Poste* [1996] ECR I-3547, paras. 34 ff; and Case T-67/94 *Ladbroke v. Commission* [1998] ECR II-1, paras. 52–3.
[62] Case T-106/95 *FFSA v. Commission* [1997] ECR II-229, paras. 178–81.

that the aid in question does not benefit the activities in the competitive sectors or exceed what is necessary to enable the undertaking concerned to perform the task assigned to it.[63]

As set out in the previous chapter, the Court of Justice has now sanctioned this approach in *Ferring* and *Altmark* and set out a four-part test to determine whether or not, in the context of Article 86(2) EC, a State aid might be involved.[64] This requires:

- a legal act conferring the public service obligations and defining the public service concerned;
- transparent and objective criteria for determining the level of compensation for this task;
- based on relevant costs plus a reasonable rate of return; and
- selection based on public procurement procedures, or at least with compensation based on best practice.[65]

If these conditions are met, there is no State aid involved. Although the clarity of these criteria does not leave much to be desired, the Commission has seized on this development to elaborate this judgment in a Notice and an Article 86(3) EC Decision, jointly constituting a framework subject to review after six years. As such, this forms the main step forward in defining the scope of services of general economic interest in many years.[66]

If, then, Article 86(2) EC can be used to exempt measures from Article 87 EC, the Court has avoided scenarios where Article 87 EC saves

---

[63] Case T-106/95 *FFSA* v. *Commission* [1997] ECR II-229, para. 192.

[64] Case C-53/00 *Ferring SA* v. *Agence Centrale des Organisms de Sécurité Sociale (Ferring)* [2001] ECR I-9067; and Case C-280/00 *Altmark Trans* [2003] ECR I-7747, paras. 89–93. Cf. Case C-451/03 *Servizi Ausiliari Dottori Commercialisti* v. *Calafiori* [2006] ECR I-2941, paras. 30 ff. See generally e.g. Boysen and Neukirchen, *Europäisches Beihilferecht und mitgliedstaatliche Daseinsvorsorge* (Baden Baden: Nomos, 2007).

[65] Case C-280/00 *Altmark Trans* [2003] ECR I-7747, paras. 89–93. In so far as the last condition seems to imply an efficiency test of sorts, it is not entirely clear how this relates to the Court's judgment in Joined Cases C-83, 93 and 94/01 P *Chronopost* v. *Commission* [2003] ECR I-6993, para. 33, where it berated the Court of First Instance for its application of the 'normal market conditions' test to an entity charged with a public service mission in Case T-613/97 *Ufex* v. *Commission* [2000] ECR II-4055, para. 75.

[66] *Community framework for State aid in the form of public service compensation*, OJ 2005 C297/04; and *Commission Decision of 28 November 2005 on the application of Article 86(2) of the EC Treaty to State aid in the form of public service compensation granted to certain undertakings entrusted with the operation of services of general economic interest*, OJ 2005 C312/67.

measures that are caught by other prohibitions. Thus the Court has held that classification as State aid of a transfer to a public undertaking does not preclude a measure from 'giving rise to abuse of a dominant position by that undertaking, contrary to Articles 82 and 86 of the Treaty'.[67] It is clearest in the free movement of goods. In early case law, the Court had seemed to suggest that simultaneous application of the rules on State aid and those on free movement could only occur by over-extensive interpretation of Article 28 EC.[68] However, in the 1990 *Du Pont de Nemours* Case, the Court held that:

Article 87 may in no case be used to frustrate the rules of the treaty on the free movement of goods. It is clear from the relevant case law that those rules and the Treaty provisions relating to State aid have a common purpose, namely to ensure the free movement of goods between the Member States under normal conditions of competition.[69]

The Italian measure at issue obliged all public undertakings to obtain at least 30 per cent of their supplies from undertakings situated in the south. The Court held this to be a measure contrary to Article 28 EC and refused to even consider the issue of State aid[70] by establishing the principle that 'the fact that national rules might be regarded as aid within the meaning of Article 87 cannot exempt them from the prohibition set out in Article 28'.[71] Measures of regional policy are thus pre-empted from being judged under State aid rules by extension of the principle of free movement.[72]

---

[67] Joined Cases C-34 to 38/01 *Enirisorse* [2003] ECR I-14243, para. 50.

[68] See Case 74/76 *Ianelli &Volpi v. Ditta Paolo Meroni* [1977] ECR 577, para. 12. In Case 91/78 *Hansen v. Haupotzollamt Flensburg* [1979] ECR 935, para. 10, the Court classified Article 37 as a *lex specialis* in relation to the State aid provisions.

[69] Case C-21/88 *Du Pont de Nemours Italiana SpA v. Unità sanitaria locale No 2 di Carrara* [1990] ECR I-889, para. 20. Cf. Case 249/81 *Commission v. Ireland (Buy Irish)* [1982] ECR 4005, para. 18.

[70] Article 87(3)(a) EC provides that, subject to review by the Commission, aid to underdeveloped regions 'may be incompatible with the common market'.

[71] Case C-21/88 *Du Pont de Nemours Italiana SpA v. Unità sanitaria locale No 2 di Carrara* [1990] ECR I-889, para. 21. In Case C-169/95 *Spain v. Commission* [1997] ECR I-135, paras. 17 and 18, the Court has held that even where Article 87(3)(a) applies, the Commission is still entitled to take the 'Community interest' into account, and assess the aid's 'impact on the relevant market or markets in the Community as a whole'.

[72] For critique, see Fernández Martín and Stehmann, 'Product Market Integration versus Regional Cohesion in the Community', (1991) 16 ELR 216.

8.7. Conclusion

The prohibition in Article 87 covers all aid granted by a Member State or through State resources and there is no necessity to draw any distinction according to whether the aid is granted directly by the State or by public or private bodies established or appointed to administer the aid.

As concerns the distinction between legislative and financial measures made in Article 87(10) EC, the Court refuses to interpret this as having any bearing on the body granting the aid, but also denies that it implies a distinction regarding the *nature* of the aid. In practice, however, it takes a strict view of financial measures and a lenient one on legislative measures.

Key to a finding of aid is the private investor test. This test is not an inflexible short-term profit maximisation standard: it is capable of taking a long-term perspective. However, the private investor test does not take financial interests that go beyond profit, albeit long term, into account: it is not a rational public authority test. The counterpart of this reasoning is that costs incurred to fulfil 'typical' obligations of a public authority, such as investments in infrastructure and training, are not considered aid.

Concerning the application of State aid to services of general economic interest, the Court has clarified four criteria which, if met, lead to the conclusion that no State aid is at stake. The Commission has clarified this rule further with an Article 86(3) EC notice and Decision, the first horizontal rules based on Article 86(3) EC since the 1988 Transparency Directive. Where free movement rules and the State aid rules are at stake, it will suffice if an infringement of the free movement rules is found.

9   Conclusion

When we started this book, we were struck by the contradiction between the assertive European law that we learned as students in the heady days of the Single European Act and the cautious approach adopted by the Court from the early 1990s onward. In short: we were challenged by the clash between *Cassis de Dijon*, when mutual recognition seemed to make short shrift of discriminatory State measures, and *Keck*, which seemed to accept barriers to trade provided only they did not entail deliberate discrimination. Almost contemporaneously similar developments appeared to take place concerning the public promotion of private restraints on competition, where the high hopes raised by *Van Eycke* were dashed by *Meng*, *Reiff* and *Ohra*.

Our original aim, therefore, was to make sense of the free movement and competition case law of the European courts, to compare the two, and to reconcile them where possible. In addition, we thought we would draw up the balance of the Court's retrenching that appeared to occur on all fronts at the time.

In the course of our writing on this topic we have discovered not only that ours was a moving target, but also that the rules of the game were far more flexible than originally thought – as evidenced, for example, by: the remarkable teleology applied in the *Albany* judgment, where the Court found an unwritten exception to the competition rules in the Treaty for the results of collective bargaining; *Wouters*, where public interest claims by private parties justified corporatist arrangements as outside the scope of the Article 81(1) EC prohibition; and *Medina*, the clearest suggestion to date that the Court is headed for a rule of reason (such as it already adopted in free movement with *Dassonville*) in competition law. The relevance of this topic and its complexity have consequently only increased.

As stated in the introduction to this book, the main question we wish to address is: what under EU law, in the case law of the Court, are the limits to legitimate governmental interference in market processes in the context of European integration today, and why? Are there fundamental differences between the ways in which the Court treats this problem under the free movement and competition rules? To what extent do these norms complement each other, or are they converging?

We have tried to formulate three (partly overlapping) questions to address this issue:

- How does the Court attribute measures to either the public or private sphere?
- How does the Court establish whether the free movement and competition rules are applicable?
- How does the Court establish whether public interest exceptions and/or justifications apply?

We will summarise our conclusions according to the two main parts in which this discussion paper is organised, before completing with a short final section that brings together some elements from both parts.

The first section has looked at the fundamental freedoms and the competition regime. First, we addressed the criteria that the Court uses to apply these rules to their original addressees, i.e. the Member States, respectively private undertakings. Next, we have reviewed cases where the original legal categories are reversed: i.e. when the competition rules are applied to State measures and the fundamental freedoms to private parties.

(i) *Free movement: (Treaty) provisions and secondary rules.* Both the vertical and horizontal scope of the free movement rules have shifted over time. When the horizontal scope of free movement in *Dassonville* and *Cassis* broadened, this was accompanied by the acceptance of new public interest exceptions under a 'rule of reason' approach, which focuses upon non-discrimination and proportionality. Taking into account the pre-existing case law on exceptions to free movement, the vertical 'withdrawal' on selling arrangements exemplified by *Keck* can also be seen as part of a trend of rationalisation with a limited material impact. This vertical realignment has been followed by a trend of horizontal rationalisation in the area of public health and social security in cases such as *Kohll* and *Decker*, with potentially more significant effects.

It is therefore not a withdrawal, but rather a rebalancing along horizontal and vertical lines that appears to have taken place. The relevant factors at play can be summarised as functionalism and subsidiarity – or perhaps more appropriately functionalism and pre-emption.

The classification of State measures and the concept of 'public bodies' under the free movement provisions confirms this interpretation. Here, the Court's horizontal advance is likewise partially compensated by a vertical retreat (as in *Hünermund*) – and vice versa. As was just noted, on balance, this involves a rationalisation of its case law along the cross-cutting lines of functionalism and subsidiarity.

Next, when looking at 'public bodies' under secondary law, we see the Court's case law on direct effect of Directives increasing the reach of Directives both horizontally and vertically.

At the same time, harmonisation itself sets limits to the functional approach: whenever possible, the Court uses the formal distinctions introduced by the Community Directives themselves as thresholds for the application of these secondary rules. Because the Court applies the EU law criteria that determine the public/private distinction in secondary legislation strictly, this can lead to divergence between economic sectors, and even within such sectors, depending on the degree of harmonisation attained in respect of specific areas of regulation.

Concerning public authority exceptions to free movement, the Court aims to limit the scope of the exceptions 'to what is strictly necessary for safeguarding the interests which that provision allows the Member States to protect'. This is simply an application of the general rule of Community law that exceptions are interpreted strictly. By employing a functional approach, the Court simultaneously aims to ensure that the scope of application is the same throughout the Community – protecting the unity of EU law.

The same trend exists concerning public authority exceptions to free movement under secondary law. The Court is willing to use a formal approach based on national legal distinctions when applying secondary law exceptions, in particular where this has a restrictive effect. The terms of explicit public service exceptions to secondary legislation are applied stringently, consistent with the objective of harmonisation and the rule of limited exceptions. Neither functionalism nor formalism affect the ground rules concerning the public interest exceptions to free movement provided by the Treaty and the mandatory requirements that the Member States may invoke.

(ii) The competition rules: The analysis on this topic has focused, first, on the key concepts that the Court uses to determine whether particular entities and/or their activities are to be subjected to the competition rules: 'undertaking', 'economic activity', 'activity typical of a public authority' and 'social function'. Next, we have looked at how the Court has, in addition, created a number of exceptions in cases such as *Albany*, *Wouters* and *Medina*, to deal with cases where there could be no doubt that economic activities and agreements between private parties were involved but where it nevertheless saw grounds to leave the measures concerned unaffected on public policy grounds.

The Court uses a functional approach when deciding whether a body should be considered an 'undertaking' subject to the competition rules. The concept of 'undertaking' in turn is based on the question of whether economic activities are carried out, meaning offering goods or services in the marketplace, for payment and while assuming the financial risks involved, as well as offering goods or services in competition, or, in its weakest form, offering goods and services that *could* be subject to competition (potential competition).

Especially where potential competition is concerned, the question of whether an activity is 'typical of a public authority' or has an exclusively social function is relevant. The Court has held that the nature and aim of an activity and the rules to which it is subject determine whether it is typical of a public authority. This appears to leave the Member States considerable freedom in defining such activities.

The relevant case law is more precise on the definition of what constitutes an exclusively social function. This means that compulsory participation and definition of benefits based on solidarity rather than contributions or returns on investment are required. Where a lesser extent of solidarity exists, the arrangements concerned may fall under the competition rules, but may for example be subject to the exceptions of Article 86 EC.

The exercise of public authority is subject to a non-discrimination and proportionality requirement, as are the exceptions to free movement, and the Article 86 exceptions. This means a similar (if not identical) standard prevails in all three cases. A degree of convergence thus seems to take place in these fields.

In the absence of formal exceptions, the Court has been creative in finding ways of letting agreements with a public interest dimension off the hook even if they have a restrictive effect on competition. In doing so, it has not only applied the more standard de minimis approach, but has found an unwritten exception in the system of the Treaty as a whole for collective bargaining agreements (*Albany*), and has stretched the ancillary restraints doctrine, respectively the new economic approach (or 'rule of reason'), to accommodate private restrictions in the legal profession (*Wouters*), and concerning anti-doping rules in professional sports (*Medina*). In these cases, it appears that the Court is willing to limit the scope of the competition rules based on de minimis, respectively pre-emption or subsidiarity grounds, possibly including a rule of reason, much more drastically than under the free movement rules. As concerns the apparent use of a rule of reason approach, there is again convergence between the free movement and the competition rules.

Finally, if public authority is delegated to an entity active in the market that combines or mixes regulatory and commercial activities, the competition rules may be applied even to the regulatory activities involved.

(iii) Public constraints on private parties and private constraints on public measures. So far, our discussion has focused on cases where the Court attempted to draw a line between activities related to the public sphere that could be precluded from the application of the competition rules altogether, and activities that should be subject to closer scrutiny. The focus of this was the application of free movement to private parties and the application of the competition rules to public bodies.

It has become clear that the Court takes a functional approach to free movement and consequently appears headed for recognising horizontal direct effect, i.e. subjecting private parties to the free movement rules. Concerning the application of the competition laws, however, in a number of cases where restrictions were self-evident and no formal public interest exceptions existed, the Court has compensated this by not applying the competition rules to certain activities with a public interest dimension. *Wouters*, *Medina* and *Albany* are prime examples of this.

As regards the application of the competition rules to public bodies, teleology is central, given that the concept of *effet utile* is based on the good faith clause of the Treaty as an agreement between Member States. Since *Meng*, however, a link with pre-existing illegal private restrictions of competition is clearly required. If a link between State regulation and concerted action is established, the question arises if the undertakings involved are protected from the application of the competition rules? The answer to this question is simple: if national legislation leaves undertakings sufficient (even limited) freedom either to compete, or to restrain competition at their own initiative, the competition rules can be infringed and therefore applied.

On balance so far the *effet utile* line of case law, which initially appeared to herald a new age with the end of corporatism and State-organised collusive practices, has proven to be a damp squib. As is demonstrated in such cases as *Librandi* and *Arduino*, the procedural guarantees required to avoid illegal forms of delegation of decision-making are by now minimal. *CIF* may give a new lease of life to *effet utile* by enabling its application by national competition authorities at least in theory, but in the absence of stronger support by the Court few authorities are likely to take up this invitation to test the limits of their credibility.

In the second part of this book, we have examined the interface between the public and private realms as it was explicitly provided for in the Treaty itself: i.e. the exceptions for public undertakings, and State aids.

(iv) Article 31 EC: commercial state monopolies. So far, the Court appears to accept that commercial monopolies can remain justified. We believe that, in accordance with pre-emption, it will strike them down only where a Community standard for the public interest concerned is available, because only that would enable it to apply a strict proportionality test to the creation or maintenance of monopoly itself. This squares with the observations concerning the scope of the public sphere under the competition rules made earlier – notably concerning the Court's approach to book price maintenance in *Au Blé Vert*.[1]

The present Article 31 EC loophole, if such it is, is to be found in the loose proportionality test applied under Article 86(2) EC and the absence of a definition of what constitutes a legitimate 'public interest' that merits exceptions to the competition and free movement rules. In any event, the 1997 *Electricity* cases indicate a convergence of applicable public interest standards on free movement and competition, which we have examined further under Article 86 EC.

(v) Article 86(1): public undertakings, special and exclusive rights. Article 86 EC on exclusive and special rights is an elaboration of the principle of Community 'good faith' set out in Article 10 EC that formed the basis of the Article 81 EC *effet utile* case law.

---

[1] Case 229/83 *Leclerc* v. *Au Blé Vert* [1985] ECR 1.

Neither the creation nor the extension of a monopoly by means of exclusive rights are incompatible with Article 86 EC. However, exclusive and special rights involving distortions of competition are illegal, barring the exceptions provided in Article 86(2) EC and elsewhere in the Treaty. If exclusive and special rights are contested as constituting (part of) an Article 82 EC abuse under Article 86(1) EC no public interest derogations exist. However, just as was found to be the case for *effet utile*, the abuse test requires the existence of a formal link between the award of the special or exclusive right and the alleged abuse. Where Article 86 (1) EC is applied in combination with Articles 28 and 49 EC (free movement), non-economic justifications in the general interest may be relevant.

The Court's reading of Article 86 EC completes the triangle that links the Treaty rules on free movement and competition across the public/ private divide:

- the Court's reading of the competition rules as intended to bar private restrictive practices replacing quantitative restrictions and measures of equivalent effect;
- the *effet utile* approach to the competition rules to bar the Member States from depriving these rules of their effect by sanctioning such private restrictions; and
- Article 86 EC forms the third link between the private and public regimes concerning the free movement and competition rules, barring restrictions by means of statutory monopolies.

In each case, the focus of the Court is on foreclosure of markets, especially by means of enforcing proportionality and non-discrimination requirements.

The effective scope of the Article 86(1) EC prohibition is determined by, on the one hand, the margins left to national public interest considerations such as allowed under Articles 28, 46 and 86(2) EC and, on the other hand, pre-emption. It is illegal to award special and exclusive rights that include regulatory duties placing an undertaking 'at an obvious advantage over its competitors' (as found in *RTT* v. *GB-INNO-BM*), and the exercise of regulatory powers can lead to a finding of an infringement of the competition rules. However, the delegation of rule-making functions is saved when the exercise of regulatory powers by the undertaking involved is justified by the public interest, and adequate procedural guarantees ensure that these powers cannot be abused. For instance, the technical complexity of a regulatory task may require it to be performed by an undertaking, provided there is adequate judicial scrutiny. Again, the standard applied here comes close to that of illegal delegation under *effet utile*.

With these observations, we now come to Article 86(2) EC on services of general economic interest.

(vi) Article 86(2) EC: derogation for services of general economic interest. The Article 86 EC standard is that creating (public or private) monopolies remains warranted, so long as their mere creation does not make abuse unavoidable, or they are otherwise clearly linked to abuse.[2] This involves both a justification of the exclusive right in public interest terms and a proportionality test. Any restrictions concerned must be proportional (necessary) both in relation to the general economic interest defined at national level and to the Community interest concerned.

Services of general economic interest are defined in line with subsidiarity and pre-emption: where there is no Community norm that has occupied the field (pre-emption), the lighter 'manifestly disproportionate' administrative law test prevails; where pre-emption has occurred, Member States may only intervene based on 'the least restrictive means'. At the same time, liberalisation creates the need for defining services of general economic interest. The spill-over of liberalisation from commercial and production monopolies of goods to network services and more recently to social services makes this an area of particular interest.

In the *Electricity* cases, the Court has been willing to accept an Article 86(2) EC defence even for import and export monopolies. One way out of this stalemate occurs where the Community can pre-empt autonomous Member State action. This would be the case where either the Commission has sufficient confidence to provide a coherent Article 86 (3) EC framework, as in the case of State aid (*Altmark Trans*), or the Council achieves political agreement on harmonised standards, as eventually occurred in the energy sector.

Moreover, finding a majority in favour of harmonisation or relying on the independent powers of the Commission may not always be necessary. As social services become increasingly difficult to fund without a significant degree of recourse to the market mechanism, in the context of liberalisation, Member States may be hampered by the competition and free movement rules in protecting core public services. This means they may eventually favour a formal legal act to bring that core within the haven of services of general economic interest.

---

[2] Case C-323/93 *La Crespelle* [1994] ECR I-5080; Case C-179/90 *Merci* [1991] ECR I-5889.

Consequently, it is submitted here that services of general economic interest may, instead of being used as an ad hoc legal defence, come to be applied as a full-fledged legal instrument, if not the main source of exceptions to market freedoms in the social sphere.

(vii) Articles 87–8 EC: State aid. The prohibition in Article 87 covers all aid granted by a Member State or through State resources and there is no necessity to draw any distinction according to whether the aid is granted directly by the State or by public or private bodies established or appointed to administer the aid.

As concerns the distinction between legislative and financial measures made in Article 87(1) EC, the Court refuses to interpret this as having any bearing on the body granting the aid, but also denies that it implies a distinction regarding the *nature* of the aid. In practice, however, it takes a strict view of financial measures and a lenient view on legislative ones.

Key to a finding of aid is the private investor test. This test is not an inflexible short-term profit maximisation standard: it is capable of taking a long-term perspective. However, the private investor test does not take financial interests that go beyond profit, albeit long term, into account: it is not a rational public authority test. The counterpart of this reasoning is that costs incurred to fulfil 'typical' obligations of a public authority, such as investments in infrastructure and training, are not considered to be aid.

Concerning the application of State aid to services of general economic interest in *Altmark Trans*, the Court has clarified four criteria which, if met, lead to the conclusion that no State aid is at stake. The Commission has clarified this rule further with an Article 86(3) EC notice and Decision, the first horizontal rules based on Article 86(3) EC since the 1988 Transparency Directive. Where free movement rules and the State aid rules are at stake, it will suffice if an infringement of the free movement rules is found.

(viii) Summary: The results of the book's exercise as a whole can be summarised as follows.

It has turned out that neither *Ordo*liberalism in its idealistic view of the Treaty as a kind of sacrosanct market-based metanorm not subject to the tug and pull of politics nor the backward looking *service public* approach, which has merely managed to stall the debate on services of general economic interest, are particularly revealing as prisms on the case law of the Court. At best they have helped to colour the incomparably greater influence of the dialectics of the Court's case law on

European integration, notably its goal-oriented character (teleology) and its functional growth in a process that might uncharitably be dubbed as contamination of new sectors that, once touched, are inexorably dragged into the universe of EU law.

It is also true that the November 1993 revolution can be described as a watershed, but not so much one which led to the curtailment of EU law as a rationalisation based on a new understanding of the limits of the possible in terms of integration by law, as a measure of healthy scepticism concerning the need to see every type of governmental action in EU law terms. Indeed, a few years later, it has become clear that private restraints on competition are much more likely not to be held to infringe the competition rules than was previously thought. In both cases, pre-emption, as it already existed in free movement, is playing an ever more central role in resolving State action issues. Furthermore, it has become clear with *Albany* that whether or not the Treaty will come to be restated as a formal constitution, the Court is already treating it as a comprehensive system.

As expected, the case law of the Court is guided in many of the borderline cases by functionalism rather than formal categories and by teleology, in other words further integration and combating foreclosure of national markets. However, horizontal widening of the scope of EU law along these lines tends to go hand in hand with vertical withdrawal.

The two key variables are proportionality and pre-emption, which are linked as follows. The Court tends to follow the more modest test of '(not) manifestly disproportionate' to rule on cases where secondary Community law has not yet occupied the field and where there is therefore less democratic legitimacy for judicial intervention. Where secondary rules exist, it tends to be more strict and use the least restrictive means test and to rely more on formal categories. Moreover, it should be emphasised that where the importance of the rule of reason is increasing, so is that of proportionality: this is the key test of both public and private restrictions of competition and free movement and as such is likely to be the subject of future developments.

Since cases like *Albany*, teleology now cuts both ways, and *Wouters* and *Medina* suggest that an even more fundamental change in the direction of a rule of reason test under the competition rules (such as already existed for free movement) may be under way. This would further increase the importance of pre-emption and proportionality. A de minimis rule likewise applies to the free movement as well as, increasingly, the competition rules. The importance of Article 86(2) EC appears to be increasing as a leading exception to free movement and competition rules, especially now that its interpretation in the area of State aid has been clarified and, if the Member States start making use of this provision proactively, rather than as a defence of last resort.

Most unpredictable is probably the future of *effet utile*. On the one hand, minor procedural public interest guarantees by now tend to suffice, and a link with anti-competitive behaviour is required that is all the less likely to be found given the tentative adoption of a rule of reason approach to private constraints of competition. This is mirrored by the link needed between the creation of a monopoly and infringements of the competition rules. The common bottom line seems to be strict checks on foreclosure based on non-discrimination and – in the presence of pre-emption – proportionality. It is clear that there is a dialectical relationship between harmonisation (including Article 86(3) EC measures) and the case law of the Court in free movement and competition moving European law on competition and free movement inexorably forward. The main new ground broken may yet turn out to be *CIF* by handing the torch of EU law activism on the borderline between the public and private spheres to those national authorities that feel up to the task – adding a new variable to the aforementioned dialectic process.

References

Amable, Bruno, *The Diversity of Modern Capitalism* (Oxford University Press, 2003).

Aman, Alfred C. Jr, 'Globalization, Democracy, and the Need for a New Administrative Law', (2002) 49 *UCLA Law Review* 1687.

Amato, Giuliano, *Antitrust and the Bounds of Power – The Dilemma of Liberal Democracy in the History of the Market* (Oxford: Hart, 1997).

Il Gusto della Libertà (Bari: Laterza, 1998).

Andenas, Mads and Roth, Wulf-Henning (eds.), *Services and Free Movement in EU Law* (Oxford University Press, 2003).

Arrowsmith, Sue, 'Deregulation of Utilities Procurement in the Changing Economy: Towards a Principled Approach?', (1997) 7 *European Competition Law Review* 420.

'The EC Public Procurement Directives, National Procurement Policies and Better Governance: The Case for a New Approach', (2002) 27 *European Law Review* 3.

The Law of Public and Utililities Procurement 2nd rev. edn (London: Sweet & Maxwell, 2005).

Ashiagbor, Diamond, *The European Employment Strategy: Labour Market Regulation and New Governance* (Oxford University Press, 2006).

Auby, Jean-François, 'La Délégation de Service Public: Premier Bilan et Perspectives', [1996] *Revue du Droit Public* 1095.

Bach, Albrecht, *Wettbewerbsrechtliche Schranken für staatliche Maßnahmen nach europäischem Gemeinschaftsrecht* (Tübingen: Mohr, 1992).

Bacon, Kelyn, 'State Aids and General Measures', (1997) 17 *Yearbook of European Law* 269.

'State Regulation of the Market and EC Competition Rules: Articles 85 and 86 Compared', (1997) 18 *European Competition Law Review* 283.

Badura, Peter, 'Die Organisations- und Personalhoheit des Mitgliedstaates in der Europäischen Union' in O. Due, M. Lutter and J. Schwarze (eds.), *Festschrift für Ulrich Everling* (Baden-Baden: Nomos, 1995), p. 33.

Baquero Cruz, Julio, *Between Competition and Free Movement: The Economic Constitutional Law of the European Community* (Oxford: Hart, 2002).

'Beyond Competition: Services of General Interest and European Community Law' in G. de Búrca (ed.), *EU Law and the Welfare State: In Search of Solidarity* (Oxford University Press, 2005), p. 169.

Barnard, Catherine, *The Substantive Law of the EU – The Four Freedoms* (Oxford University Press, 2004).

Basedow, Jürgen, *Von der deutschen zur europäischen Wirtschaftsverfassung* (Tübingen: Mohr, 1992).

Becker, Ulrich, 'Von "Dassonville" über "Cassis" zu "Keck" – Der Begriff der Maßnahmen gleicher Wirkung in Art. 30 EGV', (1994) 29 *Europarecht* 162.

Beckert, Jens, *et al.* (eds.), *Transformationen des Kapitalismus* (Frankfurt a.M.: Campus, 2006).

Behrens, Peter, 'Die Wirtschaftsverfassung der Europäischen Gemeinschaft' in G. Brüggemeier (ed.), *Verfassungen für ein ziviles Europa* (Baden-Baden: Nomos, 1994), p. 78.

'Das wirtschaftsverfassungsrechtliche Profil des Konventsentwurfs einer Vertrags über einer Verfassung für Europa' in A. Fuchs, H.-P. Schwintowski and D. Zimmer (eds.), *Festschrift für Ulrich Immenga zum 70. Geburtstag* (Munich: Beck, 2004), p. 21.

Belloubet-Frier, Nicole, 'Service Public et Droit Communautaure', (1994) 20 *Actualité Juridique – Édition Droit Administratif* 270.

Benz, Arthur, 'Postparlamentarische Demokratie? Demokratische Legitimation im kooperativen Staat' in M. Th. Greven (ed.), *Demokratie – eine Kultur des Westens?* (Opladen: Leske & Budrich, 1998), p. 201.

Bercusson, Brian, 'The Trade Union Movement and the European Union: Judgment Day', (2007) 13 *European Law Journal* 279.

Binon, Jean-Marc, 'Solidarité et Assurance: Mariage de Coeur ou de Raison?', [1997] *Revue du Marché Unique Européen* 87.

Biondi, Andrea, 'Justifying State Aid: The Financing of Services of General Economic Interest' in T. Tridimas and P. Nebbia (eds.), *European Union Law for the Twenty-First Century* (Oxford: Hart, 2004), Vol. 2, p. 259.

'Some Reflections on the Notion of "State Resources" in European Community State Aid Law', (2007) 30 *Fordham International Law Journal* 1426.

Biondi, Andrea, Eeckhout, Piet and Flynn, James (eds.), *The Law of State Aid in the European Union* (Oxford University Press, 2004).

Biondi, Andrea and Rubini, Luca, 'Aims, Effects, and Justifications: EC State Aid Law and Its Impact on National Social Policies' in M. Dougan and E. Spaventa (eds.), *Social Welfare and EU Law* (Oxford: Hart, 2005), p. 79.

Black, Julia, 'Constitutionalising Self-Regulation', (1996) 59 *Modern Law Review* 24.

Boeger, Nina, 'Solidarity and EC Competition Law', (2007) 32 *European Law Review* 319.

Van den Bogaert, Stefaan, 'Horizontality: The Court Attacks?' in C. Barnard and J. Scott (eds.), *The Law of the Single Market – Unpacking the Premises* (Oxford: Hart, 2002), p. 23.

Böhm, Franz, 'Privatrechtgesellschaft und Marktwirtschaft', (1969) 17 *Ordo* 75.

Boutayeb, Chahira, 'Une Recherche sur la Place et les Functions de l'Intérêt Général en Droit Communautaire', (2003) 39 *Revue Trimestrielle de Droit Européen* 587.

Bovis, Christopher, 'Financing Services of General Interest, Public Procurement and State Aids: The Delineation Between Market Forces and Protection in the European Common Market', [2005] *Journal of Business Law* 1.

EC Public Procurement – Caselaw and Regulation (Oxford University Press, 2006).

Boysen, Sigrid and Neukirchen, Mathias, *Europäisches Beihilferecht und mitgliedstaatliche Daseinsvorsorge* (Baden-Baden: Nomos, 2007).

Braconnier, Stéphane, *Droit des Services Publics*, 2nd edn (Paris: Presses Universitaires de France, 2007).

Bright, Christopher, 'Article 90, Economic Policy and the Duties of the Member States', (1993) 4 *European Competition Law Review* 263.

Brown, Adrian, 'The Extension of the Community Public Procurement Rules to Utilities', (1993) 30 *Common Market Law Review* 721.

Buendia Sierra, José Luis, *Exclusive Rights and State Monopolies in EC Law* (Oxford University Press, 1999).

'Article 86 – Exclusive Rights and other Anti-competitive State Measures' in J. Faull and A. Nikpay (eds.), *The EC Law of Competition*, 2nd edn (Oxford University Press, 2007).

De Búrca, Gráinne, 'The Principle of Proportionality and its Application in EC Law', (1993) 13 *Yearbook of European Law* 105.

'The Constitutional Challenge of New Governance in the European Union', (2003) 28 *European Law Review* 814.

Cassese, Sabino, *La Nuova Costituzione Economica* (Bari: Laterza, 1996).

'La Costituzione Economica Europea', (2001) 11 *Rivista Italiana di Diritto Pubblico Comunitario* 907.

Castillo de la Torre, Fernando, 'State Action Defence in EC Competition Law', (2005) 28 *World Competition* 407.

Chalmers, Damian, 'Repackaging the Internal Market – The Ramifications of the *Keck* Judgment', (1994) 19 *European Law Review* 385.

'Private Power and Public Authority in European Union Law', (2006) 8 *Cambridge Yearbook of European Legal Studies* 59.

Chevallier, Jacques, 'Regards sur une évolution', (1997) 23 *Actualité Juridique – Édition Droit Administratif*, special issue, 8.

Le Service Public, 6th ed. (Paris: Presses Universitaires de France, 2005).

Chung, Chan-Mo, 'The Relationship Between State Regulation and EC Competition Law: Two Proposals for a Coherent Approach', (1995) 16 *European Competition Law Review* 87.

Coates, Kevin and Sauter, Wolf, 'Communications (Telecoms, Media and Internet)' in J. Faull and A. Nikpay (eds.), *The EC Law of Competition*, 2nd edn (Oxford University Press, 2007), p. 1475.

Cohen-Tanugi, Laurent, *Le Droit sans l' État* (Paris: Presses Universitaires de France, 1985).

Constantinesco, Leontin-Jean, 'La Constitution Économique de la CEE', (1977) 13 *Revue Trimestrielle de Droit Européen* 244.

Craig, Paul, 'The Evolution of the Single Market' in C. Barnard and J. Scott (eds.), *The Law of the Single Market – Unpacking the Premises* (Oxford: Hart, 2002), p. 1.

EU Administrative Law (Oxford University Press, 2006).

Cross, Eugene D., 'Pre-emption of Member State Law in the European Economic Community: A Framework for Analysis', (1992) 29 *Common Market Law Review* 447.

Crouch, Colin, *Capitalist Diversity and Change: Recombinant Governance and Institutional Entrepreneurs* (Oxford University Press, 2005).

'Models of Capitalism', (2005) 10 *New Political Economy* 440.

Crouch, Colin and Streeck, Wolfgang (eds.), *Political Economy of Modern Capitalism: Mapping Convergence and Diversity* (London: Sage, 1997).

Curtin, Deirdre, 'The Province of Government: Delimiting the Direct Effect of Directives in the Common Law Context', (1990) 15 *European Law Review* 195.

Davies, Paul, 'Market Integration and Social Policy in the Court of Justice', (1995) 24 *Industrial Law Journal* 49.

Deckert, Martina and Schroeder, Werner, 'Öffentliche Unternehmen und EG-Beihilferecht', (1998) 33 *Europarecht* 291.

Dehousse, Renaud (ed.), *L'Europe sans Bruxelles? Une Analyse de la Méthode Ouverte de Coordination* (Paris: L'Harmattan, 2004).

Delacour, Eric, 'Services Publics et Concurrence Communautaire', [1996] *Revue du Marché Commun et de l'Union Européenne* 501.

Delors, Jacques, *Le Nouveau Concert Européen* (Paris: Odile Jacob, 1992).

Devolvé, Pierre, 'Les Contradictions de la Délégation de Service Public', [1996] *Actualité Juridique – Édition Droit Administratif* 675.

Devroe, Wouter, 'Privatizations and Community Law: Neutrality Versus Policy', (1997) 34 *Common Market Law Review* 267.

Drexl, Josef, 'Wettbewerbsverfassung- Europäisches Wettbewerbsrecht als materielles Verfassungsrecht' in A. von Bogdandy (ed.), *Europäisches Verfassungsrecht* (Berlin: Springer, 2003), p. 747.

Due, Ole, 'Pourquoi cette Solution? (De Certains Problèmes Concernant la Motivation des Arrêts de la Cour de Justice des Communautés Européennes)' in O. Due, M. Lutter and J. Schwarze (eds.), *Festschrift für Ulrich Everling* (Baden-Baden: Nomos, 1995), p. 273.

Duguit, L., *Law in the Modern State*, tr. H. J. Laski (London: Allen & Unwin, 1921).

Dyson, 'Cultural Issues and the Single European Market: Barriers to Trade and Shifting Attitudes', (1993) 64 *Political Quarterly* 84.

Edward, David and Hoskins, Mark, 'Article 90: Deregulation and EC Law: Reflections Arising From the XVI FIDE Conference', (1995) 32 *Common Market Law Review* 157.

Ehle, Dirk, 'State Regulation Under the US Antitrust State Action Doctrine and Under EC Competition Law: A Comparative Analysis', (1998) 19 *European Competition Law Review* 380.

Ehlermann, Claus-Dieter, 'Neuere Entwicklungen im europäischen Wettbewerbsrecht', (1991) 26 *Europarecht* 307.

'The Contribution of EC Competition Policy to the Single Market', (1992) 29 *Common Market Law Review* 257.

'Managing Monopolies: The Role of the State in Controlling Market Dominance in the European Community', (1993) 14 *European Competition Law Review* 61.

Ehricke, Ulrich, 'Zur Konzeption von Art. 37 I und Art. 90 II EGV', (1998) 8 *Europäische Zeitschrift für Wirtschaftsrecht* 1998.

Elhauge, Einer, 'The Scope of the Antitrust Process', (1991) 104 *Harvard Law Review* 667.

Eichengreen, Barry, *The European Economy Since 1945 – Coordinated Capitalism and Beyond* (Princeton University Press, 2007).

Emiliou, Nicholas, *The Principle of Proportionality in European Law: A Comparative Study* (London: Kluwer, 1996).

Enchelmaier, Stefan, 'The Awkward Selling of a Good idea, or a Traditionalist Interpretation of Keck', (2003) 22 *Yearbook of European Law* 249.

Van der Esch, Bastiaan, 'Dérégulation, Autorégulation et le Régime de Concurrence non Faussée dans la CEE', (1990) 26 *Cahiers de Droit Européen* 499.

'Die Artikel 5, 3f, 85/86 und 90 EWGV als Grundlage der wettbewerbsrechtlichen Verpflichtungen der Mitgliedstaaten', (1991) 155 *Zeitschrift für das gesamte Handelsrecht* 274.

'Loyauté Fédérale et Subsidiarité', (1994) 30 *Cahiers de Droit Européen* 523.

Evans, Andrew, 'Privatisation and State Aid Control in EC Law', (1997) 18 *European Competition Law Review* 259.

Everling, Ulrich, 'Der Einfluß des EG-Rechts auf das nationale Wettbewerbsrecht im Bereich des Täuschungsschutzes', (1994) 21 *Zeitschrift für das gesamte Lebensmittelrecht* 221.

'Wirtschaftsverfassung und Richterrecht in der Europäischen Gemeinschaft' in U. Immenga, W. Möschel and D. Reuter (eds.), *Festschrift für Ernst-Joachim Mestmäcker* (Baden-Baden: Nomos, 1996), p. 365.

Everson, Michelle, 'Adjudicating the Market', (2002) 8 *European Law Journal* 152.

Faull, Jonathan and Nikpay, Ali, *The EC Law of Competition* (Oxford University Press, 1999).

Feldmeier, Gerhard M., *Ordnungspolitische Perspektiven der Europäischen Integration* (Frankfurt a.M.: Lang, 1993).

Fernández Martín, José M. and Stehmann, Oliver, 'Product Market Integration versus Regional Cohesion in the Community', (1991) 16 *European Law Review* 216.

Fernández Martín, José M. and O'Leary, Siofra, 'Judicially-Created Exceptions to the Free Provision of Services' in M. Andenas and W.-H. Roth (eds.), *Services and Free Movement in EU Law* (Oxford University Press, 2002), p. 163.

Ferrera, Maurizio, *The Boundaries of Welfare: European Integration and the New Spatial Politics of Social Protection* (Oxford University Press, 2005).

FIW. *Weiterentwicklung der europäischen Gemeinschaften und der Marktwirkschaft* (Cologne: Carl Heymanns, 1992).

Freeman, Jody, 'Private Parties, Public Functions and the New Administrative Law', (2000) 52 *Administrative Law Review* 813.

'Extending Public Law Norms Through Privatization', (2003) 116 *Harvard Law Review* 1285.

Galmot, Yves, and Biancarelli, Jacques, 'Les Réglementations Nationales en Matière de Prix au Regard du Droit Communautaire', (1985) 21 *Revue Trimestrielle de Droit Européen* 267.

Ganten, Ted Oliver, *Die Drittwirkung der Grundfreiheiten* (Berlin: Duncker & Humblot, 2000).

Gardner, Anthony, 'The Velvet Revolution: Article 90 and the Triumph of the Free Market in Europe's Regulated Sectors', (1995) 16 *European Competition Law Review* 78.

Genschel, Philipp, 'Markt und Staat in Europa', (1998) *Politische Vierjahresschrift* 55.

Geradin, Damien (ed.), *The Liberalization of State Monopolies in the European Union and Beyond* (Deventer: Kluwer, 1999).

(ed.), *The Liberalization of Electricity and Natural Gas in the European Union* (Deventer: Kluwer, 2001).

Gerber, David J., 'Constitutionalizing the Economy: German Neo-liberalism, Competition Law, and the "New" Europe', (1994) 42 *American Journal of Comparitive Law* 25.

Law and Competition in Twentieth Century Europe – Protecting Prometheus (Oxford: Clarendon, 1998).

'The Transformation of European Community Competition Law?', (1994) 35 *Harvard International Law Journal* 25.

Gerstenberg, Oliver, 'Privatrecht, Demokratie und die lange Dauer der bürgerlichen Gesellschaft', (1997) 16 *Rechtshistorisches Journal* 152.

Van Gerven, Walter, 'The recent case-law of the Court of Justice concerning Articles 30 and 36 of the EEC Treaty', (1977) 14 *Common Market Law Review* 5.

'The Effect of Proportionality on the Actions of the Member States of the European Community: National Viewpoints from Continental Europe' in E. Ellis (ed.), *The Principle of Proportionality in the Laws of Europe* (Oxford: Hart, 1999), p. 42.

Gillingham, John, *European Integration 1950–2003 – Superstate or New Market Economy?* (Cambridge University Press, 2003).

Giubboni, Stefano, *Social Rights and Market Freedom in the European Constitution – A Labour Law Perspective* (Cambridge University Press, 2006).

Gormley, Laurence, 'Reasoning Renounced? The Remarkable Judgment in *Keck and Mithouard*', [1994] *European Business Law Review* 63.

Goyder, D. G., *EC Competition Law*, 4th edn (Oxford: Oxford University Press, 2003).

Graham, Cosmo, and Prosser, Tony, *Privatizing Public Enterprises: Constitutions, the State and Regulations in Comparative Perspective* (Oxford: Clarendon, 1991).

Grard, Loïc, Vandamme, Jacques and van der Mensbrugghe, François (eds.), *Vers un Service Public Européen* (Paris: ASP Europe, 1996).

Grimm, Dieter, 'Does Europe need a Constitution?', (1995) 1 *European Law Journal* 282.

Von der Groeben, Hans, 'Zur Wirtschaftsordnung der europäischen Gemeinschaft' in H. Von der Groeben, *Die europäische Gemeinschaft und die Herausforderungen unserer Zeit* (Baden-Baden: Nomos, 1981), p. 201.

'Probleme einer europäischen Wirtschaftsordnung' in J. F. Baur, P.-C. Müller-Graff and M. Zuleeg (eds.), *Europarecht, Energierecht, Wirtschaftsrecht. Festschrift für Bodo Börner* (Cologne: Carl Heymanns, 1992), p. 99.

Gromnicka, Ewa, 'Services of General Economic Interest in the State Aids Regime: Proceduralisation of Political Choices?', (2005) 11 *European Public Law* 429.

Günther, Klaus, '"Ohne weiteres und ganz automatisch"? Zur Wiederentdeckung der Privatrechtsgesellschaft', (1992) 11 *Rechtshistorisches Journal* 473.

Gyselen, Luc, 'State Action and the Effectiveness of the EEC Treaty's Competition Provisions', (1989) 26 *Common Market Law Review* 33.

'Anti-Competitive State Measures under the EC Treaty: Towards a Substantive Legality Standard', (1994) 19 *European Law Review* 55, p. 61.

Hall, Peter A. and Soskice, David (eds.), *Varieties of Capitalism: The Institutional Foundations of Comparative Advantage* (Oxford University Press, 2001).

Hancher, Leigh, 'Artikel 90 EEG – Minder troebel, maar nog niet helder', (1993) 41 *Social-Economische Wetgering* 328.

Hancher, Leigh and Buendia Sierra, José Luis, 'Cross-subsidization and EC Law', (1998) 35 *Common Market Law Review* 901.

Hancher, Leigh, Slot, Piet Jan and Ottervanger, T. R. (eds.), *EC State Aids*, 2nd rev. edn (London: Sweet & Maxwell, 2006).

Hancké, Bob, Rhodes, Martin and Thatcher, Mark (eds.), *Beyond Varieties of Capitalism: Conflict, Contradictions and Complementarities in the European Economy* (Oxford University Press, 2007).

Hannsler, Martin and Kilian, Matthias, 'Die Ausübung hoheitlicher Gewalt im Sinne des Art. 45 EG', (2005) 40 *Europarecht* 192.

Hatje, Armin, 'Wirtschaftsverfassung' in A. von Bogdandy (ed.), *Europäisches Verfassungsrecht* (Berlin: Springer, 2003), p. 683.

Héritier, Adrienne (ed.), *Policy-Analyse. Kritik und Neuorientierung, Sonderheft Politische Vierteljahresschrift* 24 (Opladen: Leske & Budrich, 1993).

Hervey, Tamara K., 'The Current Legal Framework on the Right to Seek Healthcare Abroad in the European Union', (2007) 9 *Cambridge Yearbook of European Legal Studies* 261.

Hirst, Paul, and Thompson, Graham, *Globalization in Question. The International Economy and the Possibilities of Governance* (Cambridge: Polity, 1996).

Hochbaum, 'Artikel 90' in Hoffmann-Riem, Wolfgang and Schmidt-Aßmann, Eberhard (eds.), *Öffentliches Recht und Privatrecht als wechselseitige Auffangordnungen* (Baden-Baden: Nomos, 1996).

Hollingsworth, J. Rogers, Schmitter, Philippe C. and Streeck, Wolfgang (eds.), *Governing Capitalist Economies: Performance and Control of Economic Sectors* (Oxford: Oxford University Press, 1994).

Hollingsworth, J. Rogers and Boyer, Robert (eds.), *Contemporary Capitalism: The Embeddedness of Institutions* (Cambridge: Cambridge University Press, 1999).

Jarass, Hans D., 'A Unified Approach to the Fundamental Freedoms,' in M. Andenas and W.-H. Roth (eds.), *Services and Free Movement in EU Law* (Oxford: Oxford University Press, 2002), p. 141.

Jickeli, Joachim, 'Der Binnenmarkt im Schatten des Subsidiaritätsprinzips', (1995) 50 *Juristen Zeitung* 57.

Joerges, Christian, 'Markt ohne Staat? Die Wirtschaftsverfassung der Gemeinschaft und die regulative Politik' in R. Wildenmann (ed.), *Staatswerdung Europas? Optionen für eine europäische Union* (Baden-Baden: Nomos, 1991), p. 225.

'European Economic Law, the Nation-State and the Maastricht Treaty' in R. Dehousse (ed.), *Europe after Maastricht* (Munich: Beck, 1994), p. 29.

'The Impact of European Integration on Private Law: Reductionist Perceptions, True Conflicts and a New Constitutionalist Perspective', (1997) 3 *European Law Journal* 378.

'What is Left of the European Economic Constitution? A Melancholic Eulogy', (2005) 30 *European Law Review* 461.

Joliet, René, 'Réglementations Étatiques Anticoncurrentielles et Droit Communautaire', (1988) 24 *Cahiers de Droit Européen* 363.

Jourdan, Philippe, 'La Formation du Concept de Service Public', (1987) *Revue de Droit Public* 89.

Judt, Tony, *Postwar – A History of Europe Since 1945* (London: Penguin, 2005).

Karydis, Georges, 'Le Principe de l' "Opérateur Économique Privé", Critère de Qualification des Measures Étatiques, en tant qu'aides d'Etat, au sens de l'Article 87(1) du Traité CE', (2003) 39 *Revue Trimestrielle de Droit Européen* 389.

Kenis, Patrick and Schneider, Volker (eds.), *Organisation und Netzwerk-Institutionelle Steuerung in Wirtschaft und Politik* (Frankfurt a.M.: Campus, 1996).

Kingreen, Thorsten, 'Grundfreiheiten' in A. von Bogdandy (ed.), *Europäisches Verfassungsrecht* (Berlin: Springer, 2003), p. 631.

Klasse, Max, *Gemeinschaftsrechtliche Grenzen für staatlich veranlasste Wettbewerbsbeschränkungen* (Baden-Baden: Nomos, 2006).

Kluth, Winfried, 'Die Bindung privater Wirtschaftsteilnehmer und die Grundfreiheiten des EG-Vertrages', (1997) 122 *Archiv des öffentlichen Rechts* 227.

Knaul, Andreas and Flores, Francisco Pérez, 'State Aid' in J. Faull and A. Nikpay (eds.), *The EC Law of Competition*, 2nd ed. (Oxford: Oxford University Press, 2007), p. 1703.

Koenig, Christian, Bartosch, Andreas and Braun, Jens-Daniel (eds.), *EC Competition and Telecommunications Law: A Practitioner's Guide* (New York: Aspen, 2002).

Kovar, Robert, 'Droit Communautaire et Service Public: Esprit d'Orthodoxie ou Pensée Laïcisée', (1996) 32 Revue Trimestrielle de Droit Européen 215, p. 493.

'Dassonville, Keck et les Autres: de la Mesure Avant Toute Chose,' (2006) 42 Revue Trimestrielle de Droit Européen 213.

Krajewski, Markus and Farley, Martin, 'Non-economic Activities in Upstream and Downstream Markets and the Scope of Competition Law after Fenin', (2007) 32 European Law Review 111.

Kurcz, Bartlomiej and Vallindas, Dimitri, 'Can General Measures Be...Selective? Some Thoughts on the Interpretation of a State Aid Definition', (2008) 45 Common Market Law Review 159.

Laigre, Philippe, 'Les Organismes de Sécurité Sociale sont-ils des Entreprises?', [1993] Droit Social 488.

'L'Intrusion du Droit Communautaire de la Concurrence dans le Champ et la Protection Sociale', [1996] Droit Social 82.

'Régimes de Sécurité Sociale et Entreprises d'Assurance', [1996] Droit Social 705.

Lane, Jennifer, 'Public Procurement, Public Bodies and the General Interest: Perspectives from Higher Education', (2005) 11 European Law Journal 487.

Linotte, Didier and Romi, Raphaël, Services Publics et Droit Public Économique, 5th edn. (Paris: Litec, 2003).

Lohse, Eva Julia, 'Fundamental Freedoms and Private Actors – towards an "Incidental Horizontal Effect"', (2007) 13 European Public Law 159.

Loughlin, Martin, 'The Functionalist Style in Public Law', (2005) 55 University of Toronto Law Journal 361.

Louis, Jean-Victor and Rodrigues, Stéphane (eds.), Les Services d'Intérêt Économique Général et l'Union Européenne (Brussels: Bruylant, 2006).

Lowe, Philip, 'Telecommunications Services and Competition Law in Europe', (1994) 5 European Business Law Review 139.

Lyon-Caen, Antoine, 'Le Financement Public d'un Plan Social est-il Condamné par le Droit Communautaire?', [1997] Droit Social 185.

'Les Services Publics et l'Europe: quelle Union?', (1997) 23 Actualité Juridique – Édition Droit Administratif 33.

Majone, Giandomenico, 'The Rise of the Regulatory State in Europe', (1994) 17 West European Politics 77.

'Paradoxes of Privatization and Deregulation', (1994) 1 Journal of European Public Policy 54.

'From the Positive to the Regulatory State: Causes and Consequences of Changes in the Mode of Governance', (1997) 17 Journal of Public Policy 139.

Mancini, G. Federico, 'The Free Movement of Workers in the Case-Law of the European Court of Justice' in D. Curtin and D. O'Keeffe (eds.), Constitutional Adjudication in European Community and National Law (Dublin: Butterworths, 1992), p. 67.

Marchegiani, Giannangelo, 'La nozione di stato inteso in senso funzionale nelle direttive comunitarie in materia di appalti pubblici e sua rilevanza nel contesto generale del diritto comunitario', (2002) 12 Rivista Italiana di Diritto Pubblico Comunitario 1233.

Marenco, Giuliano, 'Le Traité CEE Interdit-il aux Etats Membres de Restreindre la Concurrence?', (1986) 22 *Cahiers de Droit Européen* 285.

'Government Action and Antitrust in the United States: What Lessons for Community Law?', (1987) 14 *Legal Issues of European Integration* 1.

Mattera, Alfonso, 'De l'Arrêt 'Dassonville' à l'Arrêt 'Keck': l'Obscure Clarté d'une Jurisprudence Riche en Principes Novateurs et en Contradictions', (1994) *Revue du Marché Unique Européen* 117.

Matthies, Heinrich, 'Artikel 30 EG-Vertrag nach Keck' in O. Due, M. Lutter and J. Schwarze (eds.), *Festschrift für Ulrich Everling* (Baden-Baden: Nomos, 1995), p. 803.

Mavridis, Prodromos, 'Régimes Complémentaires: Droit de la Concurrence ou Droit Social Communautaire?', [1998] *Droit Social* 239.

La Sécurité Sociale à l' Épreuve de l'Intégration Européenne (Brussels: Bruylant, 2003).

Mayntz, Renate and Scharpf, Fritz W. (eds.), *Gesellschaftliche Selbstregelung und Politische Steuerung* (Frankfurt a.M.: Campus, 1996).

'Politische Steuerung: Aufstieg, Niedergang und Transformation einer Theorie', [1995] *Politische Vierteljahresschrift Sonderheft* 26, 149.

Menz, Georg, *Varieties of Capitalism and Europeanization: National Response Strategies to the Single European Market* (Oxford University Press, 2005).

Merola, Massimo and Medina, Caroline, 'De l'Arrêt Ferring à l'Arrêt Altmark: Continuité ou Revirement dans l'Approche des Services Publics, [2003] *Cahiers de Droit Européen* 639.

Mestmäcker, Ernst-Joachim, 'Auf dem Wege zur einer Ordnungspolitik für Europa' in E.-J. Mestmäcker, H. Möller and H.-P. Schwarz (eds.), *Eine Ordnungspolitik für Europa- Festschrift Von der Groeben* (Baden-Baden: Nomos, 1987), p. 9.

'Staat und Unternehmen im europäischen Gemeinschaftsrecht', (1988) 52 *Rabels Zeitschrift* 526, p. 527.

'Der Kampf ums Recht in der offene Gesellschaft', (1989) 20 *Rechtstheorie* 273.

'Die Wiederkehr der bürgerlichen Gesellschaft und ihres Rechts', (1991) 10 *Rechtshistorisches Journal* 177.

'Zur Anwendbarkeit der Wettbewerbsregeln auf die Mitgliedstaaten und die Europäischen Gemeinschaften' in J. Baur, P.-C. Müller-Graf and M. Zuleeg (eds.), *Europarecht, Energierecht, Wirtschaftsrecht: Festschrift für Bodo Börner zum 70. Geburtstag* (Cologne: Carl Heymanns, 1992).

'Zur Wirtschaftsverfassung in der Europäischen Union' in R. H. Hasse, J. Molsberger and Ch. Watrin (eds.), *Ordnung in Freiheit- Festschrift für Hans Willgerodt* (Stuttgart: Fischer, 1994), p. 263.

'On the Legitimacy of European Law', (1994) 58 *Rabels Zeitschrift* 615.

Wirtschaft und Verfassung in der Europäischen Union (Baden-Baden: Nomos, 2003).

Van Miert, Karel, 'Les Missions d'Intérêt Général et l'Article 90§2 du Traité CE dans la Politique de la Commission', (1997) 2 *Il diritto dell'economia* 277.

MonopolKommission, *Hauptgutachten 1988/1989: Weltbewerbspolitk vor neuen Herausforderungen* (Baden-Baden: Nomos, 1990).

Monti, Giorgio, 'Article 81 EC and Public Policy', (2002) 39 *Common Market Law Review* 1057.

Moral Soriano, Leonor, 'How Proportionate Should Anti-competitive State Intervention Be?', (2003) 28 *European Law Review* 112.

'Public Services: The Role of the European Court of Justice in Correcting the Market' in D. Coen and A. Héritier (eds.), *Refining Regulatory Regimes: Utilities in Europe* (Cheltenham: Elgar, 2005), p. 183.

Moran, Michael and Prosser, Tony (eds.), *Privatization and Regulatory Change in Europe* (Buckingham: Open University Press, 1994).

Mortelmans, Kamiel, 'Towards Convergence in the Application of the Rules on Free Movement and on Competition', (2001) 38 *Common Market Law Review* 613.

Möschel, Wernhard, 'Hoheitliche Maßnahmen und die Wettbewerbsvorschriften des Gemeinschaftsrechts' in FIW, *Weiterentwicklung der europäischen Gemeinschaften und der Marktwirtschaft* (Cologne: Carl Heymanns, 1992).

'Kehrtwende in der Rechtsprechung in der EuGH zur Warenverkehrsfreiheit', (1994) 47 *Neue Juristische Wochenschrift* 429.

'Wird die effet utile Rechtssprechung des EuGH inutile?', (1994) 47 *Neue Juristische Wochenschrift* 1709.

'Competition as a Basic Element of the Social Market Economy', (2001) 2 *European Business Organization Law Review* 713.

Müller-Armack, Alfred, *Wirtschaftsordnung und wirtschaftspolitik. studien und konzepte zur sozialen marktwirtschaft und zur europäischen integration* (Freiburg im Breisgau: Rombach, 1966).

Müller-Graff, Peter-Christian, 'Die wettbewerbsverfaßte Marktwirtschaft als gemeineuropäisches Verfassungsprinzip?', (1997) 31 *Europarecht* 422.

Müller-Graff, Peter-Christian and Eibe Riedel (eds.), *Gemeinsames verfassungsrecht in der europäischen union* (Baden-Baden: Nomos, 1998).

Munanza, Elisabetta, 'Privatised Services and the Concept of "Bodies Governed by Public Law" in EC Directives on Public Procurement', (2003) 28 *European Law Review* 273.

Naftel, Mark, 'The Natural Death of a Natural Monopoly: Competition in EC Telecommunications after the Telecommunications Terminals Judgment', (1993) 14 *European Competition Law Review* 105.

Napolitano, Giorgio, 'Towards a European Legal Order for Services of General Economic Interest', (2005) 11 *European Public Law* 565.

Nicolaides, Phedon, 'Compensation for Public Service Obligations: The Floodgates of State Aid', (2003) 24 *European Law Review* 651.

Nihoul, Paul and Rodford, Peter, *EU Electronic Communications Law – Competition and Regulation in the European Telecommunications Market* (Oxford University Press, 2004).

Odudu, Okeoghene, 'The Meaning of Undertaking Within Article 81', (2005) 7 *Cambridge Yearbook of European Legal Studies* 211.

The Boundaries of EC Competition Law – The Scope of Article 81 (Oxford University Press, 2006).

O'Keeffe, David, 'Judicial Interpretation of the Public Service Exception to the Free Movement of Workers' in D. Curtin and D. O'Keeffe (eds.), *Constitutional Adjudication in European Community and National Law* (Dublin: Butterworths, 1992), p. 89.

Oliver, Dawn, *Common Values and the Public/Private Divide* (London: Butterworths, 1999).

Oliver, Peter, 'Some Further Reflections on the Scope of Articles 28–30 (ex 30–36) EC', (1999) 36 *Common Market Law Review* 783.

Oliver, Peter and Enchelmaier, Stefan, 'Free Movement of Goods: Recent Developments in the Caselaw', (2007) 44 *Common Market Law Review* 649.

Oliver, Peter and Roth, Wulf-Henning, 'The Internal Market and the Four Freedoms', (2004) 41 *Common Market Law Review* 407.

Oppermann, Thomas, 'Europäische wirtschaftsverfassung nach den einheitlichen europäischen Akte' in P.-Ch. Müller-Graff and M. Zuleeg (eds.), *Staat und Wirtschaft in der EG* (Baden-Baden: Nomos, 1987), p. 53.

Organisation for Economic Cooperation and Development, *Regulatory Reform, Privatisation and Competition Policy* (Paris: OECD, 1992).

Pais Antunes, Luis Miguel, 'L'Article 90 du Traité CEE', [1991] *Revue Trimestrielle de Droit Européen* 187.

Pappalardo, Aurelio, 'Die Europäische Gerichtshof auf der Suche nach einem Kriterium für die Anwendung der Wettbewerbsregeln auf staatliche Maßnahmen' in E.-J. Mestmäcker, H. Möller and H.-P. Schwarz (eds.), *Eine Ordnungspolitik für Europa* (Baden-Baden: Nomos, 1987), p. 303.

'State Measures and Public Undertakings: Article 90 of the Treaty Revisited', (1991) 12 *European Competition Law Review* 29.

Parish, Matthew, 'On the Private Investor Principle', (2003) 28 *European Law Review* 70.

Paulis, Emil, 'Les Etats peuvent-ils Enfreindre les Article 85 et 86 du Traité CEE?', (1985) 104 *Journal des Tribunaux – Droit Européen* 209.

Pescatore, Pierre, 'Le Carence du Législateur Communautaire et le Devoir du Juge' in G. Lücke, G. Ress and M. R. Will (eds.), *Rechtsvergleichung, Europarecht und Staatenintegration. Gedächtnisschrift für Léontin-Jean Constatinesco* (Cologne: Carl Heymanns, 1983), pp. 559–580.

'Public and Private Aspects of European Community Competition Law', (1987) 10 *Fordham International Law Journal* 373.

Petersmann, Ernst-Ulrich, 'Proposals for a New Constitution for the European Union: Building Blocks for a Constitutional Theory and Constitutional Law for the EU', (1995) 32 *Common Market Law Review* 1123.

Picod, Fabrice, 'La Nouvelle Approche de la Cour de Justice en Matière d'Entraves aux Échanges', (1998) 34 *Revue Trimestrielle de Droit Européen* 169.

Pierre, Jon and Peters, B. Guy, *Governance, Politics and the State* (New York: St Martin's, 2000).

Poiares Maduro, Miguel, '*Keck*: The End? The beginning of the End? Or Just the End of the Beginning?', (1994) 1 *Irish Journal of European Law* 33.

'Reforming the Market or the State? Article 30 and the European Constitution: Economic Freedom and Political Rights', (1997) 3 *European Law Journal* 55.

We the Court – The European Court of Justice and the European Economic Constitution (Oxford: Hart, 1998).

Pontier, Jean-Marie, 'Sur la Conception Française du Service Public', [1996] *Recueil Dalloz* 9.

Prechal, Sacha, *Directives in EC Law*, 2nd edn (Oxford University Press, 2005).

Prosser, Tony, *The Limits of Competition Law – Markets and Public Services* (Oxford University Press, 2005).

'Competition Law and Public Services. From Single Market to Citizenship Rights', (2005) 11 *European Public Law* 543.

Quigley, Conor, 'The Notion of State Aid in the EEC', (1988) 13 *European Law Review* 243.

European State Aid Law, 2nd rev. edn (Oxford: Hart, 2007).

Reich, Norbert, 'Die Bedeutung der Binnenmarktkonzeption für die Anwendung der EWG-Wettbewerbsregeln' in J. F. Baur, K. J. Hopt and K. P. Mailänder (eds.), *Festschrift für Ernst Steindorff* (Berlin: De Gruyter, 1990), p. 1065.

'The "November Revolution" of the European Court of Justice: *Keck, Meng* and *Audi* Revisited', (1994) 31 *Common Market Law Review* 459.

Rhodes, Martin, '"Varieties of Capitalism" and the Political Economy of European Welfare States', (2005) 10 *New Political Economy* 363.

Rinne, Alexander, *Die Energiewirtschaft zwischen Wettbewerb und öffentlicher Aufgabe* (Baden-Baden: Nomos, 1998).

Rittner, Fritz, 'Die wirtschaftsrechtliche Ordnung der EG und das Privatrecht', (1990) 42 *Juristen-Zeitung* 838.

'Abschied vom "Öffentliche Auftragswesen" für private Unternehmen', (1997) 8 *Europäische Zeitschrift für Wirtschaftsrecht* 161.

Rodrigues, Stéphane, 'Les Services Publics et le Traité d'Amsterdam- Genèse et Portée Juridique du Projet de Nouvel Article 16 du Traité CEE', [1998] *Revue du Marché Unique Européen* 37.

Rohe, Mathias, 'Binnenmarkt oder Interessenverband? Zum Verhältnis von Binnenmarktziel und Subsidiaritätsprinzip nach dem Maastricht-vertrag', (1997) 61 *Rabels Zeitschrift* 1.

Ross, George, *Jacques Delors and European Integration* (Cambridge: Polity, 1995).

Ross, Malcolm, 'State Aids – Maturing into a Constitutional Problem', (1995) 15 *Yearbook of European Law* 79.

'Article 16 and Services of General Interest: from Derogation to Obligation?', (2000) 25 *European Law Review* 22.

'Promoting Solidarity: From Public Services to a European Model of Competition?', (2007) 44 *Common Market Law Review* 1057.

Roth, Wulf-Henning, 'Drittwirkung der Grundfreiheiten?' in O. Due, M. Lutter and J. Schwarze (eds.), *Festschrift für Ulrich Everling*, (Baden-Baden: Nomos, 1995), p. 1231.

Ruggie, John G., 'International Regimes, Transactions and Change: Embedded Liberalism in the Postwar Economic Order', (1982) 36 *International Organization* 379.

Sauter, Wolf, *Competition Law and Industrial Policy in the EU* (Oxford: Clarendon, 1997).

'The Economic Constitution of the European Union', (1998) 4 *Columbia Journal of European Law* 27.

Schaefer, D., *Die unmittelbare wirkung des verbots der nichttarifären handelshemnisse (Art. 30 EWGV) in den rechtsbeziehungen zwischen privaten* (Frankfurt a.M.: Lang, 1987).

Schäfer, Wolf (ed.), *Zukunftsprobleme der europäischen Wirtschaftsverfassung* (Berlin: Duncker & Humblot, 2004).

Scharpf, Fritz W., 'Die Handlungsfähigkeit des Staates am Ende des zwanzigsten Jahrhhunderts', (1991) 32 *Politische Vierteljahresschrift* 165.

Governing in Europe – Effective and Democratic? (Oxford University Press, 1999).

'The European Social Model', (2002) 40 *Journal of Common Market Studies* 645.

Schepel, Harm, 'Delegation of Regulatory Powers to Private Parties under EC Competition Law: Towards a Procedural Public Interest Test', (2002) 39 *Common Market Law Review* 31.

'The Enforcement of EC Law in Contractual Relations: Case Studies in How Not to "Constitutionalize" Private Law', (2004) 12 *European Review of Private Law* 661.

The Constitution of Private Governance – Product Standards in the Regulation of Integrating Markets (Oxford: Hart, 2005).

'The Public/Private Divide in Secondary Community Law: a Footnote to the European Economic Constitution', (2006) 8 *Cambridge Yearbook of European Legal Studies* 259.

Scherer, Josef, *Die Wirtschaftsverfassung der EWG* (Baden-Baden: Nomos, 1970).

Schiek, Dagmar, 'Private Rulemaking and European Governance: Questions of Legitimacy', (2007) 32 *European Law Review* 443.

Schmidt, Vivien A., *The Futures of European Capitalism* (Oxford University Press, 2002).

Schmidt-Leithoff, Christian, 'Gedanken über die Privatrechtsordnungen als Grundlage zum EWG-Vertrag', in M. Löwisch, Ch. Schmidt-Leithoff and B. Schmiedel (eds.), *Beiträge zum Handels- und Wirtschaftsrecht- Festschrift für Fritz Rittner* (Munich: Beck, 1991), p. 597.

Schroeder, Werner and Weber, Karl (eds.), *Daseinsvorsorge durch öffentliche Unternehmen und das europäische Gemeinschaftsrecht* (Vienna: Manz, 2003).

De Schutter, Olivier and Deakin, Simon (eds.), *Social Rights and Market Forces: Is the Open Coordination of Employment and Social Policies the Future of Social Europe?* (Brussels: Bruylant, 2005).

Schwarze, Jürgen, 'Das wirtschaftsverfassungsrechtliche Konzept des Verfassungsentwurfs des europäischen Konvents- zugleich eine Untersuchung der Grundprobleme des europäischen Wirtschaftsrechts', (2004) *Europäische Zeitschrift für Wirtschaftsrecht* 135.

(ed.), *Der verfassungsentwurf des europäischen konvents-verfassungsrechtliche grundstrukturen und wirtschaftsverfassungsrechtliches konzept* (Baden-Baden: Nomos, 2004).

Europäisches Wirtschaftsrecht. Grundlagen, Gestaltungsformen, Grenzen (Baden-Baden: Nomos, 2007).

Scott, Colin, 'Services of General Interest in EC Law: Matching Values to Regulatory Technique in the Public and Privatized Sectors', (2000) 6 *European Law Journal* 310.

'Private Regulation of the Public Sector: A Neglected Facet of Contemporary Governance', (2002) 29 *Journal of Law and Society* 56.

Scott, Joanne and Trubek, David M., 'Mind the Gap: Law and New Approaches to Governance in the European Union', (2002) 8 *European Law Journal* 1.

Skouris, Vassilios, 'Der einfluß des europäischen gemeinschaftsrecht auf die unterscheidung zwischen privatrecht und öffentlichem recht', [1998] *Europarecht* 111.

Slot, Piet Jan, 'The Application of Articles 3(f), 5 and 85 to 94 EEC', (1987) 12 *European Law Review* 179.

'Energy and Competition', (1994) 31 *Common Market Law Review* 511.

'The Concept of Undertaking in EC Competition Law' in O. Due, M. Lutter and J. Schwarze (eds.), *Festschrift für Ulrich Everling* (Baden-Baden: Nomos, 1995), Vol. II, p. 1413.

'Harmonisation', (1996) 21 *European Law Review* 378.

Slotboom, Marco, 'State Aid in Community Law – A Broad or Narrow Definition', (1995) 20 *European Law Review* 289.

Snell, Jukka, *Goods and Services in EC Law – A Study of the Relationship between the Freedoms* (Oxford University Press, 2002).

'Private Parties and the Free Movement of Goods and Services' in M. Andenas and W.-H. Roth (eds.), *Services and Free Movement in EU Law* (Oxford University Press, 2002), p. 211.

Snyder, Francis, 'Ideologies of Competition in European Community Law', (1989) 52 *Modern Law Review* 149.

Steindorff, Ernst, 'Drittwirkung der Grundfreiheiten im europäischen Geeinshaftsrecht' in P. Badura and R. Scholz (eds.), *Festschrift für Peter Lerche* (Munich: Beck, 1993), p. 576.

'Unvollkommener Binnenmarkt', (1994) 158 *Zeitschrift für das gesamte Handelsrecht* 149.

EG-Vertrag und Privatrecht (Baden-Baden: Nomos, 1996).

Strange, Susan, *The Retreat of the State – The Diffusion of Power in the World Economy* (Cambridge University Press, 1996).

Streeck, Wolfgang and Schmitter, Philippe C. (eds.), *Private Interest Government – Beyond Market and State* (London: Sage, 1985).

Streeck, Wolfgang and Thelen, Kathleen (eds.), *Beyond Continuity: Institutional Change in Advanced Political Economies* (Oxford University Press, 2005).

Streit, Manfred E. and Mussler, Werner, 'The Economic Constitution of the European Community: From "Rome" to "Maastricht"', (1995) 1 *European Law Journal* 5.

Symchowicz, Nil, 'La Notion de Délégation de Service Public', [1998] *Actualité Juridique – Édition Droit Administratif* 195.

Szyszczak, Erika, 'Public Services in Competitive Markets', (2001) 21 *Yearbook of European Law* 35.

'Financing Services of General Economic Interest', (2004) 67 *Modern Law Review* 982.

The Regulation of the State in Competitive Markets in the EU (Oxford: Hart, 2007).

'Competition and Sport', (2007) 32 *European Law Review* 95.

Temple Lang, John, 'The Duties of National Administrations Under Community Constitutional Law', (1998) 23 *European Law Review* 109.

Tesauro, Giuseppe, 'The Community's Internal Market in the Light of the Recent Case-law of the Court of Justice', (1995) 15 *Yearbook of European Law* 1.

Teubner, Gunther, 'The "State" of Private Networks: The Emerging Legal Regime of Polycorporatism in Germany', (1993) *Brigham Young University Law Review* 553.

'After Privatization? The Many Autonomies of Private Law', (1998) 51 *Current Legal Problems* 393.

Treheux, Michel, 'Privatization and competition versus public service', [1992] *Telecommunications Policy* 757.

Triantafyllou, Dimitris, 'Les Règles de la Concurrence et l'Activité Étatique y Compris les Marchés Publics', (1996) 32 *Revue Trimestrielle de Droit Européen* 57.

Tridimas, Takis, *The General Principles of EC Law* (Oxford University Press, 1999).

Trubek, David M. and Mosher, James S., 'New Governance, Employment Policy and the European Social Model' in J. Zeitlin and D. M. Trubek (eds.), *Governing Work and Welfare in a New Economy – European and American Experiments* (Oxford University Press, 2003), p. 33.

Trubek, David M. and Trubek, Louise G., 'Hard and Soft Law in the Construction of Social Europe: the Role of the Open Method of Co-ordination', (2005) 11 *European Law Journal* 343.

Truchet, Didier, 'État et Marché', (1995) 40 *Archives de Philosophie du Droit* 314.

Valette, Jean-Paul, *Le Service Public à la Française* (Paris: Ellipses, 2000).

Verhoeven, Amaryllis, 'Privatisation and EC Law: Is the European Commission "Neutral" with respect to Public versus Private Ownership of Companies?', (1996) 45 *International and Comparative Law Quarterly* 861.

Vickers, John and Wright, Vincent (eds.), *The Politics of Privatisation in Europe* (London: Frank Cass, 1989).

Vogel, Steven K., *Freer Markets, More Rules – Regulatory reform in Advanced Industrial Countries* (Ithaca: Cornell University Press, 1996).

Wachsmann and Berrod, 'Les Critères de Justification des Monopoles: un Premier Bilan après l 'Affaire *Corbeau*', (1994) 30 *Revue Trimestrielle de Droit Européen* 39.

Waelbroeck, Michel, 'Application des Règles de Concurrence du Traité de Rome à l'Autorité Publique', (1987) 30 *Revue du Marché commun* 25.
  'Les Rapports entre les Règles sur la Libre Circulation des Marchandises et les Règles de Concurrence Applicables aux Entreprises dans la CEE' in F. Capotorti *et al.* (eds.), *Du Droit International au Droit de l'Intégration* (Baden-Baden: Nomos, 1987), p. 781.
Weatherill, Stephen, *Law and Integration* (Oxford: Clarendon, 1995).
  'After *Keck*: Some Thoughts On How To Clarify the Clarification', (1996) 33 *Common Market Law Review* 885.
  'Preemption, Harmonisation and the Distribution of Competence to Regulate the Internal Market' in C. Barnard and J. Scott (eds.), *The Law of the Single Market – Unpacking the Premises* (Oxford: Hart, 2002), p. 41.
  (ed.), *Better Regulation* (Oxford: Hart, 2007).
Weiler, Joseph H.H., 'Does Europe Need a Constitution? Demos, Telos, and the German Maastricht Decision', (1995) 1 *ELJ* 218.
  'The Constitution of the Common Market Place: Text and Context in the Evolution of the Free Movement of Goods' in P. Craig and G. de Búrca (eds.), *The Evolution of EU Law* (Oxford University Press, 1999), p. 349.
Wernicke, Stephan, *Die privatwirkung im europäischen gemeinschaftsrecht* (Baden-Baden: Nomos, 2002).
Wesseling, Rein, *The Modernisation of EC Antitrust Law* (Oxford: Hart, 2000).
Winter, Gerd, 'Subsidiarität und Deregulierung im Gemeinschaftsrecht', (1997) 31 *Europarecht* 247.
Winter, Jan, 'Re(de)fining the Notion of State Aid in Article 87(1) of the EC Treaty', (2004) 41 *Common Market Law Review* 475.
Wright, Vincent (ed.), *Privatization in Western Europe: Pressures, Problems, Paradoxes* (London: Pinter Publishers, 1994).
Zuleeg, Manfred, 'Demokratie und wirtschaftsverfassung in der europäischen gemeinschaft', (1982) 16 *Europarecht* 21.
Zumbansen, Peer and Saam, Daniel, 'The ECJ, Volkswagen, and European Corporate Law: Reshaping the European Varieties of Capitalism', (2007) 8 *German Law Journal* 1027.

Index

CAMBRIDGE STUDIES IN EUROPEAN LAW AND POLICY

Books in the Series

State and Market in European Union Law

he EU internal market as

Court of Justice,

, the free movement of

goods, services, persons and capital and the evolution of the interpretation of the provisions.

The 'State' has been retreating from direct intervention in economic life as more goods and services, the provision of which was once thought to be a 'public' responsibility, are delivered through market mechanisms. Given the need for consistent application of EC law in internal market, a common core conception of public authority, elded from the discipline of EC competition law, is needed. The ulting realignment of public and private functions and responsi
ities is not a linear and coherent process, especially in light of the changing nature of the European legal integration project and the progressive incorporation of non-economic values in the Treaties.

WOLF SAUTER is professor of healthcare regulation at the University of Tilburg and a competition expert at the Dutch Healthcare Authority.

HARM SCHEPEL is a Reader at Kent Law School and Deputy Dean at the University of Kent's Brussels School of International Studies.

For a full list of titles published in the series, please see the end of the book.